THE ULTIMATE STUDENT COOKBOOK

TO SIG, GUY AND JAMES:

THREE GREAT COOKS OF THE FUTURE.

THE ULTIMATE STUDENT COOKBOOK

FIONA BECKETT WITH

SIGNE JOHANSEN, GUY MILLON AND JAMES RAMSDEN

ABSOLUTE PRESS **A.**

First published in Great Britain in 2009
by **Absolute Press**
Scarborough House
29 James Street West
Bath BA1 2BT
Phone 44 (0) 1225 316013
Fax 44 (0) 1225 445836
E-mail info@absolutepress.co.uk
Website www.absolutepress.co.uk

Reprinted 2009

Publisher
Jon Croft
Commissioning Editor
Meg Avent
Art Direction and Design
Matt Inwood
Design Assistant
Claire Siggery
Food Photography
Matt Inwood
Food Styling
Andrea O'Connor

A catalogue record of this book is available from
the British Library

ISBN 13: 9781906650070

Printed and bound in Italy by Printer Trento

For more information visit
www.beyondbakedbeans.com
or Facebook
BEYOND BAKED BEANS STUDENT COOKING
PAGE

A note about the text
This book was set using Helvetica Neue and
Aachen Bold. Helvetica was designed in 1957
by Max Miedinger of the Swiss-based Haas
foundry. In the early 1980s, Linotype redrew the
entire Helvetica family. The result was Helvetica
Neue. Aachen Bold was designed in 1969 by
Colin Brignall.

CONTENTS

FOREWORD BY HESTON BLUMENTHAL

I am a totally self-taught chef. I was very lucky that I fell in love with food and cooking at a young age and subsequently had boundless natural energy and enthusiasm in the kitchen. Looking back at my early kitchen days, I think that there were three things that helped me immensely: having an inquisitive mind, confidence in the kitchen and possessing a general sense of fun with cooking and eating. Many of us will shy away from cooking because of the lack of one or more of these attributes.

This book will help to build all of these. For the inquisitive cook, there is no-nonsense information that will make the recipes easier and help to develop confidence. The book is lively, vibrant and accessible. It radiates a great sense of fun and above all, does all of this on a budget. What more could a student want?

STUDENTS CAN COOK...

It's six years now since Absolute Press published my first student cookery book *Beyond Baked Beans*. Thanks to a surprise serialisation in the *Guardian* it became an instant best seller, for one brief glorious moment outstripping the celebrity chef cookbooks to top the food book charts. I think the secret of its success was that unlike most of the cookbooks out there it didn't talk down to students or assume they spent their time consuming bizarre throwbacks to the 1970s (like tuna bakes topped with crisps). It's always been my view that if you can write an essay you can follow a recipe.

In the intervening years two other books appeared: *Beyond Baked Beans Green* (for veggies, obviously) and *Beyond Baked Beans Budget*, focussing more on the student who was cooking for his- or herself. There has also been a website, **www.beyondbakedbeans.com**, and, more recently, a Facebook page where students have been able to upload their own tips, videos and recipes (with a little encouragement in the form of a rewards points scheme and assorted lavish prizes).

As a result of all this, we've learnt a lot about students that busts open the popular 'Young Ones' stereotype. Mainly that you are no different from the rest of the population – just more hard up, with worse cooking facilities. Some won't go near a cooker for their entire university career, others really want to eat healthily and are prepared to make the – let's face it, not massive – effort to do so. They enjoy cooking, enjoy being in the kitchen, enjoy sitting round a table and sharing food with friends. This book is for you.

We're fortunate this past year to have stumbled on three brilliant students who fall into just that category (see opposite) and who gave us the inspiration for this book: a compilation of the most popular recipes from the *Beyond Baked Beans* series along with their own favourite recipes. They've also commented throughout on my recipes, adding tips and – often witty – observations of their own which makes this a unique book, combining the experience of an established cookery writer (me, in case you were wondering!) with on-the-ground experience of three current students.

We've also – as the eagle-eyed among you will have spotted – finally got some flashy food photography, brilliantly executed by the lovely Matt and Andrea, which shows that student food doesn't have to be drab food.

Finally, we're more than a little proud to have the endorsement of Heston Blumenthal, a role model for all of us: a self-taught chef who has brought the lab into the kitchen and a sense of irreverent fun and playfulness to the hitherto starchy world of Michelin-starred cuisine. (Sig has been lucky enough to work with him, hence her learned treatise on making your own ice cream on pages 246-247.)

I hope, if you're coming to cooking for the first time, this book will ignite a passion for food and give you confidence. If you're a more experienced cook, I hope you will use it as a base to branch out from and experiment. Either way, I hope you will develop a love for cooking that will stay with you for the rest of your life.

FIONA BECKETT
July 2009

guy

sig

james

ESPECIALLY THESE THREE....

Since standing on a stool as a young boy, helping his mother cook and licking cake mixture off a wooden spoon, 23-year-old Yorkshireman **James Ramsden** has always been obsessed by cooking and food. In 2004, he went to Ballymaloe Cookery School in Ireland before starting his own catering company, The Hungry Caterpillar, honing the modern rustic, western European style that he loves. He has worked in France and Italy, both as chef and gardener, and has now finished his final year at Bristol University, studying, unsurprisingly, French and Italian. He writes The Larder Lout cookery blog (www.thelarderlout.blogspot.com), and has also written on food for *Sainsbury's Magazine*.

Guy Millon is a 21-year-old just-graduated psychology student at the University of Nottingham. He starts his MSc in October 2009. He grew up travelling around Europe with his food-writer-and-photographer parents who instilled in him a voracious appetite for food of all kinds. For the first nineteen years of his life he experienced dining purely from a consumer stance (and consume he did!). When the time came for him to fly the proverbial nest, he realised that he must learn to craft his own meals. Together with his partner-*en-crème*, Claire, he learnt to cook through trial and error, aided by an indispensable custom-built recipe book inherited from his parents. He continues to film regular videos for the Beyond Baked Beans Facebook site.

Signe (Sig) Skaimsgard Johansen is 28 years old. She grew up in Oslo, the daughter of a Norwegian father and a half-British/half-American mother. At the age of eight she tasted her first piece of raw fish at her Japanese best friend's house. Food has been a passion all her life; baking in particular, to which she devotes her food blog, Scandilicious (www.scandilicious.blogspot.com), and about which she learnt so much from her mother and grandmother. She trained at Leith's cookery school for a year, then moved on to freelance catering and a three-month stint as a *stagière* at Heston Blumenthal's Fat Duck Experimental Kitchen. She has a degree in Archaeology and Anthropology from Cambridge and is studying for her MA in the Anthropology of Food from the School of Oriental and African Studies (SOAS), University of London, and is hoping to continue with her PhD at SOAS.

BASICS

This is what you need to get started; the crucial kit, the must-have store cupboard ingredients, smart ways to shop and eat and invaluable advice that will safeguard your equipment, accommodation and friendships.

MUST-HAVE KITCHEN KIT

If you've already done some cooking at home the big difference you'll notice about cooking in a student kitchen is the lack of kit. Those endless bowls, pans, knives and labour-saving machines you take for granted are simply not there. At least not unless you bring them with you.

Look on the bright side – if there are fewer things to cook with there are fewer things to wash up. And there's no point in acquiring too much stuff of your own or it'll simply get nicked.

Obviously you can't actually cook properly unless you have the basics and if you're keen you'll want to add to these. That doesn't have to cost a bomb. Chances are your parents want to chuck out some stuff anyway. Or that they'll be so anxious about how you're going to look after yourself when you leave home they'll kit you out. (You can always point out magnanimously that if they give you their old toaster/kettle/mixer they can treat themselves to a new one.)

You can acquire other things – extra knives, forks, spoons, plates and glasses – bit by bit from charity shops or car boot sales. Discount stores like TK Maxx are good sources of inexpensive kitchen equipment such as pans. Or simply wait for the sales.

When I say 'must-have' someone must have it – not necessarily you. The list of kit on page 14 represents kit which, while not necessary, could further save you time and energy, and the kit on page 15 covers those slightly expensive items which it's well worth tapping up friends and family for!

☐ **Large frying pan (preferably non-stick)**
Not just for fry-ups but for quick meat and fish cooking too. It should be deep enough to be able to do a stir-fry, unless you're also going to buy a wok (see page 15). Incidentally, your frying pan is less likely to stick if you don't use washing-up liquid on it. Just rinse it under the hot tap as soon as you've finished using it and wipe it with kitchen towel.

☐ **Large-lidded saucepan or steamer**
The main purpose of which will probably be cooking pasta and making large batches of soup. The advantage of steamers – which are not too expensive these days – is that they have an inbuilt colander which you can use for straining your pasta as well as steaming veggies and fish.

☐ **Small/medium non-stick pan**
For scrambling eggs, heating up soup, making sauces, boiling eggs... (you could actually do with two but one will suffice).

☐ **Large roasting dish**
For that Sunday lunch you're going to make. Or for anything you want to bake in the oven. Like roast potatoes.

☐ **Medium-sized microwaveable dish**
Obviously essential if you have a microwave. But it should do double duty in a conventional oven, if you want to make a crumble for example, or something like a macaroni cheese.

☐ **Chopping board**
Plastic is easier to clean – and cheaper – so I'd go for that.

Small knife and a large knife

The small one for preparing vegetables and the large one for cutting and carving meat. Both knives should be kept sharp – a knife sharpener would help but isn't cheap. An old-fashioned hardware shop or kitchen shop might sharpen them for you. Or even a friendly butcher provided you buy from him occasionally.

Pair of kitchen scissors

For cutting the rind off bacon and opening those plastic packets you can't open with anything else.

Can opener

Not all cans have ring pulls.

Corkscrew

Obviously. Get an old-fashioned twist-and-pull one. Plastic corks will destroy a decent one.

Wooden spoon

Preferably two.

Fish slice or spatula

For lifting fish, fried eggs or anything else flat and floppy out of frying pans. Get one with a long handle if you intend to use it with a wok.

Grater

For cheese (Cheddar on the large holes, Parmesan on the small ones), carrots, fresh ginger. The square box-style type is easier to use.

Large and small mixing bowls

A large one will double as a salad bowl; the small one is ideal for mixing up salad dressings (unless you have a convenient jam jar), beating eggs, etc.

Measuring jug

Graded with solid measurements as well as liquid ones.

Pepper mill

Freshly ground pepper makes the world of difference. It doesn't have to be one of those flashy wooden jobs – a plastic one will do fine.

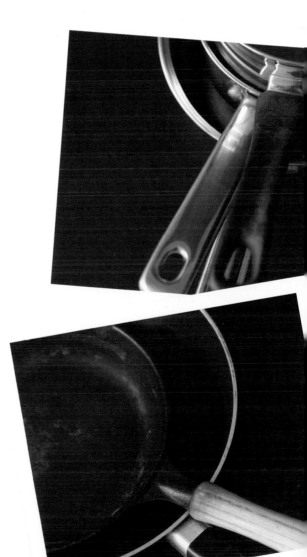

USEFUL KITCHEN KIT

☐ **Ice-tray**
Certainly if you're into cocktails. Nice for cold drinks during exam time too.

☐ **Garlic crusher**
You can of course chop it by hand but a crusher is quicker and less smelly.

☐ **Lemon squeezer**
You can stick a fork in the cut side of half a lemon and wiggle it while you squeeze but you'll get more juice out of a squeezer.

☐ **Wok**
You can cook a surprising number of things in a wok – quick stews as well as stir-fries. One with a lid is useful (though you can use a sheet of foil). You can buy them cheaply in Chinese supermarkets – though this type may rust if you don't wash and dry them immediately after use.

☐ **Colander and/or a sieve**
If you don't have a steamer you'll need something to strain your pasta (you can also use it as a steamer if you fit it on top of a saucepan and cover it with a lid). A sieve is useful for rice or for straining sauces that have lumps in them (not that yours will, I'm sure).

☐ **Measuring spoons**
Spoons are not vital but they're not expensive and they do make following recipes easier. Scales give you precision and so a bit of a safety net.

☐ **Timer**
Unless you're amazingly well organised.

☐ **Baking sheet**
Useful for heating up pizzas and for cooking pies and cookies.

☐ **Rolling pin**
Again, useful if you want to make or roll out pastry. But you can use a (clean) wine bottle at a pinch. Also useful for bashing steak.

☐ **Serrated bread knife**
If you're into unsliced bread. Quite useful for cutting tomatoes too.

☐ **Rotary whisk**
If you want to whip cream or egg whites for meringues. For basic whisking (eggs, salad dressings) a fork will do.

☐ **Vegetable peeler**
Not essential but it does make the job easier.

☐ **Potato masher**
Ditto. Worth getting if you're heavily into mash.

☐ **Metal tongs**
Very useful for turning sausages, bits of chicken, etc.

☐ **Cheese slicer**
Yes you can use a knife but a slicer makes it much easier to cut fine slices for sandwiches and as a topping for toast.

WISH-LIST KITCHEN KIT

☐ Kettle and a toaster
Though there's always a danger that everyone will bring one. Worth checking first.

☐ Handheld mixer, blender or processor
Basically something to blitz soups. Handheld blenders are the best value and take up least space. Blenders get a smoother result and can be used for smoothies too. A food processor will also make pastry and chop ingredients like vegetables and nuts. Depends how ambitious a cook you are.

☐ Cast-iron grill pan
A heavyweight ridged grill pan for quick, low-fat cooking. You get the grill really hot (about 3–4 minutes on the hob) lightly smear or spray your food with oil then quickly sear it either side. Gives a real barbecue flavour – but creates a lot of smoke. (Follow the cleaning tips for 'frying pan', see page 12.)

☐ Contact grill
A bit like a sandwich toaster without the sandwich indents so you can also grill burgers and other flat bits of meat and fish on it.

☐ Pestle and mortar
If you want to do some Jamie-Oliver-style bashing. Useful if you're into Thai, Indian or Moroccan cooking – anything which involves grinding up spices. Fun to use too. You'll find them cheapest in Asian supermarkets.

☐ Coffee maker
Real coffee is an expensive habit but once you've got the bug nothing else will do. It doesn't need to be electric though – go for a cafetière if you like a lighter style of coffee, an Italian stove-top coffee pot if you want a strong espresso hit.

☐ And a round-up of all those other things which should be to hand in any student kitchen...

Foil, Clingfilm, kitchen towel, plastic bags (for keeping fresh herbs in), oven gloves, apron, plasters (for when you inevitably cut yourself), fire blanket or extinguisher (just in case...), washing-up liquid, scourers/washing-up brush, tea towels enough to always have a clean one), sponge cloths, kitchen cleaner, Brillo pads (for stuck-on gunk, but no good for non-stick pans), bin bags, fridge thermometer (to tell if your fridge is cold enough – turn it up if it isn't!).

☐ And for the table...
Forks, knives, spoons, teaspoons, serving spoons, large plates, side plates, mugs (vast quantities of), egg cups, soup/cereal bowls, and a couple of serving plates/bowls.

OUR FAVOURITE KIT

 A wok; a rice cooker; an egg poacher (perfect for making easy starters; light lunches, breakfasts); a blowtorch (for pyromaniac moments — crème brûlée style); a corkscrew (naturally). **GUY**

 An oven thermometer – essential for gaging the actual temperature of an oven (especially when baking). Best investment for £5 a cook or baker can make; an electric whisk/hand blender; a Microplane grater, tongs for quickly flipping things, and a very good, very sharp all-purpose knife (plus a knife sharpener). **SIG**

 One good, sharp chef's knife; a large stock pan; a handheld blender; a good peeler; a Microplane or grater. **JAMES**

THE ESSENTIAL STUDENT STORECUPBOARD

No student these days can afford a well-stocked store cupboard, but there are ingredients without which you can't cook at all (salt and cooking oil for example) and others you should acquire if you want to eat well (assuming you do or you wouldn't have bought this book). It also makes sense – however tough it may be on the budget – to buy staples like pasta or tinned tuna when they're cheap. More on this in the section on shopping on a budget.

The stars of your store cupboard however should be herbs, spices and other flavourings that will transform the other cheap ingredients you have to buy into really tasty food. Which ones you pick depends on your own preferences – whether you're mad about chilli for example or more into Italian – I can only tell you what I wouldn't want to be without. Don't panic by the way if you get to the middle of a recipe and find you haven't got exactly the right ingredient. You can almost always substitute something else. Just pick them up as you can afford them.

6 MUST-HAVE INGREDIENTS

☐ Fresh parsley or coriander
They may seem like an indulgence but fresh herbs make all the difference to the look, taste and texture of your food. Buy them if you can in an Asian, Turkish or Middle-Eastern grocer where you'll find bunches twice the size and half the price of those you get in supermarkets (though you will need to wash them before you use them). Flat-leaf parsley generally has a better flavour than curly parsley, but is often more expensive.

☐ A couple of fresh lemons and a lime
A squeeze of lemon or lime juice lifts almost any dish. Once cut, keep them in the fridge wrapped in Clingfilm. Unwaxed fruit is better, particularly if you want to use the zest. They're juicier too, but they don't keep as long and you can often only buy them in packs of four, which is really annoying. To get the maximum juice out of a lemon or lime, warm it by rolling it on a work surface or chopping board under the palm of your hand for a few seconds or microwave it for 20 seconds on a very low setting.

☐ Garlic
Essential for any Mediterranean-inspired recipe, especially tomato-based sauces. You need it for stir-fries and curries too. Remember a clove is one section of a head, not the whole thing (my first major mistake when I started cooking). If you don't like handling garlic you can buy fresh garlic paste but it's pricey. Incidentally garlic should be kept out of the fridge.

☐ Freshly ground black pepper
Light years away from the beige powdery kind. Add during and after cooking.

☐ A chunk of Parmesan
Or rather Grano Padano, which is pretty well the same but comes from outside the officially recognised area, so is slightly cheaper. Freshly grated Parmesan just tastes so much better than the stuff you buy in sachets or cartons and although it's pricey a little goes a long way. Buy it from an Italian deli if you can.

☐ Extra-virgin olive oil
For salad dressings and drizzling over vegetables or pasta. Again, it's expensive so buy when there's a special offer. Use cheaper sunflower oil for frying.

AND A FEW MORE ESSENTIALS...

□ Cumin
My favourite spice. It's tangy flavour just conjures up the flavours of Morocco and the Middle East. You can buy it ground or as whole seeds (which are fabulous dry-roasted). Like all spices it's much cheaper in Asian shops than in supermarkets. Use it on its own or as the base of a Moroccan Spice Mix (see page 107).

□ Oregano
One of the most versatile of herbs, it won't give your food that horrid dried herb flavour. Invaluable for Mediterranean salads and pasta sauces. If you can't find it, use a pinch of dried marjoram or thyme.

□ Smoked paprika (pimenton)
This Spanish paprika has a fabulous smoky flavour – it comes in two strengths: Dulce (sweet) and Piccante (hot). If you can't find (or afford) it some chopped chorizo (a wonderful spiced Spanish sausage) plus a little bit of ordinary paprika will give you a similar flavour. Or use some mild chilli powder.

□ Thai sweet chilli sauce
Much more exciting than ketchup but you can use it the same way. Cheapest from Chinese supermarkets. (See also Cucumber and Sweet Chilli Salsa, page 110.)

□ Soy sauce
Useful for stir-fries. I prefer light to dark although Kikkoman is a good brand without additives.

□ Fresh ginger
Adds a hot, lemony kick to stir-fries and other Asian dishes. Buy a chunk, keep it wrapped in the fridge then peel and grate it as you need it.

□ Fish sauce (nam pla)
A sauce based on rotted fish doesn't sound like the most desirable adjunct to the student kitchen but it's brilliant for ratcheting up the fishy flavour of seafood curries, noodles and even pasta sauces and fish pies. Just a few drops will do it. Lasts forever.

□ Marigold Vegetable Bouillon Powder
Much, much better than any stock cube I've tried. Really natural tasting. A 150g tub should last you a good half-term.

□ Marmite
Even if you don't like it as a spread buy it as a gravy base or for stock (see page 149).

□ Dijon mustard
Mainly for a classic vinaigrette but you can also whip up classy tasting sauces with it. Get someone to bring you back some from France if you can. It's a fraction of the price it is here.

□ Runny honey
Useful as a sweetener or as a sweet-sour glaze.

HANDY TO HAVE TO HAND...

☐ **Half a dozen eggs**
☐ **A pack of Cheddar or other hard cheese**
☐ **A pack of bacon**
☐ **A couple of onions**
☐ **Tomato paste** (adds richness to tomato sauces; if you don't have any you can always use a little tomato ketchup)
☐ **A tin of tomatoes or a carton of passata or creamed tomatoes**
☐ **A pack of dried spaghetti or other pasta shapes** (preferably Italian)
☐ **A pack of basmati rice** (much more flavour than Easy-cook rice)
☐ **A couple of tins of cannellini beans or chickpeas**
☐ **A can of tuna**
☐ **A good curry paste and/or curry sauce** (Patak's are the most authentic)
☐ **Tabasco or other hot chilli sauce**
☐ **A jar of mayonnaise** (for salads and sandwiches)
☐ **Plain unsweetened yoghurt** (to accompany fresh fruit or stir into dips, dressings or curries)
☐ **A pack of instant mash** (flakes rather than powder)
☐ **A couple of packs of good instant noodles**
☐ **A small pack of plain flour**

AND BASICS NOT TO FORGET...

☐ **An inexpensive oil for cooking**
Sunflower or rapeseed for preference.

☐ **Butter**
Even if you don't use it as a spread, butter has a great flavour for cooking. If you can buy it on promotion use spreadable butter which kills two birds with one stone.

☐ **Red or white wine vinegar**

☐ **Fine sea salt**
Tastes much, much better than table salt.

I'm assuming you've already thought of coffee, tea, sugar, fresh and long life milk, bread, breakfast cereal, jam....

OUR FAVOURITE INGREDIENTS

Can't be without mustard, Parmesan or tinned tomatoes (a student cliché but can't live without 'em). I also need cumin seed, coriander seed and cardamom (I like to grind my own) Oh, and fresh parsley. **JAMES**

I have to have eggs, tinned fish, lemons and garlic around always. Then cinnamon, cardamom and chilli (the first two for baking and the latter because, of all the savoury spices in my kitchen, I use this the most). Mint, rosemary and thyme are the herbs I need. **SIG**

My essentials would run something like: fresh ginger, soy sauce, Chinese five-spice (for pork marinades), curry powder, basil and oregano (for pasta sauces) and rosemary for roasting meats. **GUY**

SHOPPING ON A BUDGET

Figures differ but the average UK student currently spends around £20–28 a week on food depending on whether the calculations involve eating out. That's just under £3–4 a day... quite tight if you're catering for yourself, not at all bad if you're living in a student house and pooling your resources. However, it's all too easy as we all well know to blow the lot in one supermarket visit and not have a lot to show for it. The only answer is to learn to shop – and eat – cannily so that you really make your money work for you. Bye bye impulse shopping, hello bargain hunting....

Here are the 10 golden rules of budgeting:

PLAN YOUR SHOPPING TRIP

If you really want to stick to a budget you need to make a plan. Not a totally inflexible one (you still need to be in a position to snap up a particularly good bargain) but at least have an idea before you go out of what you're going to cook. Take a look at these recipes to see what appeals to you, then make a list, taking care you don't duplicate ingredients you already have. If you're buying just for yourself, rather than a household, the key thing is to make every thing you buy earn its keep. A roast chicken, for example, can stretch to at least 3 meals if you use every scrap of the meat and make a stock with the carcass for a batch of homemade soup.

SHOP TWICE A WEEK

Don't plan too far ahead. If you try to plan a whole week's meals, chances are you'll waste at least some of the food you've bought. I find it better to plan in 3- to 4-day blocks, which also

enables you to ring the changes, varying what you eat so you don't get bored. If you've decided to have three meals based on mince you might well want to switch to stir-fries or noodles, for example.

SCRIMP AT THE START OF THE WEEK

Try and leave yourself enough money each week to give yourself a treat, perhaps a bottle of olive oil, a lump of Parmesan or a large bar of chocolate. If you eat frugally at the beginning of the week it's more likely you can splash out at the end. That's also the time to take advantage of special offers on things you eat regularly like bacon, pasta and tuna.

BUY THINGS AS YOU NEED THEM

Obviously you'll have to make an initial outlay on some basic stores, but don't go mad and buy a whole lot of stuff you may not need (unless your parents are paying of course...). Many ingredients can be substituted. For example, if you want an onion flavour, you can use onions, spring onions or leeks. If you want to make a dish hotter, you could use paprika, chilli powder, fresh chillies or chilli sauce.

LEARN WHAT THINGS COST...

That might sound an impossible task given the several hundred lines in the average supermarket, but you should at least know the price of the things you buy regularly, like pasta, tinned tomatoes or cheese so that alarm bells ring if you find them at a higher price than you usually pay or, conversely, at a knockdown price.

Remember though a bargain isn't a bargain if you don't, or can't, use it before it goes off.

...AND WHAT'S IN SEASON

If you insist on buying strawberries in January or leeks in June, you'll pay for them. Food that's in season tastes better too. Sometimes, retailers sell produce at a high price even when it's in season though. I've been shopping for root veg in winter and found parsnips at four times the price of carrots. You need to keep your wits about you.

AVOID CONVENIENCE FOODS

Well obviously not completely. I don't expect you to make your own mayonnaise, and most of us use pre-packed stir-fry veg. But do you really need to buy ready-grated cheese? Unwrapped fruit and veg also tend to be substantially cheaper than pre-packed and you only need buy the amount you're going to use.

DON'T SCOFF THE LEFTOVERS!

Behave as if you're on a diet, serve up what you're going to eat (which can be quite substantial – I'm not advocating diet rations), cool the rest down, wrap it up and put it in the fridge. OK, I know we all pick at leftovers and conduct fridge raids in the early hours, but if you really want to save money you can't afford to eat next day's food.

SAVE ON FUEL

It's cheaper to cook on top of the stove than it is in the oven. If you do use the oven try to cook more than one thing – a tray of roast peppers that could be used for sandwiches and salads for example, while you're cooking a roast.

BE MORE ADVENTUROUS!

The more types of food you're prepared to eat, the cheaper your shopping basket will be. Experiment with own-brand versions of the foods you like. Give cheap, nutritious foods like liver and sardines a try. (Not at the same time, obviously.)

WHERE TO SHOP

You might assume – as most people do – that the only place to shop cheaply is the supermarket. This is not strictly true. Of course, they often have some good bargains (see below) but they balance these by charging more for other items. Obviously, I'm not advocating that you trek round every shop in the neighbourhood comparing prices, simply that you should be aware what different kinds of food shops might have to offer. Don't make assumptions that certain kinds of shops such as independent butchers are expensive.

SUPERMARKETS

Supermarkets are highly sophisticated shopping environments. From the time you walk in through the luscious fresh produce of the fruit and veg department to the time you check out everything is designed to grab your attention.

They cater primarily for people who are cash-rich and time-poor – not you in other words. They make their money out of adding value to products – washing and pre-packing them so that you don't have to do the work. But you obviously pay for the convenience.

Next time you go to a supermarket take a look at the price of loose carrots. Next, check how much it costs to buy them pre-packed (the unit cost, i.e. price per kilo or 100g, is given on almost all products). Chances are that they will cost at least twice as much.

They also, as you'll have noticed, have several different quality levels. Ranges like 'Finest' (Tesco) and 'Taste the Difference' (Sainsbury's) at the top of the tree, 'Basics' or 'Value' at the bottom. These budget ranges are the ones you

should try. (These products are often stacked right at the bottom of the shelf rather than at eye level by the way.)

Ingredients also tend to be expensive if they're in demand. Products like chicken breasts, rump steak, salmon fillets, salads, popular cheeses like Mozzarella, feta and mascarpone – the sort of ingredients you find on TV cookery programmes – are generally pricier than their less sexy equivalents (chicken thighs, minute steak, loose lettuces, English regional cheeses, Quark and curd cheese). The same applies to the products you might need for making fashionable Asian dishes like coriander, soy sauce and fish sauce. But there can be good offers on these sort of lines at particular times of year when supermarkets want to lure customers away from their competitors – Christmas, Valentine's Day and Chinese New Year, for example.

Then there's the infamous BOGOF (buy one get one free) which can sound incredibly tempting but would you buy it if it didn't have that sticker on it? And 3 for the price of 2 may not be a good offer at all if it encourages you to buy something you can't or won't use by the eat-by date. What I look out for are special offers on products I use regularly and will keep for at least a couple of weeks like bacon, tuna or pasta.

Another good buy in supermarkets is fresh produce that's reduced. That can be any day of the week but there are usually some good offers available at the beginning of the week on produce that hasn't sold over the weekend. Some of my best bargains have been bagged at the supermarket at my local petrol station which often reduces lines by up to 80% on a Sunday evening. You need to use them up quickly though – the reason they're cheap is that they've reached their sell-by date.

The best way to use supermarkets is for basics. They're hard to beat for everyday items like tea, coffee, cooking oil, pasta and breakfast cereals and for tinned products like tomatoes, tuna and beans, particularly if you use own brands. And veggies may find certain products like honey and vegetable bouillon powder cheaper than in a health food shop (though not products like nuts and dried fruits – see page 24).

DISCOUNT STORES

The new generation of discount supermarkets are cheap, no doubt about it, but they do have a few drawbacks. The range of products they carry is typically not as wide as the average supermarket and the quality of fresh produce, particularly meat and fish isn't as good. You may also face unexpected charges for car parking or carrier bags (not much, admittedly). The big supermarkets have also responded to the competition they pose by increasing the number of items in their budget ranges so on many products they're not that much cheaper. But you do tend to find the odd really good bargain – recent finds have been very cheap bread products like naan and pitta bread and excellent German-style sausages (Aldi and Lidl are both German-owned). Worth checking out if you have one near you certainly, though don't expect to find everything you want in there.

INDEPENDENT FOOD SHOPS

The general perception is that small specialist shops are really expensive. Some, such as smart urban delis, are certainly going to be beyond your reach. But others, such as old-fashioned butchers and fish shops can provide really cheap food. What they excel at is the sort of produce that supermarkets won't touch (less expensive cuts of meat, in the case of butchers, less common types of fish or locally grown fruit and veg). Get to know the people behind the counter and you may even get great advice too on what to buy and how to cook it. A good baker is a real find; decent bread is hard to find in supermarkets.

ETHNIC SHOPS

Great bargains to be found here, especially if you're after particular types of ingredients:

Indian/Pakistani/Bangladeshi grocers
Spices, cheap pulses, fresh herbs like mint and coriander.

Greek/Turkish/Middle-Eastern grocers
Wonderful cheap herbs and veg, inexpensive lemon juice, hummus.

Chinese/Asian supermarkets
Cheap soy sauce, fish sauce, sweet chilli sauce, hoisin sauce, rice vinegar, lemon grass, chillies, lime leaves. The only place to shop for a Thai curry.

Afro-Caribbean shops
Good cheap veg.

WHERE TO SHOP

HEALTH FOOD SHOPS / CO-OPERATIVES

The best place to buy nuts and dried fruits and specialist products like miso or tofu. Can also be good value for beans and other pulses but tend to be expensive for fresh produce which can also be variable in quality if the store does not have a regular turnover.

CORNER SHOPS / CAMPUS SHOPS

Convenient if you've just tumbled out of bed on a Sunday afternoon, but rarely cheap – certainly not the place to do the bulk of your food shopping!

MARKETS

If you actually want to enjoy, rather than endure, your food shopping go to a local market. It's likely to be the cheapest place to buy your fruit and veg – so long as you don't get carried away. The big temptation is to buy more than you need, especially towards the end of the day when stallholders are trying to flog what they've got left. If you're just shopping for yourself you do need to ask yourself what you're going to do with 2 kilos of bananas even if you got them for a quid. Produce that may be worth snapping up are foods you can keep for a bit, like onions or other root veg, or ones you can cook in bulk like fresh tomatoes or peppers (if you can be bothered to do that). You may also find specialist stalls selling meat, fish, bread, health foods, or Asian stalls selling good cheap ingredients (see 'Ethnic shops', page 23). Farmers' markets are also hugely enticing but tend to be less cheap.

ONLINE SHOPPING

Much better established than it was when my first *Beyond Baked Beans* book was published and a good option for your weekly supermarket shop if you're a) buying for a student house and b) haven't got a car. If you're very well organised you could even band together with neighbours and split the cost of delivery. (That's certainly a good option with veg boxes.) The downside? It's easy to order more than you need, or forget items and then have to shop for them, ending up buying other things you don't really need. Result – a big food bill. (A useful tip though: guilt-ridden parents can sometimes be induced to put through an order for you if you sound as if you're on the verge of starvation, particularly in the first year....)

WHERE WE SHOP

In my final year, my two flat mates and I got an organic veg box, reasoning that a fiver each (or two pints) a week was worth it to eat healthily. How right we were. On the whole, we got a variety of often interesting vegetables to experiment with, and we ended up making the effort to cook every night because we had all this veg, instead of copping out and getting a pizza when we couldn't be bothered. We probably saved money in the long run! JAMES

I try to avoid the larger supermarket chains like the plague. Although they may seem cheap, I find that I impulse-buy like crazy and end up with far more food than I really need. Far better to go into a smaller, though more expensive, local shop and buy fewer but better quality items. You also won't be forced to wander

aimlessly between vast aisles when you realise that you've forgotten to pick up a key item just as you're leaving the shop and have no idea where to find it. I tend to pick up a weekly vegetable box from a local community centre which is incredibly cheap (£3.50). This is because it's run as a charity and not a money-making business venture. Often, universities run similar schemes and you won't have to pay the high prices charged by the ultra-fashionable big-name organic vegetable suppliers. **GUY**

 Rather than doing a weekly supermarket raid I'll get staples such as cleaning products and random food items (tinned food, frozen berries, beer) from a supermarket and scout around local shops for everything else. Granted, this is the luxury of living in a city, and especially my neighbourhood, where we have a variety of food shops, grocers and delis. Mostly, I'll pick up milk, yoghurt and cheese from my local deli and fill in with produce from nearby markets or health food shops. This might seem time-consuming and ridiculous but I'll swing by markets on the way home from uni' or wherever I've been, making sure to bring one of those cloth bags that squish down to nothing in my handbag for impromptu veggie or fruit purchases, so no extra time is really expended in food shopping. **SIG**

HEALTHY EATING... AND DRINKING

If you're on a tight budget it's not easy to eat healthily, I admit. But then it's not that easy on an unlimited budget either. Basically, it needs a conscious effort on your part, an effort that may seem just too tedious to make. The reason you should is not simply to do with your long term health – it's hard to focus on the possibility that you may suffer from osteoporosis when you're 70 – but about your health right now. If you don't eat a well-balanced diet you stand a much greater chance of getting ill. Not seriously ill, but subject to the kind of succession of colds and other bugs that can make you feel tired, listless and depressed. It can also, of course, make you less attractive. Overweight. Spotty. Greasy-haired.... Convinced? Here's how to do it.

THE 4 CRUCIAL FOOD GROUPS

The key to healthy eating is to incorporate something from within each of these groups every day. Yes, even fat has a part to play.

1) FRUIT AND VEG

5 portions a day is the amount the health tsars recommend but I reckon 4 is a more realistic target. If you always have some fruit juice or a piece of fruit for breakfast, a portion of veg or salad for lunch and supper and a piece of fruit some time during the day you'll achieve it but for most of us it takes a conscious effort. The key is to think about it every time you prepare food. If you make a fry-up, add a tomato. If you make a sandwich, cram in some cucumber or lettuce. If you heat up a lasagne or other ready meal, make sure you have a salad too (although the tinned tomato in lasagne counts, certainly in a homemade version). If you have a nibble of

cheese, accompany it with an apple, pear or a stick of celery. Use fresh herbs wherever possible in your cooking. If the cost daunts you, remember frozen and canned fruit and veg count too. The ones in fruit or natural juice are obviously healthier than the ones in syrup or with added sugar.

2) BREAD, POTATOES, PASTA AND RICE

A crucial source of energy that you may be tempted to skip if you're trying to lose weight. (But don't – just go easy on the butter or rich sauces you put with them). Obviously, wholemeal products are better (higher in fibre and B vitamins – the ones that stop you feeling stressed) but if you don't enjoy the taste don't torture yourself. Even bog standard white bread is fortified with calcium. About 50% of your diet (5–6 helpings a day) should be made up of carbohydrate but that doesn't mean you have to live off sandwiches and pasta. Grains like couscous, bulgur wheat and polenta count too. As do breakfast cereals (which are also fortified with B vitamins and iron).

3) RED MEAT, CHICKEN, FISH, EGGS AND VEGGIE ALTERNATIVES

Protein provides iron and zinc which are vital for cell health and renewal. The easiest way to absorb it is by eating meat, but vegetarians can get it from beans and lentils, nuts, seeds, soy products, egg yolks, fortified breakfast cereals and dark green veg like spinach and cabbage. Even meat-eaters should vary their sources of protein and not just rely on bacon sarnies to do the job. Remember, the amount of actual meat in many processed foods and ready meals can

be quite low. Aim for 2–3 small servings a day*
– and a couple of portions of oily fish like
mackerel or tuna a week (good for your heart).
If you are a vegetarian, drinking a vitamin C-rich
drink like orange or cranberry juice with a meal
or following it with fruit, like oranges,
strawberries or kiwi fruit will help you absorb
iron more effectively.

* You don't need as much as you might think.
A skinless chicken breast will actually provide
almost all your daily protein requirements.
A small 50g chunk of cheese would provide
about a third of it.

4) MILK, CHEESE AND YOGHURT

Important for the calcium they contain which
keeps your teeth and bones healthy. You should
aim for 2–3 servings, some of which will
obviously be accounted for by the milk you have
in tea and coffee. The downside is that full-fat or
sugary versions can also pile on the pounds so
stick to semi-skimmed milk, low-fat cheeses
such as Quark and fromage frais and plain,
unsweetened yoghurt if you're trying to keep
your weight down but don't skip them
altogether. (Plain yoghurt is more flexible than
flavoured yoghurt anyway as you can also use it
in savoury dishes.) Vegans should make sure
they have enough non-dairy sources such as
calcium-enriched soya milk and tofu, green leafy
vegetables, brazil nuts and dried apricots.

LEARN TO LOVE...

☐ **Lentils** Rich in B-vitamins, iron and fibre
☐ **Liver** Rich in iron
☐ **Sardines, mackerel (at least try it smoked)
and other oily fish** Rich in omega 3 fatty acids
which offer protection against heart disease
☐ **Spinach, watercress and other dark
leafy veg** Rich in iron, beta-carotene, vitamin C
☐ **Carrots** Rich in beta-carotene and vitamin A
☐ **Kiwi fruit** More vitamin C than oranges
☐ **Mangoes** Rich in fibre and vitamin C and E
☐ **Tofu** High in protein, helps lower cholesterol
☐ **Wholemeal bread** Rich in iron, selenium
and other minerals

HEALTHY EATING... AND DRINKING

SHOULD I TAKE VITAMIN SUPPLEMENTS?

If you know your diet is deficient in crucial vitamins such as C and B (which can easily happen if you're a smoker), I think you should, especially if you're going down with a cold. Sure, it's much better to eat the right foods, but if you haven't been eating that well supplement your diet until you're back on track. If you do feel seriously run down you should of course consult a doctor.

LIQUID REFRESHMENT

I'm not going to get preachy about how much you should drink other than to remind you that the recommended daily maximum is 3 units for women and 4 for men. And that's really, really easy to exceed. A small (125ml) glass of 13.5% Chardonnay is about 1.8 units alone and most glasses you pour will be a lot bigger than that. One cocktail or a double vodka and you're almost at the limit. Alcohol is also fattening – anything from about 90 calories to 120 calories a glass, so don't be surprised if a lot of partying piles on the pounds. What you should be drinking is water. Lots of it – about 2 litres or 8 large glasses – a day. Coffee and tea don't count (they contain caffeine which increases the heart rate and can make you feel jittery), but fruit squashes and herbal and fruit 'teas' are OK.

SNACKING ISN'T BAD...

Or it needn't be provided it doesn't consist solely of fatty or sugary foods. Supplies of nuts, raisins and other dried fruits like apricots provide iron and other essential vitamins and minerals, a low-fat yoghurt will boost your calcium intake, a banana will give you energy. Keep a supply of sliced peppers, celery and carrots in the fridge for when hunger strikes or dunk in hummus for a more substantial snack.

WHEN YOU FEEL ROUGH

Whether it's self-inflicted or you've succumbed to a bug there are times when you need to give your system a break and recharge your batteries. The easiest way to do this is by following a liquid – or near liquid – diet for 24 hours. And I don't mean booze. Soup is the obvious starting point (see pages 70–75 and pages 126–128), but if you're feeling under par you're not going to want to start making it from scratch. Most instant soups are pretty disgusting – you'd actually be better to make a simple broth with a decent chicken stock cube (kosher ones such as Telma are best), or vegetable bouillon powder. If you find it bland you can infuse the hot broth for 5 minutes with flavourings such as lime leaf, ginger and garlic. Instant miso soup is also really comforting and filling but improved with a finely sliced spring onion floated in it.

If you're feeling a bit brighter you could move on to a roughie (pages 50–51). Roughie? Roughies are what to make when you fancy a smoothie but haven't got a blender... or if you have but can't be bothered to wash it up.

LIGHT EATING

Once you do start eating proper meals again stick to light, non-fatty foods. Eggs are perfect, though boil or scramble rather than fry them. Fish is more digestible than meat especially if microwaved or steamed, and eat as much fresh fruit and raw or plainly cooked veg as you can. Pasta is fine if you avoid rich creamy or cheesy sauces, and if you're recovering from a bout of gastroenteritis a simple dish of boiled rice and peas won't tax the system too much. Nor will a few pieces of vegetarian sushi.

PREVENTING THAT HANGOVER...

You know this already I'm sure but you shouldn't drink on an empty stomach. Even a glass of milk will stop the alcohol going straight into your bloodstream and making you drunk. Better still would be a glass of milk and a banana or a couple of pieces of toast. Once you do start drinking, dilute the effect by having regular glasses of water – one for every drink you have. Down a couple more before you go to bed. And if you want to avoid a splitting headache don't mix wine and spirits.

EXAM TIME

Good eating habits tend to go out of the window during exam time, essay deadlines or other periods of stress, but you don't actually do yourself any favours if you starve your body – or brain – of essential nutrients. Staying up all night fuelled by caffeine may make you feel like you're on top of things but a Horlicks or herbal tea-induced night's sleep would make you function a lot better.

Keep yourself going with nourishing snacks, a bowl of cereal, a health bar, a yoghurt, a piece of fruit. This is the sort of time ready-meals do come in handy, so be prepared to overspend your budget if necessary to save yourself the bother of having to think about meals. Drink plenty of water too.

Before an exam try and eat something even if you're sick with nerves – a bowl of cereal, some fruit and yoghurt if it's first thing, a bowl of soup and a sandwich or a plate of pasta before an afternoon exam. Or a smoothie if you can't face anything solid.

If you're having trouble sleeping, stick to herbal teas such as camomile and lemon verbena or milky drinks rather than coffee.

TOP STUDENT TIPS

There is no such thing as a hangover cure. It's like suggesting there's an 'illness cure' – every hangover is different. There's the 'churny-churny', the 'eye-jiggler', the 'head-exploder' the 'head-down-the-toilet-er', the 'ooh-I-think-I've-got-away-with-it-until-it-creeps-up-at-lunchtime-er'. And that's just to barely scrape the surface. The best 'cures' are pre-emptive. My advice is to force 2–3 pints of water down before bed, along with 2 Nurofen. This way, at least the 7am loo dash shouldn't be accompanied by a stinking headache. A slightly parental one, but no less true, is just to avoid mixing your drinks – that even means trying to stay on the same make of wine, if that's what you're drinking (though if you're supping from the Morrison's bargain bucket you'll know what you've got coming to you). One method I tried, and it was effective, if hard to maintain, is to drink the same volume in water every time you get a drink. Pint of cider? Pint of water too, please. It really pulls the birds as well. They love it. **JAMES**

HOW NOT TO POISON YOUR FRIENDS

There are an awesome number of cases of food poisoning every year, most of them perpetrated by dodgy restaurants and fast food traders. If you don't want to add to those statistics you need to be at least vaguely aware of what constitutes food hygiene.

• Always wash your hands thoroughly before starting to prepare food. With soap. And dry them with a hand towel or kitchen towel rather than your tea towel.

• Keep your working surfaces clean. Or use a clean chopping board if they're not. Give them a good blitz every couple of days with an anti-bacterial cleaner.

• Keep the sink clean and free from teabags, potato peelings, leftover pasta and other grot.

• Wash your tea towels regularly and replace the washing up brush and/or scourers before they get too squalid.

• Keep the food you store in the fridge wrapped or covered – partly to avoid cross contamination, partly to stop them drying out.

• Don't store fresh and cooked meat side by side or put fresh meat or fish where it can drip onto cooked food (no wonder so many people are vegetarian). Wash any utensils or chopping board you have used for preparing raw meat before using them for anything else.

• Don't refreeze frozen food that has thawed, especially ice cream.

• If you're using frozen chicken or other joints defrost them completely before cooking them.

• If you cook something to eat later or have perishable food left over cool it then refrigerate it (NEVER put warm food in the fridge). If you're going to eat it hot always reheat it thoroughly – that means simmer it for at least 5 minutes.

• Make sure your fridge is set at a cold enough setting for the amount of food it has in it. (Afraid there's no other way to check than buying a fridge thermometer). Defrost and clean it thoroughly at least once a term.

• Refrigerate perishable food as soon as you can after buying it. Don't lug it round warm lecture rooms and coffee bars.

• Store the contents of half-finished tins like canned tomatoes or fruit in china, glass or plastic containers. Tins that are left open to the air can corrode.

• Get rid of anything that smells rank or shows obvious signs of decay – spots of mould, furry growths or generally unappealing squishy bits. Also potatoes that have sprouted or developed green patches. And anything that has passed its eat-by date. If in doubt, chuck it out.

TOP STUDENT TIPS

 Few things raise the Johansen heckles quite as much as a sink of dirty dishes, grimey work surfaces or sticky tables. A kitchen after a fun evening cooking with your mates will invariably be messy and that's fine. What is not fine is living with recalcitrant flatmates or neighbours in halls of residence who seem to think it's their God-given right to live in filth and squalor, even if they share a communal kitchen with you. So, what to do with a kitchen slob? It can be tricky to galvanise those you live with to join in with the cleaning, but instead of simmering with passive-aggression (as I usually do, and then erupt in a fit of rage throwing all their junk out) make light of it, gently hint that the kitchen's a mess and suggest a group effort at cleaning – it needn't take long if you work together. Entice them with a meal if need be, and should they still seem oblivious to bio-hazards, then throw all their stuff out. Very cathartic, I promise you.

You don't have to buy expensive branded kitchen cleaners. Kitchen ingredients such as vinegar, bicarbonate of soda are more eco-friendly E-cover surface spray is just as effective. The latter's good for everyday cleaning, vinegar is brilliant for adding shine to just about everything and acts as a deodoriser when you've been cooking fish or curries. Place vinegar in a small bowl and leave overnight: the next day all those cooking smells will have disappeared. Bicarb is an old family staple – put a few tablespoons in a jar and place in your fridge. It will absorb nasty fridge smells and you can also use it to clean sinks and loos and help remove stains from clothes. **SIG**

HOW LONG THINGS KEEP IN THE FRIDGE

Obviously it depends when and where you bought them and how quickly you put them away. Produce bought loose, especially from small shops will generally need to be eaten sooner than pre-packed produce which has been chilled, though it also depends on the sell-by date. If you buy things cheap because they've reached or are nearing the end of their shelf life you should generally eat them the same day.

EAT WITHIN 24 HOURS

High-risk foods such as shellfish and other fresh fish, mince, offal, pre-prepared salads, stir-fries and beansprouts.

EAT WITHIN 1–3 DAYS

Chicken and other meat, sausages (if wrapped), mushrooms, soft fruit such as strawberries, leftovers.

EAT WITHIN 4–6 DAYS

Soft cheese, yoghurt, milk, tomatoes and other fresh veg.

EAT WITHIN A WEEK TO 10 DAYS

Bacon and ham (though consume within a couple of days once you open the pack) hard cheese, eggs.

STORE FOR UP TO A MONTH OR MORE

Butter and spreads (check the use-by date). Frozen foods (but ice cream should never be refrozen once thawed).

AND REMEMBER...

Always read the instructions on jars once you've opened them. Many products such as mayonnaise and cook-in sauces need to be kept in the fridge.

KEEP OUT OF THE FRIDGE

Garlic, onions and melons (will taint the other food you've got stored there, especially butter). Bananas and avocados go black and soggy. Potatoes are best stored in a paper bag. If you buy them in a plastic bag, tear it open so the air can get to them.

FOOD ALLERGIES

Quite a few people are allergic or intolerant to ingredients these days, most commonly wheat and dairy products made from cow's milk. But it's nuts and shellfish (even if fresh) that can make them seriously ill. Most of them will be aware of the risk but never include either ingredient in a dish without telling your friends you've done so. Especially peanuts which can be fatal.

OTHER KITCHEN HAZARDS

There are a number of other hazards that can befall you when you're cooking. More fires start in the kitchen, for example, than any other room in the house – usually when someone just wanders off and forgets that they've left something on the hob. So...

DON'T:

- buy dodgy second hand appliances with frayed cords
- Leave kitchen towel, tea towels or oven gloves near the hob where they can catch fire
- cook with floppy sleeves
- cook when you're legless
- leave pan handles sticking out from the stove
- leave the hob, oven or appliances like sandwich toasters on when you've finished cooking
- use a metal or foil container in a microwave

BUT DO:

- keep electrical leads away from water
- clean out your toaster occasionally so it's not full of crumbs. And keep your grill pan clean and free from fat

WHAT TO DO IF THE OIL IN A PAN CATCHES FIRE

Throw a damp towel over it to exclude the air. (Wring it out under the tap) Never throw water on a fire. If it's out of control get everyone out of the kitchen, shut the door and call 999.

GUY'S AWFUL ACCIDENT:

 In the excitement of preparing a delicious meal, it's easy to forget how dangerous the kitchen can be. I personally had a very nasty accident involving boiling water. It was a lazy Sunday afternoon soup-making session (winter vegetable) and I had made up a bowl of stock using water from a kettle. As I was transferring this into the soup pan, I spilt some onto my pouring hand. I instinctively moved my hand away, and in the process dropped the bowl of boiling stock all over my stomach and legs. It was the most painful sensation I have ever experienced. I was only wearing pyjamas, which I rapidly kicked off while running around screaming. My girlfriend put me in a cold shower immediately, which although causing me to faint due to the extreme temperature change of my skin, was in hindsight the best possible course of action. As soon as I could think clearly, we went to A&E where my bright red, blistered skin was heavily bandaged and I was put on a cocktail of painkillers. For months afterwards, I could barely walk and had to have my dressings changed most days by my patient girlfriend, mother and a series of nurses. This meant I was out of the kitchen for a long time, and my appetite for soup remains (partially) diminished.

Since then, I have always cooked with a thick waterproof apron, and have a new measuring jug with a handle that I use whenever preparing a stock. The incident really taught me to be so much more careful with boiling water and with cooking in general, even with seemingly innocuous ingredients and techniques. However, I've since worked up the nerve to use my crème brûlée blowtorch so I seem to be back in the culinary saddle! **GUY**

HOW TO READ RECIPES AND OTHER USEFUL TIPS

• Read any new recipe through in full before you start cooking. Laying out and preparing the ingredients you need also helps.
• If you're buying pre-packed foods make sure you read the instructions.
• Most recipes in this book can be halved or doubled but spices and seasonings don't usually need to be changed that much.
Use a little bit less or a little bit more, tasting as you go.
• Vegetables take different times to cook. Account for this when you're timing a meal.
• Ovens – particularly student ovens – are temperamental and can be slightly hotter or cooler than the norm'. (In a gas oven the top of the oven is always hotter than the bottom.) If you find your food is generally overcooked use a setting lower than I recommend. If it's undercooked turn it up a setting. Don't keep opening the oven door while food is cooking.
• Always preheat the oven before you put the food in.
• Remember what time you put the food on to cook (a timer helps).
• Don't use the same cooking fat continuously – it will taste rank. And don't pour fat down the sink – it'll block it. Cool it, then pour it into a disposable container like a yoghurt pot and put it in the bin.
• Plates and pans are easier to wash when you've finished using them rather than three days later. If you have got to that stage soak them first.
• It's much easier (and more hygienic) to wash up in hot water than lukewarm or cold.
• If you use a metal spoon, scourer or Brillo pad on a non-stick pan you'll ruin it.

TOP STUDENT TIPS

 Dishes that are familiar, such as a beloved chilli recipe, can be improvised but that's not the case for dishes which are unfamiliar, or for those that require a certain order of cooking or a chemical reaction. Take baking, for example: there is a logic to recipes for cakes, cookies and bread that requires due diligence before you start. Too much bicarbonate of soda will result in a soapy-tasting cake. Too much butter and you'll have a greasy, dense texture. Adding eggs at the wrong juncture can mean disaster. Pastry requires carefully calibrated ratios of ingredients because too much liquid will strengthen the gluten in flour, resulting in a tough shortcrust. Try free-wheeling with choux pastry and you might as well make rock cakes. **SIG**

A GUIDE TO THE SYMBOLS

The top of each recipe page features some cryptic-looking symbols. Here's what they mean:

| VEG | £ | 5m | 5m |

The green box will tell you if it is suitable for vegetarians (see the index for a list of vegan recipes). **The orange box** will give you a rough indication of cost; **£** being a real budget recipe, **££££** a wantonly extravagant one. Most will depend on what ingredients you already have in your fridge or storecupboard. **The two red boxes** refer to time: the first box to preparation time and the second one to cooking time. Those recipes which don't require cooking or next-to-no preparation may only have one figure. You may also need to allow time for resting, cooling or chilling, so read the recipe carefully.

DO MEASUREMENTS MATTER?

Some of the best cooks cook without measuring anything so why bother with measurements? Because while chefs are used to measuring things by eye, feel and taste, if you haven't cooked much before you're more likely to succeed if you know roughly how much of what to put in. That said you don't have to take what I say as gospel. If I recommend using 400g of onions and you only have 350g that's not going to make a big difference. But doubling the quantity of a strongly flavoured spice like chilli powder is. Some measurements are approximate, leaving it up to you how much to add – one or two cloves of garlic for instance. Others take account of the fact that you may not have a set of measuring spoons, a measuring jug or scales. When I say 'teaspoon', an ordinary teaspoon will do but keep it level (i.e. the ingredients should be level with the rim of the spoon). A rounded teaspoon would be slightly more than that. There are 3 teaspoons in a tablespoon. If you haven't got a tablespoon use a large serving spoon. This is quite a useful way to measure out butter, particularly soft butter. The amount you would cut off with a tablespoon is about 15g. Sometimes with herbs or greens like spinach I'll recommend a handful. Which is exactly that – the amount you can pick up and hold in your hand (without trying overhard to cram it in). An ordinary mug is a reasonably good measure for liquid. If you fill it up to the level you'd normally fill it for a coffee, it'll hold about 225–250ml.

So far as cooking terms are concerned I've tried to keep it simple but if a phrase has slipped in you don't understand or if something goes horribly wrong you can e-mail me at **fiona@beyondbakedbeans.com**

TOP STUDENT TIPS

As a fledgling cook, it's pretty essential that you have a recipe to work from. It's unlikely that you are going to know instinctively how much of this or that is needed to make a dish taste good, or how much time it takes to cook. But the real fun in cooking comes once you are familiar with certain techniques, and you can start trusting your instincts. I adore cookbooks for the ideas they give me, but it's much more satisfying to be able to cook a meal without having to slavishly follow one. No recipe is a divine rule. So just because your flatmate does something differently to you, don't be bullied into thinking they are right. The most important thing to do when you cook is think and taste. Before you add an ingredient, ask yourself whether you are adding it because you think it will improve the flavour, or if you're adding it for the hell of it. Then taste. And taste again. Before long you will know instinctively what works and what doesn't. **JAMES**

QUICK & EASY MEALS FOR 1 OR 2

There are times when you need to eat quickly. On your own or maybe just making enough for you and a flatmate. It's certainly not worth putting on the oven so these are mainly things you can make in a saucepan or a wok. Some of them are more complicated than others, but you can do them all in under 30 minutes. And they'll taste a lot better than pot noodles. Promise.

HOW TO COOK EGGS

Eggs, let's face it, are a lifeline. For a couple of pounds you can make yourself three meals and never have them the same way twice.

BOILED EGGS

Start with the eggs at room temperature (if you prick the base with a pin or special egg pricker it will lessen the risk of them cracking). Bring a small pan of water to the boil. Place each egg in a spoon and lower it carefully into the water. Boil for 3$\frac{1}{2}$–4 minutes (medium eggs) and 4–4$\frac{1}{2}$ minutes (large eggs) for a yolk runny enough to dunk toast in. (A timer helps.) For hard-boiled eggs continue to boil for 10 minutes in total. Remove the eggs and transfer them to a pan or bowl of cold water. To peel, crack them gently against a hard surface and peel off the shell under running water.

FRIED EGGS

Heat a frying pan for a couple of minutes until moderately hot then add 3 tablespoons of (clean!) cooking oil. Crack the egg(s) on the side of the pan (or on the edge of a cup if you feel a bit nervous about it) and break the egg(s) into the pan. Cook for a couple of minutes then add a small lump of butter to the pan, tilt it, holding the handle, and spoon the hot butter and oil over the eggs so the yolks cook thoroughly and the whites puff up.

POACHED EGGS

Not the easiest of techniques without a poacher. I've tried various different ways of doing it but I don't think you can beat the Delia method. Which basically is to boil a kettle of water and pour it into a saucepan or frying pan to a depth of 2.5cm. Put the pan over a low to moderate heat and when the water looks as if it's about to boil (little bubbles will appear on the base of the pan) slide the egg in. (This is easier if you break it into a cup first.) Let the egg cook for a minute – the water should be trembling rather than boiling – then turn off the heat and leave it in the pan for another 10 minutes. Scoop it out with a slotted spoon, place it on a piece of kitchen towel to mop up the water then serve on buttered toast, spinach or whatever. The considerable advantage of this method is that you can; a) poach more than one egg at once; b) the egg white doesn't go flying all over the place like it does when you attempt to slip it into fast-boiling water (provided your egg is scrupulously fresh – very important, that); and, c) it doesn't taste of salt or vinegar – the traditional additions to the poaching water. The one downside is that it takes 10 minutes. Can you wait? If not, fry it.

SCRAMBLED EGGS

Break 2 large fresh eggs into a bowl and beat them with a fork. Add a little milk and season with salt and pepper. Place a small, preferably non-stick, pan on a gas or electric ring, set on a very low setting. Add the butter and let it melt, then tip in the eggs. Stir them continuously till the mixture starts to solidify (anything from 3–5 minutes), then keep stirring till you have a rich creamy golden mass. Serve on hot buttered toast. (If you want to add mushrooms to your scrambled egg it's better to cook them first then set them aside, wipe the pan then make your scrambled eggs from scratch, otherwise you'll find you have dirty grey eggs, which will taste fine but just look pretty yucky.)

MUSHROOM OMELETTE

SERVES 1

There's a great deal written about how difficult it is to make a perfect omelette but don't let that put you off. It's a doddle really.

2–3 large fresh eggs, preferably free-range
salt and freshly ground black pepper
25g butter
5–6 button or chestnut mushrooms (about 100g), rinsed and sliced

Crack the eggs into a bowl and beat them with a fork till the yolks and whites are well amalgamated. Add salt, pepper and a dessertspoon of water and beat again. Heat a small non-stick frying pan and add half the butter. When it starts foaming, tip in the mushrooms and stir-fry them for about 3 minutes until beginning to brown. Scoop them out of the pan, wipe the pan with a scrunched up piece of kitchen towel and place it back on the heat. Add the remaining butter and pour the beaten egg into the pan. Working quickly, keep lifting the egg away from the edges of the pan so that the liquid egg runs underneath and solidifies. When almost all the liquid egg has disappeared tip the mushrooms back onto the omelette, let it cook for another 30 seconds, then with a plate ready, ease a spatula under one side of the omelette and fold it over, tipping the pan as you do it so that the omelette rolls onto the plate. (Don't worry if it isn't very neat the first time you do it. It gets easier with practice.)

• You can put all kinds of other fillings in an omelette – grated cheese, tomato or fresh chopped herbs, for example.

TOP STUDENT TIPS

 Eggs, you might be surprised to learn, should not be stored in the fridge. Having the porous shell that they do, eggs will absorb other flavours, which, unless you have a fridge full of truffles, is probably not a good thing. On top of that, they should always be cooked from room temperature – if you've ever struggled with baking, it might well be because your eggs are too cold. **JAMES**

 Soft-boiled eggs are true comfort food. Ignore the losers who don't eat egg yolks because they contain fat – it's good fat! **SIG**

 I strongly recommend buying an egg poacher. They make poaching so much easier and can be bought for about £10. Cook the eggs in a slither of butter to make them really luxurious and season well. I use my egg poacher at least twice a week for quick lunches and weekend breakfasts. **GUY**

'eggs: your versatile friend'

ULTIMATE FRY-UP

SERVES 1

You probably know how to cook a fry-up but here's a good basic recipe.

Heat the pan and the oil for at least a couple of minutes before you start. Buy small chipolata sausages (they cook more quickly) and get them on first. Next the tomatoes: cut them in half, season with salt and pepper and put them in the pan, cut side down. Turn them after about 3 minutes. If you're using cheap bacon it helps to microwave it briefly first to get rid of the goo that otherwise oozes into the pan. To do this lay 2–3 rashers on a plate, cover loosely with a sheet of kitchen towel and cook on HIGH for a minute. Then pat them dry before you fry them – they'll be crisper. Crack the eggs into a saucer before you add them to the pan – you're less likely to break the yolk. Tilt the pan and spoon the hot fat over them as you cook them to set the yolks. If you only have a medium-sized frying pan cook the sausages, tomatoes and bacon, then put them aside on a warm plate. Wipe the pan, add a little more oil or some oil plus butter and cook the eggs.

TOP STUDENT TIPS

Hash browns are also a good addition: grate some onion and potato and squeeze out all excess water. Season, from into little cakes and then fry in a little butter. **GUY**

'what student doesn't love a fry-up?'

SPRING VEGETABLE FRITTATA

SERVES 2

A frittata is a great way of using up the previous night's veg – and any other bits and pieces in the fridge. You can either make a deep one and cut it into wedges or make it thinner, more like an omelette, and use it to stuff a pitta bread or roll.

1 tbsp olive oil
$\frac{1}{2}$ bunch of spring onions, trimmed and finely sliced or a small onion, peeled and finely chopped, or a trimmed and finely chopped leek
175g cooked new potatoes, cut into small cubes
60g cooked or thawed frozen peas or podded and skinned broad beans
60g lightly steamed purple sprouting broccoli or broccoli
5 large, fresh, free-range eggs
1 heaped tbsp finely chopped parsley (optional)
salt and freshly ground black pepper

Preheat a grill on medium heat. Heat the oil in a small (20 cm) frying pan and fry the chopped onion gently for a minute or two until softened. Add the cubed potatoes, peas and broccoli, stir and heat through without browning for another 3–4 minutes. Beat the eggs and season with salt and pepper. Turn the heat up under the vegetables for a minute then pour in the egg mixture. Using a palette knife, or round-bladed knife, lift the sides of the frittata so the liquid egg falls back underneath. Cook for about 3–4 minutes until the underside of the frittata is nicely browned then pop the pan under the grill for another 4 minutes or so, until the remaining liquid egg has puffed up and browned and the top is firm. Cool for 10 minutes then serve warm or cool and refrigerate.

TOP STUDENT TIPS

 The perfect springtime meal! Alternatives to broccoli could be a small chopped courgette or some peeled and chopped up asparagus stalks. If you want to make it more substantial and meaty you could add a roughly chopped thick slice of ham, cooked sausage or chorizo, or some crisply fried and crumbled bacon. Flaked cooked or smoked salmon and smoked haddock are also good with eggs. If you whizz it up from your leftovers the night before, it means you've got a ready-made light lunch or packed lunch to take to uni' the following day. **SIG**

BANANA & HONEY PORRIDGE

If you find regular porridge a bit bland, try this indulgent version.

1 small, ripe banana, sliced
3 tbsp porridge oats (25–30g)
100ml semi-skimmed milk
2 tsp clear honey or about 1 tbsp soft brown
   sugar, Demerara sugar or ordinary sugar

Peel and slice the banana and put it in a small non-stick saucepan with the oats, milk and honey and bring slowly to the boil. Turn the heat down and simmer for 3–4 minutes. A spoonful of double cream is particularly yummy stirred in at the end. You could also add a few chopped nuts if you have some. Almonds would be especially good.

TOP STUDENT TIPS

If you make extra porridge you can reheat it the next day. All you do is add a little bit of liquid (milk or water will do), place the porridge in the microwave or in a saucepan on the hob and you can re-heat it in a minute. **SIG**

APPLE & RAISIN MUESLI

SERVES 1

If you don't have a pack of muesli you can make it with porridge oats and a few raisins.

3 tbsp porridge oats
100ml apple juice or milk
a handful of raisins
a few chopped nuts if you have some
1 tsp soft brown sugar
1/2 crisp apple, cored and peeled
plain or soy yoghurt, to serve

Spoon the oats into a cereal bowl. Pour over the apple juice or milk, stir in the raisins, and nuts if you have some, add the sugar and leave for 5 minutes. Grate the apple into the bowl, adding a little more liquid if you think it needs it. Serve with yoghurt.

HOW TO MAKE YOUR OWN MUESLI

You may not save much cash by making your own muesli, but the motivation for making it lies in knowing exactly what goes into your breakfast cereal. Commercial granola-style mueslis often have more sugar and fat than you'd expect from a 'healthy' breakfast option, and a lot of Swiss-style mueslis taste like sawdust or are too sweet. So, here's my muesli mix that can be eaten on its own with yoghurt or milk, or soaked overnight as 'bircher' muesli in milk or apple juice. Come wintertime it can be cooked to make a tasty porridge too. **SIG**

For 2–3 weeks' worth of muesli you will need
500–750g jumbo oats (preferably organic) or any mix of grains you like (such as rye, barley, millet, spelt)
a large handful of dried cranberries that have been sweetened in grape juice (not sugar)
a large handful of dried cherries or blackcurrants
a large handful of dried coconut shavings
a large handful of hazelnuts/almonds/pecans/cashews (all unsalted)
a large handful of linseed and/or hemp seeds
if you like some sweetness in your muesli, then a generous sprinkling of chopped, dried dates or good old raisins also work a treat
if you're feeling adventurous, add some cinnamon, cardamom or nutmeg to this mix (coriander seeds are also surprisingly satisfying, but not to everyone's taste)

All you do is mix these ingredients in a large tupperware container, shake a few times to distribute all the fruit, nuts and seeds and seal so they keep for a few weeks.

To make bircher muesli take a portion of muesli and place in a bowl, grate in half an apple then pour in milk or fruit juice. Cover and refrigerate your bircher mix overnight, eat as it is the next day or with some fruit compôte or cream.

'apple and raisin muesli'

AMERICAN BREAKFAST PANCAKES

SERVES 2

Don't be daunted if you've never made pancakes before. These are a doddle.

125g plain flour
2 level tsp caster sugar
1/4 level tsp fine sea salt
1 1/2 level tsp baking powder
1 large fresh free-range egg
150ml whole (i.e. not skimmed or semi-skimmed) milk
40g of butter, melted
1 x 125g carton blueberries and/or raspberries
a small carton of Greek yoghurt or plain low-fat fromage frais
some clear honey

To make the pancakes, mix the first 4 ingredients together in a bowl leaving a hollow in the centre. Lightly beat the egg, mix with the milk and a tablespoon of the melted butter and gradually pour into the flour stirring with a wooden spoon until it is mixed in. Don't worry if it looks a bit lumpy.

Heat a non-stick frying pan over a moderate heat, pour in a little of the remaining melted butter and spread it over the pan with a piece of kitchen towel. Place four tablespoons of the pancake mixture into the pan, leaving a space between them. Let them cook for about a minute until bubbles begin to appear on the surface, then flip them over with a spatula and cook them for 45 seconds on the other side. Stack them on a plate covered with a clean tea-towel and repeat the process until all the mixture is used up, greasing the pan with melted butter before you cook each batch. Place three or four pancakes on each plate, with a mound of blueberries and a dollop of fromage frais or yoghurt, drizzled with a little honey.

TOP STUDENT TIPS

 I like my pancakes flecked with blueberry, adding not only colour but also texture to your pancake. This can be quite simply achieved by finely chopping half of your blueberries and stirring them into your batter mix. Another heavenly and super-traditional addition to pancakes is maple syrup, yet I often find that you end up with a syrup-drenched top pancake while the rest stay bone-dry. Well those days are over, my friend. Take a knife and cut down the centre of the pancakes, gouging out a hole the size of a two-pence piece in the middle, and pour the syrup into it all the way to the top, so that the sweet ambrosia permeates every level of pancake.
JAMES

OTHER IDEAS FOR FRUITY BREAKFASTS

BRAMLEY APPLE & BLACKBERRY COMPOTE

SERVES 4

One of the reasons, we're convinced, that students don't eat more fruit is that half of it is unripe and sour, but you can get round this by cooking it in a little water and sugar. Fruits that respond to this treatment are Bramley apples, rhubarb, berries like blackberries and blackcurrants and stone fruits like plums and apricots. (You can use a mix of fresh and frozen fruit.) Bramley apples are the best to use for cooking. They have a great flavour and go fabulously fluffy.

2 large Bramley apples
125g blackberries, picked wild or bought in season (late summer) or 125g mixed frozen fruits
about 3 tbsp caster sugar (preferably unrefined)

Quarter, peel, core and slice the apples and put them in a saucepan. Tip in the berries and add 3 tablespoons of sugar and 2 tablespoons of water. Put a lid on the pan and heat over a moderate heat until the fruit softens and collapses (about 10–15 minutes), stirring it occasionally. Pull the pan off the heat and check for sweetness, adding more sugar if you think it needs it. Give it a vigorous stir if you want a purée, rather than chunky fruit. Cool and refrigerate. To make your own fruit yoghurt, mix a good tablespoon of the compôte with 2–3 tablespoons of plain yoghurt.

WINTER RASPBERRY COMPOTE WITH YOGHURT AND TOASTED OATMEAL

Frozen raspberries – like other berries – are frequently cheaper frozen than fresh and provide a touch of summer sun in the depths of gloomy winter.

SERVES 4

250g raspberries or frozen mixed berries
2 tbsp unrefined caster sugar
200g plain or Greek yoghurt
40g toasted oatmeal (see below) or muesli

Tip the fruit into a saucepan, add the sugar, bring to the boil and simmer for two minutes. Take the pan off the heat, cool for 10 minutes then mix roughly with yoghurt to create a streaky, marbled effect. Spoon into tumblers or glass dishes and sprinkle with toasted oatmeal or muesli. To toast oatmeal, tip coarse (pinhead) oatmeal onto a baking tray and cook in a moderate oven (about 180C/350F/Gas 4) for 8–10 minutes.

TOP STUDENT TIPS

 Warm leftover compôte can turn back-of-the-freezer vanilla ice cream into a more interesting dessert. The fruit salad, opposite, can also be used as either a pudding or a light starter before a more substantial main course. *GUY*

STRAWBERRY & APRICOT FRUIT SALAD WITH ORANGE AND MINT

A great way of stretching a small punnet of strawberries and/or jazzing up a cheap can of apricots. Looks pretty too!

SERVES 4

250g fresh strawberries, hulled
1 tsp caster sugar
1 x 400g tin apricot halves in apple juice
1 orange
4–6 mint leaves (optional)

Slice the strawberries into a glass bowl and sprinkle over the sugar, stir and leave for 5 minutes. Drain the apricots, reserving the juice for another use (like a smoothie).

Halve the apricot halves and add them to the bowl. Squeeze the orange juice and strain over the fruit and gently mix together. Chill for an hour if possible. Tear or shred the mint leaves and scatter them over the salad.

MORE FRUIT (AND NUT) TIPS

• One of the best snacks you can have in the winter are clementines – they're easy to take with you to lectures, won't make a mess when you eat them (but be sure to throw the peel away rather than leave them in lecture halls!), and are full of vitamin C. Look for the ones with a slight green-yellow tinge as this will indicate they were recently picked. Also, go for the smaller clementines which give a bit when you squeeze them, the rock-hard ones are usually lacking in juice.

'a simple fruity breakfast'

TOP STUDENT TIPS

 To jazz up clementines, or any other citrus fruit for that matter, slice them, sprinkle on some cinnamon, along with a drizzle of honey and then add some walnuts or almonds: a simple, nutritious snack, breakfast or even a light dessert.

Dried fruit can also be stewed and added to your porridge or eaten with a bowl of plain yoghurt. All you do is take some apricots and prunes (or any combination of dried fruit you happen to have), place in a small saucepan and cover with water. Add some spices like cinnamon, nutmeg or cardamom, or a dash of vanilla extract or essence. Tea also adds a nice flavour, especially if you have some Earl Grey or Lady Grey, but regular builders' or Rooibos also gives a great taste. You just have to simmer the fruit for 5–10 minutes and the sugars will leach out of the fruit, creating a delicious syrup. Let the syrup reduce until it's sticky (be careful it doesn't burn) then pour over your porridge or yoghurt. **SIG**

SUPER SMOOTHIES (AND ROUGHIES...)

If you can't face anything substantial first thing in the morning (or before an exam) smoothies are a great way to boost your energy levels and get your essential nutrients on board. If you haven't got a blender, make a roughie....

A SUPER-SIMPLE SMOOTHIE

SERVES 1

Basically, what you need for a smoothie is a banana, some yoghurt and some other sharp fruit or fruit juice plus a bit of honey to sweeten to taste. This is the business.

125ml good quality orange juice (preferably the freshly squeezed type)
1 medium ripe banana
2 large spoonfuls of yoghurt
1 tsp runny honey

Peel and slice the banana and put in the blender or food processor along with the yoghurt and honey. Whizz until smooth, then add the orange juice and whizz again. Pour into a large glass. Remember to clean the blender once your exam is over!

SIG'S ENERGISING RASPBERRY & GINGER SMOOTHIE

Sig's recipe is more sophisticated. The oats and peanut butter will give you an extra energy boost.

a handful of frozen raspberries (or fresh, if cheap)
200ml plain bio yoghurt or soy yoghurt
2–3 tbsp porridge oats
1 banana, peeled

1–2 tsp grated fresh ginger (optional, but gives it a kick)
juice of 2 oranges
1 tsp peanut butter

Blitz everything together in a blender and drink.

BANANA, YOGHURT & HONEY ROUGHIE

SERVES 1

Just add everything together. Easy peasy.

1 ripe banana
1 large dollop plain, low-fat yoghurt
a little runny honey, to sweeten
a handful of muesli (optional)

Peel and slice the banana into a bowl and mash thoroughly with a fork. Add the yoghurt and a little honey to taste (I suggest about half a teaspoon). Mash again. That's it. If you want a bit more crunch add a handful of muesli.

TOP STUDENT TIPS

You can also add a teaspoon of peanut butter (or any nut butter) to this roughie – a great source of protein and essential fatty acids, both of which the brain needs on a daily basis. Try adding cinnamon and/or freshly grated ginger for a spicy twist too. **SIG**

RASPBERRY RIPPLE ROUGHIE

SERVES 1

$^1/_2$ small punnet of raspberries or around 60g
   of frozen raspberries, thawed
$^1/_2$–1 tsp caster sugar
2 tbsp of plain, low-fat yoghurt

Put the raspberries in a bowl and mash
thoroughly. Sweeten to taste with sugar. Half-stir
in the yoghurt leaving it streaky (yes, I know
you're only making it for yourself but it still looks
more appealing than making it bright pink). As
with the previous roughie, add a handful of
muesli if you fancy it.

VARIATIONS

• Instead of raspberries, try other summer
berries such as blueberries or blackberries.
Other fruit, such as mangoes and peaches in
summertime, are also great. Passionfruit is
always a winner, but kiwi most definitely not
(goes a horrible sludgy colour when mixed with
orange juice, etc.).

'raspberry & ginger smoothie and
banana, yoghurt & honey
roughie'

EASIEST EVER CHEESE ON TOAST

SERVES 1

My patented method of making cheese on toast which stops the cheese going hard and stringy and keeps the bread crisp rather than going soggy. Halfway to a Welsh rarebit but quicker and easier.

**a good chunk (about 75g) mature Cheddar
or Lancashire cheese
1 tsp flour
1 tsp brown sauce or $\frac{1}{2}$ tsp Dijon mustard
or $\frac{1}{4}$ tsp English mustard
2 tbsp milk
a couple of thick slices of wholemeal bread**

Grate the cheese and put it into a small saucepan. Mix in the flour and the milk. Heat gently, stirring, while you make the toast. As soon as the cheese mixture is smooth, stir in the brown sauce or mustard. Pour over the toast.

TOP STUDENT TIPS

 My favourite version of this dish hops back and forth across the Channel, incorporating Dijon mustard but also the quintessentially British Cheddar cheese. Not one for the short-on-time, this, but I promise it is worth the wait. Take a couple of large onions and peel and slice them. Cook them slowly – I'm talking like an hour – over a very low heat in 25 grams of butter, with some fresh thyme leaves and some salt and pepper, until they are golden and gooey and slippery. Spread a couple of lightly toasted pieces of bread with Dijon mustard and crème fraîche, top with a generous spoonful of onions, then lay a few slices of Cheddar cheese on top. Toast under a grill until lightly browned and oozing.
JAMES

PAN-FRIED CHEESE AND ONION TOASTIE

SERVES 1

Here's how to make a toastie without using a sandwich maker. Use decent quality bread, otherwise the whole thing will just be a soggy mass. This works well with a green salad.

2 medium-cut slices of wholemeal or good quality white bread
soft butter or butter-based spread
4–6 thin slices of mature Cheddar cheese – depending on the size of your bread
1 small onion, peeled and very finely sliced
freshly ground black pepper or a few drops of hot or mild pepper sauce

Butter both sides of one slice of bread and one side of the other slice. Lay the slice that only has one side buttered on a plate with the buttered side downwards. Top with a layer of cheese and a layer of sliced onion and season with pepper or pepper sauce, then place the other slice of bread on top. Heat a small frying pan over a moderate heat for about 2 minutes (without any oil) then place the sandwich in the pan. Let the bottom side cook for about $1^{1}/_{2}$ minutes then carefully turn the sandwich and let the other side cook, pressing down firmly on the top of the sandwich with a spatula. Flip the sandwich over a couple more times till the outside is nice and brown and the middle deliciously gooey.

TOP STUDENT TIPS

 Toasties are the perfect snack to eat before going out for the night. Quick, filling and full of alcohol-absorbing goodness. Use a generous amount of butter to stop any charring. Bacon and blue cheese is also a deliciously salty filling. Serve with a dressed green salad; the vinaigrette really cuts through. GUY

BRIE AND MUSHROOM MELT

SERVES 1

You might not think of using Brie for cheese on toast but it works really well, especially with mushrooms. Brie's a good cheap buy.

1 tbsp oil
a little butter
100g mushrooms, rinsed and sliced
1/2 small baguette or 1/4 of a longer one
50g of Brie, thinly sliced
salt and pepper

Preheat your grill. Heat a small pan and add the oil, then, after a few seconds, the butter. When the butter has melted, tip in the mushrooms and stir-fry for 2–3 minutes. Take off the heat and season with salt and pepper. Split the baguette and put the bottom slice on a grill pan, cut-side upwards. Pile the mushrooms on top and cover with slices of Brie. Grill until the Brie melts. Put on a plate and top with the other piece of baguette, pressing down well. (You could, of course, simply make this on toast rather than as a sandwich.)

SEXED-UP TOMATOES ON TOAST

SERVES 1

Tomatoes on toast can be quite a feast if you use good bread, ripe tomatoes, olive oil and balsamic vinegar – all affordable luxuries.

2 tbsp olive oil
2 thick slices of sourdough bread or
    traditional French country bread or
    wholemeal bread (see footnote)
3 medium-sized ripe tomatoes, halved
a handful of washed rocket or watercress
    leaves (about half a small pack)
balsamic or wine vinegar
salt and freshly ground black pepper

Heat a ridged grill pan or frying pan until almost smoking (about 3 minutes). Rub a little oil into either side of the bread slices then lay them down on the pan. Turn them after a couple of minutes then keep turning until nicely browned. Put them on a plate. Add a tablespoon of oil to the pan. Season the tomatoes with salt and pepper then put them in the pan cut side down. Cook for about 2–3 minutes then turn them over and cook for another couple of minutes on the other side until soft. Arrange the rocket or watercress leaves on top of the bread and lay the tomatoes on top. Trickle over a little extra olive oil and a few drops of balsamic or ordinary wine vinegar.

• It actually helps with this recipe to have a bread that's a day or two old. Griddled toast is also good for fried and scrambled eggs.

ITALIAN BREAD 'PIZZA'

SERVES 2

If you've got some leftover french bread or ciabatta this is a good way to jazz it up. It works with muffins too. (If you're into pizza do read James' rant on page 211 as to why you should make your own.)

(If you're into pizza do read James' rant on page 211 as to why you should make your own.)

1/2 a ready to bake ciabatta or a small
  baguette
4–5 tbsp The Easiest Ever Pasta Sauce
  (see page 77) or other tomato-based pasta
  sauce or 2 sliced, ripe tomatoes
1/2 tsp oregano or herbes de Provence
1/2 a pack (about 125g) grated Cheddar,
  Lancashire or other medium to strong
  English cheese
freshly ground black pepper

(see page 77)

Cut the piece of ciabatta or baguette lengthways into two. (If using a baguette, press each half down firmly with the heel of your hand to make a flat surface.) Toast lightly on both sides. Spread the cut side with the pasta sauce or tomatoes, sprinkle over the oregano then cover with the cheese. Put back under a hot grill and grill for about 2–3 minutes until the cheese has melted. Grind over some black pepper.

VARIATIONS

Add some chopped up ham or salami or a bit of flaked tuna before you top with cheese.

TOP STUDENT TIPS

This faux pizza is a good fallback for time-short cooking before going out. It's great with pesto and sundried tomatoes. Don't put too much tomato sauce on the bread, or it will go overly soggy.
GUY

'a great cheat pizza recipe'

GARLIC MUSHROOMS ON TOAST

SERVES 2

One of the simplest, most delicious ways to eat mushrooms.

a small pack (about 250g) button mushrooms
1 tbsp olive oil
a small chunk of butter (about 15g)
1 small clove garlic, crushed or finely chopped or ½ tsp fresh garlic paste
1 tbsp double cream or crème fraîche (optional)
salt and pepper
squeeze of lemon juice (optional)

Rinse the mushrooms under cold water, removing any dirt and slice roughly. Heat a small frying pan over a moderate heat, add the oil, then the butter.

Once the butter melts, tip in the mushrooms and stir them around. Add the garlic then continue to cook for 4–5 minutes until browned. Stir in the cream, if using, and season with salt and pepper and a little lemon juice if you've added cream. Serve on hot buttered toast.

TOP STUDENT TIPS

Total comfort food. The cream or crème fraîche adds an extra richness. A bit of fresh parsley would dress up the mushrooms and... um... soften the blow of the garlic. If you don't fancy toast, try converting this to a pasta or rice dish – mushrooms cooked in this way will also work well as a side dish for roast chicken. **SIG**

SARDINE TARTINES

SERVES 1

If you shudder with revulsion at the thought of sardines, try this. (And remember it's boosting your brainpower!)

1 small can of sardines
1 thick slice of wholemeal bread
1 clove of garlic, peeled and cut in half
1 tsp fresh or Jif lemon juice
1 tbsp finely chopped fresh parsley
black pepper

Drain the oil or brine from the can. Cut each sardine in half lengthways, split it open and remove the backbone. Toast the bread and rub

with the cut garlic. Arrange the sardines on top of the toast and scatter over the parsley. Squeeze over the lemon and grind some black pepper. Good with a green salad.

TOP STUDENT TIPS

Not everyone digs sardines, but if you're a keen fish-eater and looking for ways to save money then this is a genius recipe. Look for sardines in chilli-infused oil – delicious. You'll never look at tuna in the same way again. As with the garlic mushrooms, above, adding a sprig of parsley or oregano is tasty but not essential. The squirt of lemon juice is! **SIG**

THOROUGHLY VERSATILE MUSHROOM & BACON SAUCE

SERVES 1-2

A cheap and easy sauce that goes well with rice or pasta. It can be used as a topping for toast or baked potatoes and makes a good pancake filling. Use small white or chestnut mushrooms, rather than the big flat ones which will turn your sauce a dirty grey.

2 tbsp vegetable, sunflower or olive oil
2 rashers of back bacon or 3–4 rashers of streaky, rind removed and chopped
1 small onion or $^1/_2$ medium onion, peeled and roughly chopped
1 small clove of garlic, peeled and crushed (optional)
125g button or chestnut mushrooms, rinsed and sliced
$^1/_4$–$^1/_2$ tsp paprika
1 tsp plain flour
100ml milk
3 tbsp double or whipping cream or crème fraîche
freshly ground black pepper and lemon juice to taste
1 tbsp chopped parsley (optional)

Heat the oil in a small pan and add the chopped bacon. Fry until it begins to brown then add the chopped onion, turn the heat down and cook for about 5–6 minutes until the onion starts to soften. Add the garlic and mushrooms, stir and cook for another 3 minutes. Stir in the paprika and flour, cook for another minute then pour in the milk and bring to the boil. Turn the heat down, add the cream and simmer for another 2–3 minutes. Season to taste with pepper and a good squeeze of lemon and stir in the parsley, if using.

TOP STUDENT TIPS

If you prefer your bacon crispy then it is essential that you buy the streaky variety. For a long time I couldn't work out why back bacon didn't get crispy – duh! Less fat to render means less crispiness (and less flavour). That said, sometimes back bacon fits the bill better – tucked between two chunky slices of white bread and with a liberal dollop of brown sauce, I think back bacon is a far superior cut of meat for the bacon sarnie.
JAMES

HOMEMADE SUBS

SERVES 2

We know Subway has amazingly cheap deals but let's face it, they're not particularly healthy. Make your own and taste the difference!

1 small baguette
Soft or spreadable butter or other spread
1 tsp Dijon mustard
1 pack salami, garlic sausage or mortadella – whatever's cheap
1/2 a pack of Jarlsberg, Emmental or Cheddar (about 125g)
a large pickled cucumber or some gherkins
freshly ground black pepper
1 tbsp mayonnaise

Cut the baguette vertically in half then split each half lengthways. Spread each cut surface lightly with butter or butter substitute. Spread the two bases with mustard then top with slices of salami, cheese and pickled cucumber or gherkins. Season with freshly ground black pepper, spread the cut side of the other 2 pieces of baguette with mayo and then press them down firmly on top to close the sandwich.

TOP STUDENT TIPS

Being part-American, I have a great affection for sandwiches and these 'hero' ones always remind me of New York. There's an hilarious episode in 'Seinfeld' wherein one of the characters discovers the aphrodisiacal qualities of a sandwich. Pickles, needless to say, are essential, as is good mustard. You want sharp, tangy flavours to really balance the blandness of cheese such as Emmental, and meat such as Mortadella. Try pastrami instead of sausage and extras such as olives, grilled red peppers, etc. If you have some salad that needs using up, chuck a few leaves in too. **SIG**

'make your own subs and taste the difference!'

ULTIMATE TUNA SANDWICH FILLING

SERVES 1

This is my daughter Kate's favourite sandwich filling (along with homemade BLTs!). It makes enough for 1 generously filled sandwich, a large wholemeal bap or pitta bread or two smaller rolls.

1/2 a medium (200g) can of tuna*
1 tbsp very finely chopped onion
1 heaped tbsp French-style mayonnaise
freshly ground black pepper
a little grated lemon rind or a small squeeze
   of lemon juice (optional but good)
1 small pickled cucumber or half a larger
   one, finely chopped (again optional, but
   pickled cucumbers are quite cheap)

Drain the tuna and tip into a cup or bowl. Break it up with a fork then mix in the onion and mayo. Season with freshly ground black pepper (you shouldn't need salt) and a little finely grated lemon rind or a small squeeze of lemon juice if you have some. Stir in the chopped pickled cucumber then fill your sandwich or roll(s) – having spread them first thinly with a soft butter (or other) spread. If you don't have any pickled cucumbers just top the tuna filling with thin slices of fresh cucumber, some snipped cress or some sprouted seeds.

* There is a debate about whether we should be eating tuna at all given the current state of the fishing stocks, though it's such a student staple I know many of you will find it hard to give up. If you can afford it, go for sustainable tuna approved by the Marine Stewardship Council (MSC).

LEFTOVERS

Pickled cucumbers are great in all sorts of sandwiches and rolls – smoked ham, salami, corned beef or pastrami and cream cheese (with smoked salmon if you feel like splashing out). After you've opened the jar keep them in the fridge.

TOP STUDENT TIPS

It's the lemon rind that really lifts this filling out of the ordinary; the sharpness cuts through the creamy mayo. I would argue that the pickled cucumbers are entirely essential as they bring a slight crunch that is great in between two slices of bread. Spring onions are less strong than regular onions when uncooked, so use whichever you prefer. **GUY**

I always opt for wholemeal bread instead of white bread for sandwiches – not only is wholemeal a slower-releasing source of energy but, IMHO, it tastes better than white. Admittedly a really good baguette or ciabatta is not to be under-estimated. Mayonnaise should be banned from all sandwiches. **SIG**

STUFFED PITTA BREADS
WITH FALAFEL, SALAD AND GARLICKY YOGHURT DRESSING

SERVES 2

Pitta bread, particularly wholewheat pitta bread, is one of the best, inexpensive breads you can buy. And one of the most versatile. You can not only stuff it, dunk it in dips like hummus and make brilliant croûtons with it (see below) but you can also use it as an instant pizza base. To make croûtons for soup or salads, cut the pitta breads (garlic ones are particularly good) into thinnish strips then across into squares (not too small otherwise it's a pain to turn them over when you fry them). Heat a large frying pan for 3–4 minutes then add about 6 tablespoons of oil and heat for another minute or so until really hot. Test the temperature by dropping a piece of pitta bread in the oil. It should sizzle but not burn. Tip the pitta squares in the oil, fry them for about 30 seconds then turn them over so that both sides are nice and brown. Remove them with a slotted spoon or a tablespoon and put them on a plate lined with kitchen paper to absorb any excess oil. Cool for 10 minutes before you use them.

For the dressing
2 large spoonfuls very low-fat yoghurt
1 small or ½ large clove of garlic, peeled and
   crushed
a pinch of cumin
salt

2 tbsp oil
200g pack falafel
3 plain or wholewheat pitta breads
½ an onion, peeled and thinly sliced
2 medium tomatoes, thinly sliced or a chunk
   of cucumber
some iceberg lettuce leaves or other salad
   leaves

To make the dressing, combine the yoghurt with the crushed garlic and cumin. Season with salt. Heat the oil in a frying pan and fry the falafel for about 5 minutes, turning them regularly so they cook evenly.

Turn them onto a plate and squash them slightly with the back of a fork. Heat the pitta breads under a grill or pop them in a toaster on a low setting. (You want them warm and puffy rather than hard.) Cut them in half, open up each half and stuff with the falafel, onion, slices of tomato, a few lettuce leaves and spoon over the yoghurt.

VARIATIONS

Other good pitta bread fillings include Mexican-style refried beans, spiced chickpeas, leftover dhal and grilled or barbecued veg and goats' cheese or hummus.

TOP STUDENT TIPS

 Ahh... falafel. Good falafel is the friend of veggies and carnivores alike, bad falafel – bah! Predictably the best ones can be found in Middle-Eastern delis or shops, but M&S does a decent version. If you have a grill, you could grill both the falafel and the pitta. Opt for wholewheat pitta if you have the choice; fibre definitely helps keep you going for longer. Being a total philistine, I would also add a dollop of ketchup. **SIG**

WHOLEMEAL WRAPS
WITH GRATED CARROT AND PEANUT BUTTER

SERVES 2

An easy but substantial packed lunch to make when you're revising.

2 large chapattis or wholemeal wraps
crunchy peanut butter, preferably organic
   (I like Whole Earth)
1 medium carrot (about 100g), peeled and
   grated
2 lemon wedges or some freshly squeezed
   lemon juice
1 good chunk of cucumber (about 100g),
   finely sliced
1 spring onion, trimmed and cut into fine
   short strips or a few finely sliced red onion
   rings
a few mint or coriander leaves (optional but
   good)
sweet chilli sauce, to serve (optional)

Heat a frying pan without any oil for about 2 minutes. Freshen the chapattis by warming them for a minute each side in the pan. Turn off the heat and let the chapattis cool while you prepare the vegetables. Spread one side of the chapattis with a layer of peanut butter, cover with grated carrot, squeeze over some lemon juice cover with a layer of sliced cucumber, a layer of sliced spring onion and a few mint or coriander leaves if you have some. Squeeze over a bit more lemon juice and trickle over some sweet chilli sauce. Roll up the wrap and eat or wrap in cling film to eat later.

VARIATIONS

You could also use this filling to stuff wholemeal pitta breads or wholemeal rolls.

TOP STUDENT TIPS

Anyone who has eaten a Magic Roll in Bristol will know the benefits of a good veggie wrap – crunchy and healthy(ish). Remember to use only the freshest vegetables, as anything less than throbbing with freshness will lack the crunch and flavour that is so essential. While optional, some mint or coriander (or a generous handful of flat-leaf parsley) will really perk this wrap up, and will work particularly well with the lemon juice. A dollop of garlic mayonnaise would be good too. **JAMES**

EASY ITALIAN TUNA AND BEAN SALAD

SERVES 1

The easiest salad in the book – the classic *tonno e fagioli*.

¹/₂ large tin of tuna (it's invariably better value to buy a large can of tuna than a small one; they're always on special offer)
¹/₂ a small/medium onion, finely sliced
¹/₂ a 400g tin of cannellini beans
2 tbsp Italian-Style Oil, Lemon and Parsley Dressing (see page 68)

Drain and flake the tuna. Drain and rinse the beans. Mix the two together with the onion and the dressing.

VARIATIONS

If you don't like raw onion substitute 2 sticks of celery, finely chopped.

TOP STUDENT TIPS

For some extra colour, add cherry tomatoes. Boiled eggs are also good with tuna, as in a Niçoise salad (below). **GUY**

EASY FRENCH TUNA AND BEAN SALAD

SERVES 1

What to do with the other half of your tin... the classic *salade Niçoise*.

¹/₂ a large tin of tuna
a small can of green beans
5–6 cherry tomatoes
5–6 black olives (optional)
2–3 chopped anchovies (optional)
2 tbsp French-Style Mustard Dressing (see page 68)

Drain and flake the tuna. Drain the beans, rinse under the cold tap and pat dry with kitchen paper. Halve the tomatoes. Mix them all in a bowl with the olives and anchovies, if using. Pour over the French dressing and toss together. Good with warm new potatoes

VARIATIONS

Obviously you could substitute fresh or frozen beans for the tinned ones – about 75–100g. Once cooked, refresh them under cold water and pat dry.

MIXED BEAN & CRUMBLY WHITE CHEESE SALAD

SERVES 2

An easy salad that makes a substantial meal.

400g can of mixed beans
2 spring onions, trimmed and finely chopped
    or 2 heaped tbsp finely chopped onion
100g Caerphilly, white Cheshire or
    Wensleydale cheese, cut into small cubes
1 portion Italian-style oil, lemon and parsley
    dressing (see page 68)
extra chopped parsley, to serve

Tip the beans into a sieve or colander and rinse well under the cold tap. Shake off the excess water and put in a bowl. Add the chopped onion and cubed cheese to the salad. Pour the dressing over the salad and toss everything well together and sprinkle with extra chopped parsley. Good with warm pitta bread.

TOP STUDENT TIPS

Beans are so versatile – I love them. What gives them the edge is that they're incredibly good for you, but also fill you up much better than a green salad might. An elegant and oh-so-Provençal accompaniment to grilled meat or fish is to drain some flageolet beans and warm them gently with a little chopped parsley, garlic, lemon juice and olive oil. Just remember that any leftovers should not be stored in the tin, for fear of giving your flatmates botulism – not fun. **JAMES**

GREEKISH SALAD

SERVES 1

'-ish' because I suggest you use Caerphilly or Wensleydale rather than twice-the-price Feta. 'British Salad' wouldn't sound as sexy!

a good chunk (75–100g) crumbly white
    cheese such as Caerphilly or Wensleydale
1/4 of a cucumber
5–6 cherry tomatoes
2–3 slices of raw, peeled onion
5–6 black olives (optional)
1/2 tsp dried oregano (optional)
2 tbsp Italian-Style Oil, Lemon and Parsley
    Dressing (see page 68) plus extra salt and
    lemon, to taste

Cut the cheese and cucumber into small chunks. Halve or quarter the cherry tomatoes, depending how big they are, and roughly chop the onion. Mix together all the ingredients in a bowl with the dressing. Taste and add extra salt or lemon juice if you think it needs it (the original would be quite salty because of the Feta but it's up to you). Good served with (or even stuffed into) warm pitta bread.

TOP STUDENT TIPS

You could also add some anchovies to this, though they're not to everyone's taste. Toasting or grilling some croûtons and adding them to the salad will stretch it even further as would adding cooked pasta shells or twists. But then you've got Greekish Pasta Salad, a slightly different affair. **SIG**

6 VEG + 1 FRUIT = 6 SALADS

Tomato + cucumber + pepper + celery + onion + carrot + apple

Most student fridges, I think it's fair to say, don't have a salad drawer crammed with fabulous ingredients. In my experience the contents are most likely to be tomatoes, peppers and cucumber with perhaps an onion and a couple of carrots in the veg rack, and a still unwrapped bag of apples lying around on a work surface. Add a bunch of celery, a few other inexpensive ingredients, and you can make any one of the following easy salads.

CARROT AND APPLE SLAW

Peel and grate a medium-sized carrot and put into a bowl. Add half an apple, grated and tossed in one tablespoon of lemon juice (to stop it going brown). You could also chuck in one or more of the following: a couple of finely shredded spring onions, some finely sliced celery or green pepper, a few raisins or sultanas or some cashew nuts if you have some. Add two tablespoons of sunflower oil or light olive oil, toss together and season to taste with salt and pepper and more lemon juice if it needs it. (You could also spice it up with a teaspoon of Moroccan Spice Mix, see page 107.)

TOMATO AND ONION (OR PLAIN TOMATO) SALAD

Slice a couple of ripe tomatoes and put them in a bowl. Take a couple of slices off a mild onion (preferably a red onion, or a large Spanish one), break it up into rings and add to the tomato, along with a little chopped parsley if you have some. Pour over a couple of spoonfuls of Budget Salad Dressing (see page 68) and mix well together. Leave for 5–10 minutes for the flavours to infuse.

TZATZIKI

Pronounced, 'zatziki', this is a simple Greek cucumber salad, similar to Indian raita.

Cut off a quarter of a cucumber, peel it and then grate it coarsely into a sieve or colander. Squeeze the grated cucumber with your hands to extract as much liquid as possible and transfer to a bowl. Add one crushed clove of garlic or a tablespoon of finely chopped onion, two heaped tablespoons of plain unsweetened yoghurt, a few drops of lemon juice or vinegar, one tablespoon of oil and a little chopped fresh mint if you have some. Mix. Good with spicy sausages or burgers – unless you're a veggie, of course – or with fried courgettes.

CHEESE, CELERY AND APPLE SALAD

Wash, trim and slice 2 sticks of celery. Quarter and chop a small apple and sprinkle the pieces with lemon juice. Add a good chunk of Cheddar cheese, cut into small cubes. You could also add a few leaves from a crunchy lettuce like a little gem or a small handful of walnuts if you have some. Mix 1 heaped tablespoon of yoghurt with 1 heaped tablespoon of mayo and mix with the salad. Check the seasoning, adding salt, pepper and more lemon juice to taste. Good with cold ham.

ARAB SALAD

Most middle eastern and Turkish restaurants offer something like this simple fresh salad which is almost more like a salsa. Peel, de-seed and finely chop a $1/4$ of a cucumber and place in a bowl. Add 1–2 chopped ripe tomatoes (depending on size), $1/2$ a small red pepper and 1–2 finely sliced spring onions, or a couple of slices of mild onion, all finely chopped. Whisk together 1 dessertspoon of lemon juice with $2 1/2$ dessertspoons of sunflower or light olive oil and season with salt and a pinch of chilli pepper and/or cumin if you have some. Add to the chopped vegetables (with 1 heaped tablespoon of chopped parsley, if available) and toss together.

CRUDITES

Cut all or any of the following – cucumber, carrot, celery and peppers – into strips and serve with garlic mayo, made by crushing $1/2$ a clove of garlic into 1 heaped tablespoon of mayonnaise mixed with 1 heaped tablespoon of low-fat yoghurt. Or use the Bang Bang dressing on page 118.

TOP STUDENT TIPS

I like this – the endless variations you can make work with a limited selection of veg, deploying just a bit of imagination. The Arab Salad is especially good. **SIG**

'some of these lurking in your salad drawer?'

'...or these?'

SALAD DRESSINGS

Even if you buy a bag of salad leaves it's well worth making your own dressing. Cheap bottled dressings are just as nasty as cheap cook-in sauces. The key thing is to use decent oil, preferably olive or sunflower oil. Vegetable and corn oil won't do anything for your salads.

ITALIAN-STYLE OIL, LEMON AND PARSLEY DRESSING

SERVES 1-2

1 dessertspoon fresh lemon juice
3 dessertspoons olive oil
$1/2$ clove of garlic, crushed (optional)
a little sugar, salt and freshly ground black pepper
1 tbsp finely chopped parsley

Shake the ingredients together in a jam jar or whisk in a bowl with a fork. Suits lettuce, mixed leaf and rocket salads, tomato salads and chickpea salads.

FRENCH-STYLE MUSTARD DRESSING

The classic 'vinaigrette'.

SERVES 1

$1/2$ tsp Dijon mustard
a little salt and freshly ground black pepper
1 dessertspoon wine vinegar
4 dessertspoons olive oil

Prepare as with Italian-Style. Suits lettuce and dark leaves like watercress and spinach, bean salads and potato salads.

BUDGET SALAD DRESSING

2 tsp wine vinegar or lemon juice
$2^1/2$ tbsp sunflower oil or, better still, olive oil
$1/2$ a clove of garlic, peeled and crushed (optional)
salt, pepper and a pinch of sugar

Put all the ingredients in a jam jar and shake well together, or whisk in a bowl with a fork. If you have some Dijon mustard, add $1/4$ of a teaspoon of that too.

ASIAN-STYLE LOW-FAT DRESSING

SERVES 1

Rice vinegar is not as acidic as wine vinegar so you don't need so much oil. If you can find organic sunflower oil at a reasonable price, snap it up – it has a much nicer, nuttier taste.

1 tbsp sunflower oil
1 tbsp seasoned rice vinegar
1 tsp soy

Shake or whisk together with a fork. Serve with a crunchy salad or with cold noodles.

TOP STUDENT TIPS

For most side salad dressings, I tend to use a simple olive oil/balsamic vinegar dressing. However, sometimes something creamier is called for. Mix olive oil, cider vinegar, plain yoghurt, Dijon mustard and seasoning for a versatile creamy dressing that doesn't use unhealthy mayo or cream itself. **GUY**

If you have any salad dressing left over keep it in the fridge otherwise the oil can go rancid. Take it out 15 minutes before you need it to allow it to come to room temperature and give it a good shake or whisk before you use it. **SIG**

'asian-style low-fat dressing'

'italian- and french-style dressings'

CARROT & CORIANDER SOUP

MAKES 4 BOWLS

Carrots make really, really good soup. To make soup velvety smooth you obviously need a machine like a blender or food processor to whizz it in – or to whizz in it. Those handheld blenders do a good job and are really cheap (see Kitchen Kit, page 15). You also need to base them on a vegetable with a dominant flavour or colour otherwise they can look like brown sludge. Swirling in a spoonful of yoghurt or cream at the end and sprinkling on some herbs will improve the appearance too.

2 tbsp sunflower oil or olive oil
1 medium onion, peeled and chopped or a
    couple of leeks, cleaned and roughly
    chopped
4 medium or 3 large carrots (about 350g),
    peeled and cut into rounds
1 medium potato, peeled and roughly
    chopped
a couple of sticks of celery (optional)
1 rounded tsp ground coriander or crushed
    coriander seeds
750ml vegetable stock made with 1 tbsp
    vegetable bouillon powder or a stock cube
salt and pepper
fresh coriander or parsley, chopped

Heat the oil in a large pan, add the onion, stir and cook over a low heat until soft (about 5 minutes). Add the carrots, potato and celery if using and stir again. Cover the pan with a lid or a piece of foil and cook very slowly for about 10 minutes. Stir in the ground or crushed coriander and pour in the stock. Bring to the boil and cook for about 20–25 minutes until the vegetables are soft. Blitz the soup with a hand held blender or put it through a blender or a food processor. Return to the pan and check the seasoning. Add salt and pepper to taste and a little extra water if you think it's too thick. Serve sprinkled with chopped fresh coriander or parsley.

VARIATIONS

You can replace the potato with a small can of butterbeans.

TOP STUDENT TIPS

Homemade soups are so simple and warming, great to have on cold evenings when you come back home from a day at uni'. Carrot and coriander go really well together. This soup should be smooth and creamy in texture. A hand blender is a really great bit of kitchen kit to have on hand to blitz soups and sauces. Add some good granary bread and a hunk of farmhouse Cheddar and this makes a full meal. **GUY**

Carrot cake, carrot and gherkin salad and cinnamon-glazed carrots are all good things to make with any carrot leftovers. **SIG**

PEA, BROCCOLI & MINT SOUP

MAKES 4 BOWLS

Eating your greens can sometimes seem a bit of a tyranny but one of the answers is to cunningly plunge them into a pea soup. The slight bitterness of the greens offsets the sweetness of the peas perfectly.

1 small head of broccoli (about 225–250g)
1 tbsp oil plus a small chunk of butter or 2 tbsp oil
1 small to medium onion, peeled and roughly chopped or 5–6 spring onions, trimmed and chopped
225g frozen peas
500ml stock made with 2 tsp vegetable bouillon powder or a chicken or vegetable stock cube
the leaves from a couple of sprigs of fresh mint or a small handful of fresh coriander or parsley
a small carton of single cream (optional)

Cut the florets of broccoli off the stalk then chop them roughly. Warm the oil in a large saucepan then add the butter and the onion, stir and cook over a gentle heat for about 5 minutes until soft. Add the peas and broccoli, pour in the stock and bring to the boil. Simmer until the vegetables are soft (about 6–8 minutes). Spoon the veg into a blender or food processor and whizz until smooth, gradually adding the rest of the liquid (you may have to do this in two batches). Pour the soup back into the saucepan and season with salt and pepper to taste. Finely chop the herbs and stir in just before serving. You could also add a swirl of cream.

VARIATIONS

You can cook the soup even more quickly if you microwave the broccoli first. Place the florets in a dish with a little boiling water, cover it with cling film, pierce the film, then cook on high for 3 minutes. Add to the soup with the peas and cook for about 2–3 minutes.

Alternatively, make the soup with a bunch of watercress or a handful of spinach instead of broccoli. Wash it, break off the tougher stems, chop it roughly and cook with the peas for about 2 minutes.

TOP STUDENT TIPS

 It is a fine line, and one I have oft erred the wrong side of, between careful cooking to keep the fresh green colour, and undercooking, leaving you with a bitty soup. A couple of minutes too early and the vegetables won't be sufficiently cooked to blend fully. Too late and you will end up with a beautifully smooth but less vibrantly coloured soup. So it's important to taste the broccoli before whizzing – it should not be al dente, but nor should it be entirely denture-friendly – essentially you want it to yield to the prod of a knife without dissolving into mush. Simple eh? Then blend thoroughly in batches, to make sure it is smooth and silky.
JAMES

SAD UNLOVED VEGETABLE SOUP

MAKES 4 BOWLS

Every so often you find sad, unloved vegetables lurking in the bottom of the fridge or the veg rack. Here's what to do with them providing they're not too far gone to be edible (i.e. not actually wizened, rotting or mouldy). This is more a strategy than a recipe. Here's how it goes....

1. Dig out whatever veg you have. A good basic combination is onions and/or leeks, carrots, and potato. Celery is fine too (a couple of sticks). Courgettes and broccoli are less good for this kind of soup – if you're adding them chuck them in a bit later, otherwise they'll go a nasty sludgy green.

2. Remove any skanky bits, yellowing outer leaves, etc. Leeks need washing thoroughly as they can have grit between the leaves so slice them finely and rinse them. Peel the carrots and onions and chop or slice.

3. Find a big saucepan, put a couple of tablespoons of oil in it and some chopped streaky bacon if you have some and fry until it starts to crisp. Then tip in the onions and/or leeks and carrots, give them a stir, put a lid on the pan and cook over a low heat for about 8–10 minutes, stirring occasionally. Peel and very finely slice the potato, if using, and stir into the other veg. (If you don't have any potatoes you could add some canned beans at the end.)

4. Make up 750ml of stock with a stock cube or 1 tablespoon of Marigold vegetable bouillon powder (I'd go for the latter which has a much more natural flavour and is considerably less salty; you can find it in most supermarkets). Pour the hot stock over the vegetables. Bring the soup to the boil then turn the heat down and simmer (cook slowly, letting the soup bubble away gently) until the vegetables are tender (probably about 15 minutes). If you haven't used a potato, drain and rinse a tin of cannellini or borlotti beans and add that instead.

5. Root around to see if you can find a handful of fresh parsley or some spinach or cabbage leaves. (If the latter, cut away the tough central rib on each leaf.) Shred or chop them and add them to the soup and cook for another 2–3 minutes. Season to taste with salt and pepper. That's it, although you could drizzle over a little olive oil or sprinkle over some Parmesan if you want.

If you want actual quantities I'd suggest a large onion, a large leek, a couple of carrots and a potato.

TOP STUDENT TIPS

 Nothing sad about this recipe – onions, carrots, leeks and potatoes make a brilliant base for tasty soups. In wintertime, try using other root veg such as swede, parsnips or turnips. Jerusalem artichokes are also great, though they're fiddly to peel. Other alternatives include cauliflower, sweet potato, pumpkin and squash. Frozen broad beans are useful to have on hand for soups like these, adding a bit of springtime green to an otherwise autumnal/winter soup. Lentils would make a hearty addition to the beans, as would barley or good old pasta twists or shells. **SIG**

THAI-STYLE SWEETCORN & SPRING ONION CHOWDER

SERVES 2-3

This is an odd but to my mind wholly successful integration of Thai flavours into an American chowder. Unless you're like my husband who likes neither sweetcorn nor coconut milk. Use fresh corn in season (July–September). It's cheap and has a really good flavour.

3 medium or 2 large whole corn on the cob or 200g frozen sweetcorn or a 325g can of sweetcorn, drained
1 bunch of spring onions or 1 medium onion, peeled and finely chopped
2 sticks of celery
2 tbsp sunflower or light olive oil
1 clove of garlic, crushed
1/4 tsp ground turmeric
2 mild fresh chillies, deseeded and finely sliced
1 medium potato, peeled and cut into small cubes
250ml vegetable stock made with 1 tsp Marigold vegetable bouillon powder
200ml coconut milk
1 tbsp lime or lemon juice
salt to taste
3 tbsp chopped fresh coriander

Cut the base off each cob and peel off the husks. Propping it upright on its base, cut off the kernels, cutting downwards with a small sharp knife, then go over the cob with a small teaspoon scraping off the rest of the corn and the milky juices. Cut the top half of the leaves and the roots off the spring onions and chop the rest roughly. Clean the celery and chop it into rounds. Heat the oil in a large saucepan for a minute or two, then add the corn, onions, celery, crushed garlic and turmeric and chilli. Stir, cover the pan and cook on a low to moderate heat for 5–6 minutes. Add the diced potato and hot vegetable stock, bring to the boil and simmer for about 20 minutes or until the vegetables are soft. Add the coconut milk and heat through then add the lime or lemon juice and season with salt to taste. Stir in the coriander and serve.

TOP STUDENT TIPS

 My dad, who is American, makes a really great New England chowder; but I prefer this one. It's really zingy and fresh and much lighter than the traditional chowder. You could also add clams, smoked haddock or mussels to dress it up or make a more substantial meal. **GUY**

HOW TO COOK PASTA

Pasta has to be the easiest, cheapest, quickest meal there is. You may well know how to cook pasta already but, if not, here's how. The tomato sauce opposite is a brilliant and simple accompaniment.

PASTA FOR ONE

The quantity of pasta depends on how hungry you are. The Italian brands are best; don't bother with fresh. The most common mistake people make is not using enough water – you need a litre for every 100g of pasta you cook.

100g–125g of dried pasta

Boil a full kettle and tip the water into a large pan. Bring back to the boil, add the pasta and about $^1/_2$ teaspoon salt, stir then cook for the time recommended on the pack. To check if the pasta is done hook a strand or piece out of the pan and bite into it. It should be neither hard nor soft and soggy. Drain it in a colander or sieve, saving a little of the cooking water to add to your sauce. Tip the pasta onto a plate or into a bowl and spoon over the sauce, or return the pasta to the pan then toss with enough sauce just to coat it lightly. Don't drown it.

TOP STUDENT TIPS

If you're into saving the planet and your pennies (as you should be, and as I'm sure you are), then follow this handy trick I picked up from the brilliant Richard Ehrlich (who I think got it from American food scientist Harold McGee): add the pasta, stir it, and when the water comes back to the boil stick a lid on and turn the heat off. The pasta will take a minute or two more than it says on the packet, but you've saved a good 10 minutes of gas. Whatever you do though, don't boil with the lid on, as I once did in a hurry – you'll end up with gluey, stodgy pasta. **JAMES**

'one of the quickest, easiest meals'

THE EASIEST EVER PASTA SAUCE

SERVES 1 (PLUS 1)

Given that there are dozens of different ready-made pasta sauces, you might wonder why bother to make your own. Simple: it's cheaper and it will taste better. Fresh herbs are always nicer than the dried ones they use in jars. This makes enough sauce for two meals – a plate of pasta plus enough left over to make a pizza topping or anything else for which you need a bit of tomato sauce.

2 tbsp olive oil
1 clove of garlic, peeled and crushed
1 x 400g tin of tomatoes in their own juice
salt, pepper and sugar to taste
2 tbsp chopped fresh parsley (optional)
Parmesan or Grana Padano, freshly grated

Heat the oil in a large frying pan. Add the garlic. Tip in the tin of tomatoes and crush with a fork or a wooden spoon. Season with salt, pepper and a pinch of sugar and simmer for about 10 minutes till thick and jammy. Stir in the parsley and cook for a minute. Spoon half the sauce over a plate of freshly cooked pasta and grate over some Parmesan.

VARIATIONS

You could also try adding:
• Half a can of tuna and either a few black olives or 1 tablespoon of capers rinsed and roughly chopped (this tastes better without cheese).
• A chopped red pepper fried in a little olive oil and a little chilli sauce.
• A small aubergine, cubed and shallow-fried.

TOP STUDENT TIPS

 When tomatoes are ripe in the summer you can use skinned chopped tomatoes instead. Take 4–6 tomatoes (about 400g) make a little cut in the skin near the stem, put them in a bowl and cover them with boiling water. After a minute, drain the tomatoes, pour cold water over them and peel off the skins. Heat a large frying pan over a moderate heat, add 2 tablespoons of oil, heat for a minute then add a crushed clove of garlic and a tablespoon of tomato paste. Stir, tip in the tomatoes and simmer over a low heat while you cook your pasta, following the recipe opposite. You can also add some drained, tinned tuna or fresh or frozen prawns or mixed seafood or top the sauce with crumbled goats' cheese. Fresh basil is also fab if you can find some at a reasonable price. **SIG**

BASIC BOLOGNESE

MAKES 3–4 MEALS FOR 1

A simple Bolognese sauce you can serve with spaghetti or other pasta or as a baked potato topping.

1 tbsp oil
400–500g beef mince
1 heaped tbsp concentrated tomato purée
1–2 cloves of garlic, peeled, crushed or finely chopped
1 level tsp oregano or herbes de Provence
1 x 400g tin of tomatoes
salt and pepper

Heat a frying pan over a moderately high heat for 2–3 minutes. Add the oil, swirl round the pan then add half the mince spreading it around. Fry until beginning to brown then turn it over with a wooden spoon or spatula. Keep frying until all the mince is browned (about 1¹/₂–2 minutes). Tipping the pan away from you so the fat runs away, scoop out the mince onto a large plate. Pour the fat that has accumulated in the pan into a cup or bowl to discard later. Put the pan back on the hob and repeat with the remaining mince, discarding the fat again at the end. Turn down the heat a little and return all the meat to the pan without any further oil. Add the tomato paste and stir into the meat until it is well distributed, stirring it all the time. Add the garlic, herbs and the tinned tomatoes, breaking them up with a fork. Season with salt and pepper, bring to a simmer then turn the heat right down and leave to cook gently for about 15 minutes. Spoon out a quarter to a third of the sauce to make Spaghetti Bolognese (see page 80), then divide the remaining sauce into 2 or 3 portions, cool and refrigerate them (ready to be used for the meal ideas on page 80).

TOP STUDENT TIPS

 A trick I learnt from my mother is to add a generous quantity of chopped green pepper to Bolognese sauce. This was something her mother always did and has now entered family lore as the best Bolognese trick ever, adding a whole other dimension of flavour. Lots of veggies are the key to making a good Bolognese stretch further: onion, celery, carrot, and of course that green pepper. Marmite gives an extra umami hit on top of tomatoes and deepens the Bolognese flavour. Don't shy away from pouring in a good glug of red wine too, especially if you're enjoying a glass whilst preparing the Bolognese. Cacao (pure unsweetened chocolate), and, while you're at it, a few anchovies, also won't go amiss. Italians might regard the addition of Marmite and chocolate as heresy, but IMHO they transform Bolognese from a humble meat and tomato sauce to '*ne plus ultra Bolognese*'. *Basta*. SIG

 Italian ragù – meaty tomato sauce – is a staple of my repertoire and should be of yours too. This recipe is a good jumping-off point, but the more you attempt it, the more personal touches you will add. I add a pack of minced pork along with the beef, other times Italian sausages get crumbled in to the mix. The cooking should be started a good few hours before you are ready to eat, so that the tomato sauce has plenty of time to reduce on a low heat. Pour any leftover sauce over *penne* and bake in the oven for a quick meal the next day. GUY

OTHER BOLOGNESE VARIATIONS

All of these recipes are great ideas for using up the extra portions of Bolognese you made on page 78.

WITH SPAGHETTI OR PASTA

you need 75–100g dried spaghetti or pasta shapes and some grated cheese

Cook the spaghetti according to the pack instructions. Top with a quarter to a third of the Bolognese and sprinkle with grated cheese – Parmesan if you have some, otherwise Cheddar.

A MINI SHEPHERD'S PIE

you need a medium to large potato and some Marmite

Cut a medium to large potato into 6–8 pieces, cover with cold water and bring to the boil. Cook for about 12–15 minutes until you can easily insert a knife through the potato pieces. Drain the potato, cut it up roughly and mash with a fork. Add a little warm milk and butter and season with salt and pepper. Meanwhile take a quarter to a third of the Bolognese mixture and put it in a small saucepan. Stir in half a teaspoon of Marmite (no more – it'll be too salty) dissolved in a tablespoon of hot water. Bring to the boil and simmer for 5 minutes. Heat up the grill. Put the mince in a small heatproof bowl or dish and cover with the mash. Pop the pie under the grill and brown. Serve.

CHILLI CON CARNE

you need half a pepper, a tin of red kidney beans and some mild chilli powder

Cut the pepper into small pieces. Heat a small frying pan, add a little oil (about 1 tablespoon) and fry the pepper for 3–4 minutes until beginning to soften. Add a teaspoon of mild chilli powder and $1/4$ teaspoon of ground cumin, if you have some, and stir. Mix in a quarter to a third of the Basic Bolognese. Drain a 400g tin of red kidney beans and rinse the beans under cold running water. Add half the beans to the mince (you can save the remainder for a salad.) Add 2 tablespoons of water, stir, and heat through until boiling. Turn the heat down and simmer for 5 minutes. Serve on its own or with boiled rice (see page 100).

KEEMA (SPICY MINCE WITH PEAS)

you need some curry paste and frozen peas. Fresh coriander is a good addition if you have some

Take a quarter to a third of the Bolognese mixture and put it in a small saucepan. Add half a mug of frozen peas, $1/2$–1 teaspoon of curry paste and 2 tablespoons of water and heat through until boiling. Turn the heat down, simmer for 5 minutes, then stir in some fresh coriander if you have some. Serve with rice or naan and an onion or cucumber raita (see page 171).

SPAGHETTI CARBONARA

SERVES 1

A pasta dish that is incomparably better made from scratch than spooned from a jar. It really is worth investing in some fresh Parmesan (or the slightly cheaper Grana Padano) for this; it's a luxury, but it keeps well in the fridge and a little goes a long way. Cheddar doesn't quite hit the spot for this recipe.

1 tbsp cooking oil
4–5 streaky bacon rashers, or 2–3 back rashers, rinds removed and chopped (about 75g in total)
1 small to medium onion, peeled and finely chopped
2 eggs, preferably free-range
2 tbsp freshly grated Parmesan or Grana Padano plus extra for serving
75–100g dried spaghetti
2 tbsp double or whipping cream
salt and ground black pepper

Heat the oil in a frying pan over a medium heat and fry the bacon until the fat begins to run. Add the onion, turn the heat down low and fry for another 5 minutes or until soft. Beat the eggs with 2 tablespoons of the Parmesan and season with pepper and a little salt. Cook the spaghetti in plenty of boiling water following the instructions on the pack. Once it's cooked, drain it thoroughly, saving a bit of the cooking water and return it to the pan off the heat. Quickly tip in the bacon, onion and beaten eggs and mix thoroughly so the egg 'cooks' in the hot pasta. Add the cream and a spoonful or two of the cooking water, add extra seasoning if needed then serve immediately with extra Parmesan.

TOP STUDENT TIPS

Everyone has their own spin on carbonara. This recipe is as close as it gets to my own except I add some chopped parsley after folding in the sauce. A tip on the order of adding eggs and cream: if your pasta is piping hot and you add the egg mixture you'll run the risk of scrambling the eggs. To be safe, add the cream before the egg which cools the spaghetti enough to stop the eggs scrambling. **SIG**

SPAGHETTI WITH BACON & COCKLES

SERVES 2

This recipe might sound a bit weird but cockles are basically like clams, which makes this a Welsh *spaghetti alla vongole*... with bacon... and Thai fish sauce, which sounds odd but just accentuates the fishiness of anything you add it to.

2 tbsp olive oil, plus extra for drizzling
3 rashers of streaky bacon, rinded and finely chopped
1 medium onion, peeled and finely chopped
1 small clove of garlic, peeled and crushed
1/2 a small glass of dry white wine or water (about 75ml)
1/2 tsp of Thai fish sauce (slightly more if you use water)
100g cockles (if you can't get fresh ones you could use a jar, though drain and rinse them before you add them to the sauce)
200g spaghetti
a small handful of parsley, finely chopped
freshly ground black pepper

Heat the oil in a frying pan over a moderate heat and add the bacon. Cook for a minute until the fat starts to run then add the onion, stir, turn the heat down and cook for about 10 minutes until the onion is soft and beginning to brown. Stir in the crushed garlic, cook for a minute then turn the heat up a bit and add the white wine and fish sauce. Bubble up for a minute then take the pan off the heat, tip in the cockles and set aside. Cook the spaghetti in boiling water for the time recommended on the pack. Spoon off 2–3 tablespoons of the cooking water into the bacon and cockles then drain the spaghetti. Return to the pan, heat the sauce through, tip it over the spaghetti along with most of the parsley and toss together. Divide the spaghetti between two warm shallow bowls, drizzle over a little olive oil, add a few grinds of pepper and sprinkle with a little more parsley.

TOP STUDENT TIPS

 While far from kosher, the combination of fish (and shellfish in particular) and pig is a classic one. When splashing out on occasion (or more usually catering for people who can afford it) I love the combination of seared scallops with black pudding and Jerusalem artichoke purée.
This rich man/poor man style of cookery is a joy, and works in a way that goes beyond simple ingredient pairing – it has a soul. Another excellent piggy number that goes well with fish is chorizo. Lightly fried in chunks until crisp on the outside (I'm talking about chorizo sausage here, not paper-thin vac-packed slices), it is a delight nestled around a (responsibly sourced) cod fillet, or tossed into a paella. JAMES

GUY'S SPAGHETTI WITH TUNA, TOMATOES & CAPERS

SERVES 2

My girlfriend Claire and I ate this dish in a restaurant in Venice and had a go at recreating it at home. It's completely delicious and pretty cheap and easy to prepare. Make sure you drink the leftover cooking wine with your meal!

6 tbsp olive oil
1 small onion, peeled and finely chopped
2 garlic cloves, peeled and finely chopped
handful of chopped parsley, plus a few chopped leaves to garnish
3 tbsp capers, rinsed
10 cherry tomatoes, halved
200ml white wine
300g tinned tuna or fresh tuna, roughly flaked
300g spaghetti
salt and freshly ground black pepper

Heat the oil in a pan and then add the onion and the garlic. Fry gently until the onion becomes translucent. Next, add the parsley, the capers and the tomatoes, followed by the wine. Bring to the boil until the liquor has reduced by half. Add the tuna, reduce the heat and cook lightly for a further 10 minutes.

Meanwhile, bring a separate pan of water to the boil, add the spaghetti and then cook it for the amount of time recommended on the packet.

Drain the pasta, mix in the sauce and then serve with a garnish of parsley. Enjoy!

FIONA SAYS

The Italians know best! This is a much better way of cooking tuna with pasta than a creamy pasta bake (hot tuna is much nicer with tomatoes than with cheese sauce), let alone with crisps crumbled on the top – a student favourite when I was at uni'. Don't be tempted to skip the capers – they really make the dish and you can add them to all sorts of other pasta sauces or pizza toppings for extra pizazz.

You can also make the following lemony tuna sauce for pasta. Trim the ends and top off the leaves from half a bunch of spring onions and cut in half or quarters lengthways depending on how thick they are, then cut across into 4 or 5 pieces to give fine, short shreds. Heat 2 tablespoons of olive oil in a small pan, add the onion and cook gently for a minute or two until softened. Add a drained can of tuna and the grated rind of half a lemon rind and some chopped parsley, stir and leave over a low heat until your pasta is cooked, adding a little of the pasta cooking water. Drain the pasta and toss with the tuna sauce adding a little extra olive oil, pepper and possibly salt to taste (though the tuna may be quite salty). Any leftovers will taste great the next day as a pasta salad.

PENNE WITH COURGETTES & LEMON

SERVES 1

One of my most used and popular recipes. This light, fresh pasta sauce makes really good summer eating.

100g dried penne, fusilli or other short pasta shapes
2 medium courgettes (about 200–250g)
a good slice of butter (about 25g)
1 small clove of garlic, peeled and crushed
3 tbsp double cream
1–1$\frac{1}{2}$ tbsp lemon juice
2 tbsp chopped fresh parsley
salt and freshly ground black pepper
freshly grated Parmesan or Grana Padano

Bring a pan of water to the boil, add $\frac{1}{2}$ teaspoon of salt then cook the pasta for the amount of time recommended on the packet. Meanwhile, cut the top and bottom off the courgettes and grate them coarsely. Heat a large frying pan or wok, add the butter, then stir-fry the courgette and garlic for 2 minutes until just cooked through. Drain the pasta, saving a little of the cooking water and return to the pan. Pour over the cream and lemon juice, tip in the courgettes and chopped parsley and fork through the pasta. Add a spoonful or two of the cooking water to lighten up the sauce. Check the seasoning, adding salt, pepper and extra lemon juice to taste, then serve sprinkled with grated Parmesan.

TOP STUDENT TIPS

Grating the courgettes is the key to this dish. Courgettes have a subtle flavour but a slippery texture that can sometimes result in mushiness when cooked. Stir-frying the vegetable in butter gives a lovely richness that coats the pasta. The double cream is strictly a luxury that can be left out when eating this dish as a light lunch. As an alternative to penne, use spaghetti: the noodle-like consistency of the grated courgettes blends perfectly. **GUY**

'penne or fusilli both work well'

JAMES' TAGLIATELLE
WITH LEEKS, MUSHROOMS AND CREME FRAICHE

SERVES 1

 There is a theory in Italy that a pasta sauce should take no longer than it takes for the pasta to cook. I'm not convinced by this for two reasons. Firstly, in the north, where fresh pasta is prevalent, the stuff only takes a couple of minutes to cook so you're going to be seriously racing to knock out a sauce in that time. Also, a proper *ragù alla Bolognese* requires hours of gentle simmering, hardly a swift sauce. Either way, this puppy can be done in a matter of minutes – no excuses about too much work to cook with this one.

100g tagliatelle
1 medium leek, trimmed, washed, and cut
   diagonally in thick slices
1 large field mushroom, sliced
1 tablespoon finely chopped parsley
1 tablespoon reduced fat crème fraîche
a squeeze of lemon juice
salt, pepper and olive oil
freshly grated Parmesan

Bring some salted water to the boil and throw in your pasta.

Heat a little oil in a large sauté or saucepan. Add the leeks, mushrooms and parsley, season and stir over a medium-high heat for 5 minutes. Reduce the heat and add the crème fraîche and lemon juice. Simmer for a minute or two. Drain the pasta when cooked, and toss into the sauce. Season with more pepper (it likes pepper, does this) and serve with some freshly grated Parmesan.

FIONA SAYS

 This is really quick and easy – a great beginner's recipe. The only thing I might suggest is using button mushrooms (about 6) rather than field or Portabella ones which can turn a creamy sauce a murky shade of grey if you're not careful. But field mushrooms do have more flavour. Oh, and a tip about cleaning leeks. Trim off the darker, coarser top leaves (if it still has any) then slit it down the middle lengthways and wash it under running water to get rid of any grit. Then slice as James suggests.

BROCCOLI, CHILLI & GARLIC PASTA

SERVES 2

This spicy recipe is based on the classic Italian recipe – *spaghetti con aglio, olio e peperoncini* (spaghetti with garlic, oil and hot pepper) but it's a good way to sneak in those good-for-you greens without too much pain.

half a head (4–5 large cloves) of garlic, peeled
4 tbsp olive oil
$1/2$–1 tsp dried crushed chillies or $1/2$–1 tsp hot chilli sauce
1 head of broccoli or a small pack of broccoli florets
250g wholewheat or ordinary spaghetti or pasta shapes
salt

Slice the garlic thinly then put it in a small saucepan with the oil and the crushed chillies. Place over a ring or gas burner and cook on the lowest possible heat for about 15 minutes until the garlic is soft and transparent. Meanwhile, cut the broccoli up into very small florets and microwave, steam or cook for 3 minutes in boiling water until just tender. Drain thoroughly. Cook the pasta following the instructions on the pack and reserve a little of the cooking water. Drain, tip in the broccoli and garlicky oil, season with salt and chilli sauce, if you haven't already added chilli, and toss together. Pour in a little of the pasta cooking water (about 2 tablespoons) and place back on the hob for a minute or two to warm through, then serve.

TOP STUDENT TIPS

If you want to make this even more virtuous, try wholewheat instead of regular pasta. The extra fibre will keep you full longer, and wholewheat pasta tastes surprisingly good. Broccoli has a natural affinity with anchovies – if you're not a committed veggie, try adding a few for a serious umami kick. A bit of grated lemon zest will give a citrus twist and balance out the robust flavours of garlic and chilli. If you're not a fan of broccoli, try cauliflower – caramelise it slightly before adding it to the dish so that it's not quite so bland. Wilted spinach also lends itself well to garlic and chilli flavours. **SIG**

'the robust flavour of garlic'

JAMES' HOT AND SOUR PRAWN DETOX NOODLES

SERVES 2

This is a really cracking detox dish – full of lip-smacking sharpness and soothing depth.

2 tbsp cooking oil
a small red chilli, deseeded and finely sliced
zest (grated peel) and juice of a small lime
a small chunk of ginger, peeled and grated
a plump clove of garlic, peeled and crushed
750ml chicken or fish stock
125g rice noodles
100g raw king prawns
100g purple sprouting broccoli, halved
2 tbsp fish sauce
3 finely sliced spring onions
1 tbsp chopped coriander

Heat some oil in a large pan. Add the chilli, lime zest, ginger and garlic. Stir over a high heat for one minute and add the stock. In a separate bowl, soak the noodles in boiling water for 3 minutes and then refresh them quickly in cold water. Once the stock is boiling, add the prawns, broccoli, fish sauce and the juice of your lime. Simmer gently for 3 minutes. Pour over the noodles and garnish with the spring onions and chopped coriander.

FIONA SAYS

I can vouch for this dish – it's just the kind of food you need the day after a late, heavy meal (or student drinking session). Raw prawns might strike you as expensive but you need very few and – along with the fish sauce – they do boost the fishy flavour. You can buy them frozen in most big supermarkets now. If you prefer a drier noodle dish simply cut down the amount of stock.

A WORD ON NOODLES

Noodles should really be as popular as pasta. They're just as cheap, quicker to cook and can be combined with a stir-fry just as easily as pasta with a sauce. They tend to stick together much more than pasta, so you'll need to keep separating them with a fork while they're cooking. They're also extremely versatile – you can serve them dry like pasta or wet like soup. Maybe that's the problem. There are just too many recipes from too many cooking traditions (Chinese, Japanese and Thai, to name just three) involving too many different types of noodles to be able to get to grips with them easily. (Oh yes, and they're slithery too.) So – a quick guide. The most common types of noodles are:

Instant noodles
Flavoured ones aren't a great deal better than pot noodles with the exception of authentic Japanese brands (see below). Unflavoured ones (e.g. Blue Dragon Express) are quite useful though they don't have as good a texture as egg noodles.

Egg noodles
Look and taste very similar to pasta. Best for stir-fries.

Soba noodles
Made partly from buckwheat these are the most tasty noodles – similar to wholewheat pasta. Good for Japanese-style soups and salads.

Rice noodles
The kind to use in Pad Thai and other Thai stir-fries and soups. Useful if you're wheat-intolerant.

Pot noodles
This is not the best way to feed yourself for the next 3 years.

ASIAN-STYLE CHICKEN BROTH WITH CORIANDER AND NOODLES

SERVES 1-2

Much as I love chicken soup there are times when I feel like something punchier and more invigorating. This is it.

350ml homemade chicken stock (or, *in extremis*, stock made from a good chicken stock cube such as Telma)
1 large clove of garlic, peeled and very finely sliced
a small chunk of fresh ginger, peeled and very finely sliced
a fresh red or green chilli, de-seeded and finely sliced (or add a dash of chilli paste or chilli sauce at the end)
a few crushed coriander stalks and/or a couple of roots, well washed and roughly chopped
about 125g–150g shredded cooked chicken meat – whatever you have
a handful of finely shredded pak choi or spinach
light soy sauce and lime or lemon juice, to taste
50g rice noodles, cooked following the instructions on the pack
1–2 heaped tbsp coriander leaves

Put the chicken stock in a saucepan and add the garlic, ginger, chilli and coriander stalks if using. Bring to the boil, then leave over a very low heat for 20–30 minutes. Strain the stock then return to the saucepan with the chicken meat and shredded pak choi or spinach, bring back to the boil and simmer for 2 minutes. Season to taste with the soy sauce and lemon juice adding a dash of hot chilli sauce if you haven't used a chilli. Put the cooked noodles in a large, deep bowl (or half the noodles in a smaller bowl) and pour over the hot stock. Sprinkle over some fresh coriander leaves.

TOP STUDENT TIPS

Coriander stalks, a traditional ingredient of Thai curry pastes, are worth keeping as they have more flavour than the leaves. They can be added to any soup, stew or curry which you would finish with coriander leaves and simply be removed at the end of the cooking period.

Instead of chicken try some thinly sliced pork, beef or seafood such as squid, prawns, mussels or even seafood cocktail. If you're using seafood, replace the soy sauce with nam pla. For a creamy *laksa*-style soup, try making this soup with a can of coconut milk or some coconut cream – and a bit of finely chopped lemongrass will also add to the soup's overall zestiness. **SIG**

SMOKED MACKEREL,
CUCUMBER & SOBA NOODLE SALAD

SERVES 2

Smoked mackerel lends itself really well to this Japanese-style salad.

100g soba noodles or wholewheat spaghetti
1 smoked mackerel fillet
4 spring onions
1/4 of a cucumber, peeled, deseeded and
    diced
2 tbsp Asian-Style Low-Fat Dressing (see
    page 69) plus extra rice vinegar to taste
salt and pepper (unless you use a peppered
    mackerel fillet)
sesame oil (optional but good)

Cook the soba noodles or spaghetti, drain and rinse with cold water (break the spaghetti in half before you cook it). With a knife and fork ease the mackerel off the skin and break into rough chunks. Trim the roots and half the green tops off the spring onions and discard. Cut the onions into four lengthways, then chop into short lengths. Tip the noodles into a bowl, pour over the dressing and mix well. Add the cucumber, spring onions and smoked mackerel and mix together again. Add a little extra rice vinegar to taste and season with salt and pepper. Add a few drops of sesame oil if you have some.

TOP STUDENT TIPS

A great recipe combining the rich, smokiness of mackerel – a fish we should all be eating more of – and crisp cucumber. Soba noodles are a fab storecupboard ingredient. Look out for the really buckwheat-y ones in Asian or Japanese stores, they taste much better than the wheaten ones you often find in health food shops.
A splash of Thai fish sauce wouldn't go amiss in the dressing as a flavour-enhancer but then I tend to put fish sauce in everything! SIG

'a fish we should all be eating more of'

GUY'S (AND CLAIRE'S) LIME & PEANUT NOODLES

SERVES 2

A great recipe from Guy's girlfriend Claire who invented it for our 'Not Pot Noodle' recipe challenge last year.

For the sauce
olive oil
1 clove of garlic, chopped
1 red chilli
2 tbsp of chunky peanut butter
1 mug of water
1 tablespoon of honey
2 tbsp of soy sauce
1 small chunk of fresh ginger, finely chopped
pinch of piri piri flakes
1 teaspoon of toasted sesame seeds
1 lime

For the noodles
olive oil
1 chicken breast, diced (you could use prawns, salmon fillets or tofu instead)
1 onion, finely chopped
1 green pepper, sliced
handful of beansprouts
2 x 125g packs egg noodles
2 eggs, beaten
2 tbsp crushed peanuts

Heat a small amount of olive oil in a small pan, and add the chopped garlic and the chilli. When the garlic starts to brown, remove the chilli and discard. Add the chunky peanut butter and allow a few minutes for it to start melting. Then add up to a mug of water to keep the sauce from sticking and thickening up too much. Continually stir (adding a little more water if you need to) and add the honey, soy sauce, ginger, piri piri flakes, ginger and sesame seeds. Cut the lime in half, and squeeze the juice from one half and add it to the sauce. Set aside.

Pre-heat a wok and, when hot, add a little olive oil. Tip in the chicken, along with the onion, pepper and beansprouts and stir-fry until cooked through (about 5 minutes). Add the noodles straight to the wok and then mix in the sauce. Cook on a high heat for another 5 minutes and add the beaten egg. Cook for a further couple of minutes and then serve straight into bowls with the crushed peanuts and a wedge from the spare half lime on top.

FIONA SAYS

Peanut butter is a surprisingly good addition to savoury recipes, especially noodles and dips. You can also use it to make great cookies. It's high in fat so you shouldn't overdo it but it's also very nutritious – a good source of protein and vitamins and minerals including vitamin E and iron.

HOW TO STIR-FRY

You might think a stir-fry is one of the easiest things in the world to cook – and you'd be right but there are good and bad stir-fries just like everything else, so it's worth polishing up your technique.

There are **five** really important things to remember:

1. Get everything ready beforehand. That's a good idea generally when you're cooking but essential in the case of a stir-fry because the whole process takes place so quickly and you don't want to stop in the middle.

2. Cut everything up the same size. Unless you've bought a bag of stir-fried veg you need to make sure that you cut your meat and veg into even-sized pieces so they cook at the same time. Then sort them into groups depending how long they will take to cook. Onions and carrots, for example, will take longer than vegetables like mange-tout and beansprouts.

3. Start with a hot wok. The mistake most people make is to have their wok too cool. It wants to be almost smoking before you add your vegetables – you should almost be able to see a haze shimmer over the surface so allow at least a couple of minutes for it to heat up. DON'T heat the oil as you heat the wok, add it at the last minute. And give the whole process your full attention. Don't drink and stir-fry!

4. Cook any meat first. If you're stir-frying meat it's best to cook it on its own while the wok is at its hottest and without vegetables in the pan which will bring the temperature down. Remove it from the wok once it's seared then return it to the pan once the vegetables are cooked to heat it through in whatever sauce you've added.

5. Don't use a commercial stir-fry sauce. They're nasty, gloopy and expensive. For a simple stir-fry all you need is a mixture of light soy sauce and water. For more elaborate sauces try one of the following recipes.

'keep it moving!'

GUY'S HONEY-SESAME STIR-FRY

SERVES 2

This stir-fry tastes really fresh and clean. The crunchiness of the vegetables and the salty, sweet sauce go really well together. I like using soft, fat udon noodles as they absorb flavours well, but ribboned rice noodles are also good. It's a fun dish to cook and only takes a few minutes to actually stir-fry once the chopping is finished. There are so many different vegetables in it that you should feel really healthy after eating it!

a little olive oil
3 spring onions, chopped
2 cloves garlic, finely chopped
2¹/₂cm piece of ginger, finely chopped or grated
1 pepper, sliced
3 button mushrooms, sliced
small handful of bean sprouts
2 small packs straight-to-wok udon noodles
75ml soy sauce
1 tbsp runny honey
¹/₂ tbsp chilli flakes or chilli sauce
1 tbsp toasted sesame seeds
small handful of coriander leaves, washed and chopped
1 lime, quartered

Pre-heat a wok until hot and then add the oil, followed by the spring onions, garlic and ginger and fry them gently for a few minutes, being sure to keep moving them around the wok. Add the peppers, mushrooms and bean sprouts and increase the heat. Cook for 10 minutes, continuing to move the vegetables around the wok.

Add the noodles and cook for a further 3 minutes. Meanwhile, mix the soy sauce, honey, chilli and sesame seeds together in a bowl, then pour the mix over the contents of the wok, along with half of the coriander and stir in.

Serve into bowls and garnish with the remaining coriander and a quarter of lime.

FIONA SAYS

Although it's tempting to buy a pack of ready-sliced vegetables, as I suggest overleaf, you really will get a much better result if you cut your veg freshly just before you stir fry them. (They're more nutritious that way too.) If you find the soy flavour too strong you can always add some water to the stir fry sauce. There will probably be plenty of veg left over so make sure you use them up before they go off. Beansprouts in particular don't keep that long but can be surprisingly tasty in an omelette along with the rest of the spring onions, and a bit of chopped coriander and a splash of soy sauce.

EXTREMELY EASY STIR-FRY

SERVES 2

In general I'm not in favour of buying pre-prepared veg but if you're short of time stir-fried veg are a boon. And, it has to be said, you wouldn't get the selection of vegetables you get in a pack for the same price if you bought them individually. The best value ones are the basic vegetable stir-fries which are usually under a pound. You can also save money by simply using a light soy sauce rather than a ready-made stir-fry sauce, most of which tend to be pretty vile.

2 tbsp oil
1 cooked chicken breast*, skin removed and
　cut into thin strips (optional)
1 x 300g bag stir-fry vegetables
1 crushed clove garlic
a little grated fresh ginger or 1 tsp ginger
　paste (optional)
2 tbsp light soy sauce

Heat a wok or large frying pan until hot (about a minute or two). Pour in the oil and immediately tip in the chicken, vegetables, garlic and ginger if using. Cook for a couple of minutes, stirring them so they don't burn. Add about half a small glass (50ml) of water and cook until evaporated. Add the soy sauce and cook for a few seconds more. Taste, adding more soy if you think it needs it. Serve with boiled rice (page 100).

• You could, of course, use raw rather than cooked chicken, in which case fry it in the oil first for a couple of minutes and then add the veg.

VARIATIONS

You can make this with frozen prawns instead of chicken or for a veggie version, replace the chicken with a handful of cashew nuts.

TOP STUDENT TIPS

 A really easy way of giving this extra oomph is to slice the chicken and marinade it for a couple of hours in a couple of tablespoons of Lingham's Chilli Sauce (a minor addiction in our digs) and some chopped coriander. The chilli sauce gives the chicken an amazing caramelised texture and spicy edge, while the coriander works its magic by giving the stir-fry a real zip. Just be careful to keep the pan moving the whole time (hence 'stir-fry'), as the temperature required is so high that the ingredients will burn very easily. JAMES

HOW TO COOK RICE

We often hear students moan that their rice always ends up soggy. It could be you're using the wrong type of rice or cooking it the wrong way. Here's a rundown on the different types of rice and what they're best for, plus our tried and tested method for making perfect fluffy rice.

Basmati rice
Well worth the extra money, especially to go with a curry (see Perfect Fluffy Rice, right), it has the best flavour and texture of any rice.

Easy-cook rice
Cheaper, but doesn't have nearly such a good flavour. Works well for flavoured rice, though I prefer Basmati or ordinary long-grain rice.

Instant rice
Frozen rice is fine though expensive. 'Express' sachets are less appetising, though they are useful for late night fuel.

Thai jasmine rice
The authentic rice to accompany Thai dishes. Slightly sticky, which always makes you feel that you haven't cooked it properly. Again, you can substitute Basmati.

Brown rice
Like wholemeal flour or wholewheat pasta, brown rice contains the whole grain which gives it a distinctive nutty flavour. Good for salads but takes at least twice as long to cook as ordinary rice.

Short-grain or pudding rice
For traditional English rice puddings. Don't bother – buy a tin. And don't use it for savoury dishes or risottos.

Risotto rice
Also labelled Arborio, Carnaroli and Vialone Nano. Pricey but essential if you want to make an authentic risotto (see page 184).

Sushi rice
Perfect for making sushi, obviously (if you can be bothered).

PERFECT FLUFFY RICE

The best type of rice to go with a curry. The key to making it fluffy is to cook it in lots of water like pasta. Measure out about 60g of Basmati or other long grain rice per person, tip it into a saucepan of boiling, salted water, stir once then boil for 10 minutes. Drain in a colander or sieve then balance the sieve over the saucepan and cover it with a piece of kitchen towel. After 5 minutes, pour away any water that has accumulated in the pan, tip in the rice and fork it through to fluff it up.

FLAVOURED RICE

If you want your rice flavoured with spices, onions or other flavourings you need to measure the water you put in it exactly and cook it in a pan with a lid on until it has absorbed. The easiest way to do this is to measure both the rice and the liquid in a measuring jug (twice as much liquid as rice).

LEFTOVER RICE

If you have rice leftover at the end of a meal you can make a rice salad with it (add the dressing while the rice is still warm) or use it for egg-fried rice.

EGG-FRIED RICE

SERVES 1

A brilliant cheap storecupboard meal and the perfect way to use up leftover boiled rice. But two crucial things to remember! One is that the rice should be fridge-cold otherwise the dish will go soggy and the other is that it should have been refrigerated soon after cooking (i.e. not left out in a pan all night) and be no more than 24 hours old. Cooked rice is a potent source of food poisoning.

1 large or 2 medium eggs, preferably free-range
2 tbsp sunflower or vegetable oil
2–3 spring onions trimmed and finely sliced or 1 small onion, peeled and finely chopped
a portion of cooked basmati rice (see opposite)
50g frozen peas, cooked or thawed
about 1 tbsp light soy sauce

Break the eggs into a bowl and beat them lightly. Heat a wok or large frying pan over a moderate heat and pour in the oil. Tip in the onions and stir-fry for 2–3 minutes until beginning to soften. Add the eggs and stir until almost all the liquid egg has disappeared (a few seconds). Add the rice and peas and stir-fry for a couple of minutes until hot through. Sprinkle over soy sauce to taste.

VARIATIONS

To make this more substantial you could add a few frozen prawns, chopped ham or some sliced button mushrooms when you add the spring onions.

TOP STUDENT TIPS

 Quite a controversial one this – there are some who would say that eggs scrambled into rice is just wrong. I'm not one of them, in spite of not being the biggest fan of Chinese food, but I suppose this is a good reminder of the fact that you just can't please everyone. It's easy to be offended when someone doesn't like your food, but more often than not it won't be your cooking that they don't like – just a fussy palate. If you prefer to play it safe, rice is always good flavoured with butter or garlic, some chopped fresh herbs, or with a few cardamom pods added at the beginning of cooking. JAMES

PRAWN & PEA PILAU

SERVES 1-2

A light fresh Indian-style rice dish which you could eat on its own or as an accompaniment to a fish curry. I don't normally go for ready-made spice mixes but Schwartz's pilau rice seasoning is a good one.

3 tbsp sunflower or olive oil
1 small onion, finely chopped
1–1$\frac{1}{2}$ tsp pilau rice seasoning or
   mild curry powder
125ml Basmati rice (measured in a jug)
1 small clove of garlic, peeled and crushed
100g fresh or defrosted frozen prawns
50g defrosted frozen peas
salt and freshly squeezed lemon juice to
   taste

Heat 2 tablespoons of the oil in a saucepan. Cook the onion over a medium heat for about 7–8 minutes stirring occasionally until it starts to brown. Add a heaped teaspoon of the pilau rice seasoning, stir and cook for a minute. Then add the rice, stir, cook a further minute and pour in 500ml of boiling water. Stir once, cover the pan tightly with a lid or a piece of foil, turn the heat down and cook for about 15 minutes until the water has been absorbed. Meanwhile, heat the remaining oil in a small frying pan. Add the remaining teaspoon of pilau rice seasoning, cook for a minute then add the crushed garlic and prawns. Stir-fry for a couple of minutes then add the peas and leave on a low heat. When the rice is cooked mix the prawn and pea mixture into the rice, replace the lid and leave off the heat for 5 minutes. Check the seasoning, adding a squeeze of lemon juice and salt to taste.

TOP STUDENT TIPS

 My friend Prema recently tipped me off to the existence of 'ghee' and its flavour-enhancing potential for rice. Ghee is a type of clarified butter that is a staple of Indian cooking, and it has an intense and unusual flavour. By using ghee instead of vegetable oil to fry the onions, the rice will gain a creamy and delicious taste. **GUY**

SPICY CASHEW & MUSHROOM RICE

SERVES 2-3

A slight adaptation of a wonderfully simple rice recipe from cookery writer Vicky Bhogal, author of a great book called *Cooking Like Mummyji* (Simon & Schuster). You can vary it – and Vicky does – depending on what you have available. Here's my vegan version.

2 tbsp oil
75g cashew nuts
1 tsp cumin seeds
1/2 onion, peeled and thinly sliced or half a bunch of spring onions, trimmed and sliced
1/2 tsp dried red chilli flakes or 1/4 tsp chilli powder or hot sauce
1/4 tsp salt
1/2 tsp ground coriander
250g button mushrooms, wiped or rinsed clean and sliced
2 fresh tomatoes, skinned (see tip, page 77) and diced
a small handful of fresh coriander leaves, roughly chopped
1/2 a mug (150ml) basmati rice

Heat the oil in a medium-sized saucepan or frying pan, tip in the cashew nuts and stir-fry for 1 minute until beginning to brown. Remove from the pan with a slotted spoon or tablespoon, draining the oil back into the pan. Return the pan to the heat and add the cumin seeds. Once they start sizzling, add the onion and fry until translucent (about 2–3 minutes). Stir in the chilli flakes or chilli powder, salt and ground coriander then add the sliced mushrooms, chopped tomatoes and fresh coriander. Cook for 30 seconds then return the cashews to the pan, add the rice, stir and cook for 30 seconds then pour in about 2/3 of a mug of boiling water. Bring to the boil, put a lid on the pan, turn the heat right down and cook for about 15 minutes until all the liquid is absorbed. (If you find it absorbs more quickly add a little extra water but be careful as the mushrooms give off quite a lot of liquid.) Turn the heat off and let the rice stand for 5 minutes. Serve with onion raita (below) and mango chutney or another Indian chutney.

TO ACCOMPANY: A SIMPLE ONION RAITA

Take 3 tablespoons of soy or plain yoghurt and spoon into a bowl. Peel a small onion and finely grate about 1 tablespoon into the yoghurt. Season with salt and serve.

VARIATIONS

You could make a non-veggie version with prawns. Add them at the same time as the tomato.

TOP STUDENT TIPS

This genius vegan recipe really packs a punch – the cumin, coriander and onion add spice and flavour, the dish is quick to make and can easily be scaled up for a crowd (perfect for vegans and non-vegans alike). You could add other spices such as turmeric, cinnamon or cardamom for a change, and I'd always be inclined to add garlic but it's not essential in this dish. You could replace the rice with barley, quinoa or large Israeli couscous for a change of grain – though make sure you check the cooking times for these alternatives, as they may take longer to cook. If you're not a fan of cashews, try lentils, chickpeas or some Spanish fried *habas* (beans) for a similar crunch. **SIG**

SPANISH-STYLE BEANS

SERVES 1-2

This simple combination of onions, peppers and smoked pepper is typical of the Basque regions of northern Spain and south-west France.

2 tbsp light olive oil or sunflower oil
1 small to medium onion, peeled and thinly sliced
125g frozen peppers or a small red pepper, deseeded and cut into strips
1 clove of garlic, peeled and crushed
1/2 tsp paprika (preferably Spanish pimenton)
a small (200g) tin of tomatoes or 1/2 a 400g tin
1 x 400g tin of butter beans or chickpeas, drained and rinsed
salt and freshly ground black pepper
a heaped tbsp chopped fresh parsley (optional)

Put a large frying pan or wok over a medium heat, add the oil, heat for 30 seconds then add the onion. Fry for 2–3 minutes until beginning to soften then add the peppers, garlic and paprika. Continue to stir-fry for another couple of minutes then add the tomatoes and their juice, breaking them up with a wooden spoon or spatula. Cook the vegetables for another 2 minutes then add the drained butterbeans and cook for another 3–4 minutes until heated through. Season to taste with salt and pepper, stir in the parsley if you have some, then serve in a large soup bowl (or bowls).

VARIATION

Without the beans this also makes a great sauce for pasta or a topping for a baked potato. You could also serve the sauce with a couple of fried eggs.

TOP STUDENT TIPS

One of my favourite store cupboard ingredients is smoked paprika. It's easily found nowadays, and pretty cheap considering that it will last you a long time. You will find it (and it is certainly worth buying both variants) labelled *dulce* and *piccante*; the *dulce* variety adding a sweet, roundness to a tagine or marinade, the *piccante* giving a mayonnaise some real zip, or a spicy edge to a bean stew such as this one. Don't be put off by the fact that it's a little dearer than your average spice – you only need the smallest pinch to give a dish a wonderful, smoky, Middle Eastern note. **JAMES**

MOROCCAN-SPICED CHICKPEAS WITH SPINACH

SERVES 1-2

This spicing is one of my favourites – worth making in a big batch so you just have it to hand when you need it. To make Moroccan Spice Mix, mix together 2 tablespoons each of ground cumin and coriander, 1 tablespoon of ground turmeric and 1–2 teaspoons of chilli powder depending on your own personal taste. Use 2–3 teaspoons of the mix at a time. Note the sneaky inclusion of fresh greens which together with the tomatoes really makes this quite a healthy dish.

2 tbsp light olive or vegetable oil
1 medium onion (about 110g), peeled and
   roughly chopped
2 cloves of garlic, peeled and crushed
2 rounded tsp Moroccan spice mix
1 x 200g can or $\frac{1}{2}$ a 400g can of tomatoes
1 x 400g can of chickpeas, drained and rinsed
a handful of roughly chopped fresh spinach
   or cabbage leaves and/or 1 heaped tbsp
   chopped fresh coriander leaves
salt
a small carton of natural, unsweetened
   yoghurt or soy yoghurt (optional)

Heat the oil in a frying pan and fry the onion for about 4–5 minutes until soft. Stir in the garlic and spice mix and fry for a few seconds then tip in the tomatoes and break them up with a wooden spoon, spatula or fork. Bring to the boil, add the drained, rinsed chickpeas, cover the pan and simmer for 7–8 minutes. Chuck in the spinach or cabbage leaves and coriander (if using) and cook for another 2 minutes. Add salt to taste. You could serve this with a dollop of yoghurt and some pitta bread or naan.

LEFTOVERS

This also tastes great cold. Mash any leftover chickpeas and use them to fill a pitta bread.

TOP STUDENT TIPS

 Chickpeas are a veggie's friend, but even a committed omnivore like me digs them. Tasty, healthy and endlessly versatile – if you're cooking dried chickpeas, add a pinch of bicarbonate of soda to them when soaking the night before and also while cooking. The bicarb' creates an alkaline environment for the peas to soak up more water and cook better, try it when making hummus from scratch – see page 178). Turmeric, incidentally, is a brilliant spice – reputed to be good for weight loss and warding off dementia, so up the quantities of turmeric whenever a recipe calls for it. If you can get a hold of some fresh turmeric, even better. An Indian friend of mine swears by dabbing turmeric on wounds or spots as it apparently has great healing properties. Be wary though: it's a potent dye that can stain your skin and clothes. **SIG**

STUFFED PITTA POCKETS WITH MEXICAN BEANS

SERVES 2–4

This is an adaptation of an oddly named Mexican dish called 'Refried Beans' which isn't really refried at all. It's boiled (or canned) beans, fried up with onions and chilli. One tin makes a surprising amount – enough for a good meal with leftovers for the next day.

1 tsp cumin seeds or ground cumin
2 tbsp olive or other light cooking oil
half a bunch of spring onions, trimmed and sliced or 1 medium red onion, peeled and roughly chopped
2 cloves of garlic, peeled and crushed
1/2–1 tsp mild chilli powder or a few drops of hot pepper sauce or a small fresh chilli, deseeded and finely chopped
1 large or 2 medium tinned tomatoes plus 2 tbsp of their juice or 2 fresh tomatoes, skinned and roughly chopped (see tip page 77)
1 x 400g can of red kidney beans
2 heaped tbsp chopped fresh coriander leaves
salt and lemon juice, to taste
4 pitta breads
any salad ingredients you fancy or have available – avocado, fresh tomatoes, sliced cucumber, iceberg lettuce or other salad leaves, raw onion

If you're using cumin seeds, heat a pan over a moderate heat and dry-fry them for a couple of minutes to release their aroma. Tip them out of the pan once they begin to change colour and set aside. Add the oil to the pan and then the spring onions or chopped onion. Fry for a couple of minutes then add the garlic, chilli powder or sauce and cumin. Stir and add the tomatoes, breaking them down with a spatula or wooden spoon. Tip in the beans, cover the pan and cook for about 5–6 minutes until the liquid has evaporated. Take the pan off the heat and mash the beans roughly with a fork. Stir in the coriander and season with lemon juice and a little salt. Leave to cool for 10 minutes. Meanwhile, toast the pitta breads lightly and let them cool too. Halve the pitta breads and stuff with the fried beans and salad.

LEFTOVERS

Any leftovers make a great sandwich. Just toast the pitta bread lightly, cool, then stuff as above.

TOP STUDENT TIPS

 These are a real staple of Mexican food and you can eat them with fajitas, burritos or enchiladas. Squidgy, mushy and perfect with rice, pickled jalapeños and ice-cold Mexican beer. To make quesadillas, spread tortillas or wraps with refried beans and white cheese, fold over and fry both sides in very little oil. Serve with salsa (page 110), sour cream, guacamole (page 179) and more jalapeños. GUY

FRENCH-STYLE BRAISED LENTILS

MAKES 4 HELPINGS

This is a great recipe to make in a batch for a couple of days' eating. As well as being a substantial veggie main you can serve it with sausages or pork chops or even dress it with a bit of vinaigrette and add some other veg for a lunchbox salad.

175g Puy lentils
1 medium carrot, peeled and chopped into small dice
550ml vegetable stock, made with 2 rounded tsp vegetable bouillon powder or an organic vegetable stock cube
3 tbsp olive oil
3 cloves of garlic, peeled and finely sliced
1 medium to large onion, peeled and roughly chopped
1/2 tsp sweet Spanish paprika (pimenton)
2 heaped tbsp chopped flat-leaf parsley
salt and freshly ground pepper, to taste

Rinse the lentils and put them in a pan with the chopped carrots and stock. Bring to the boil and simmer for 20–25 minutes until the liquid has evaporated.

Heat 2 tablespoons of the oil in a pan over a low heat, add the sliced garlic and let it cook gently for a couple of minutes until beginning to colour. Add the onion, stir and cover the pan and leave to cook slowly until the lentils are ready.

Stir the paprika into the onions and cook for a minute then tip in the lentils, stir well, cover and leave over a very low heat. Season the lentils with salt and pepper to taste, then stir in the chopped parsley and remaining olive oil. Serve as a veggie main with cabbage or other greens or with sausages.

TOP STUDENT TIPS

Not only are lentils really good for you, but prepared this way, extremely tasty – even the most lentilphobic will love this dish. You could also add some crumbled goats' cheese and some cooked or pickled beetroot and *voila!*: a virtuous and delicious lunch or easy supper. Lentils will keep for a few days once cooked, and what you don't use you can add to a vegetable soup. You can also make a scaled-down version with a can of brown lentils (if you're short of time though, rinse them first to get rid of the slightly gloopy liquid you find in canned pulses). **SIG**

'even the most lentilphobic will love this dish'

FISH FINGERS 4 WAYS

The automatic accompaniment for fish fingers – or any other breadcrumbed fish or chicken – doesn't have to be chips. Partner them instead with a healthy salsa, salad or some veg.

WITH CUCUMBER AND SWEET CHILLI SALSA

SERVES 2

1/3 of a cucumber
1–2 spring onions, trimmed and finely sliced
juice of 1/2 a lemon (about 1 1/2 tbsp)
2 tbsp sweet chilli sauce
a dash of nam pla (fish sauce) or a little salt
1 tbsp roughly chopped coriander leaves

Cut the cucumber in four, lengthways, remove the seeds and cut into small dice. Mix with the onion. Mix the lemon juice, sweet chilli sauce and nam pla together and taste, adding a little more of any of the ingredients you fancy. Pour over the cucumber. Stir in the coriander leaves just before serving.

WITH FRESH TOMATO SALSA

SERVES 2

Only really worth making in the summer when tomatoes are ripe – and cheap.

4–5 ripe tomatoes (or a small pack of cherry tomatoes)
1/2 a small onion or 1/4 medium onion, finely chopped
1 mild green chilli, cut lengthways, seeds removed and finely chopped
juice of 1 lime
1 heaped tbsp chopped fresh coriander
salt

Remove the tomato skins by making a small cut in the top of each tomato, placing them in a bowl and pouring boiling water over them. After a minute drain off the water and plunge them into cold water. The skins should come away easily. Finely chop the tomato flesh and seeds and place in a bowl with the chopped onion, chilli and lime juice. Season with salt and stir in the fresh coriander.

WITH GARLIC MAYO AND BUTTERED SPINACH

SERVES 2

Don't hesitate to use frozen spinach for this dish. It's much better value and quicker to prepare than the fresh stuff.

350g frozen leaf spinach (not chopped spinach which is just like baby food)
a small slice of butter (about 15g)
salt, freshly ground black pepper and lemon juice
2–3 heaped tbsp garlic-flavoured mayonnaise (or plain mayonnaise mixed with either a clove of garlic, peeled and crushed or 1 tsp garlic paste)

Defrost the spinach in the microwave with 1 tablespoon of water or heat gently in a small pan with a lid on. When it's completely thawed, strain it in a sieve then return it to the pan with the butter and cook over a low heat till the butter has melted. Season with salt and pepper – and a little nutmeg if you've got it. Mix the mayonnaise with the crushed garlic or garlic paste and season with salt, pepper and a squeeze of lemon juice. Serve the fish fingers with a good dollop of the mayo and a portion of buttered spinach on the side.

FISH FINGER 'TACOS' AND SPICY SLAW

SERVES 1–2

A variation on the fish finger sarnie. Great for making Southern Californian-style fish finger tacos.

a quarter of a small white cabbage
1/2 a small onion or 3–5 spring onions, finely chopped or sliced
1 small carrot, peeled and grated
1/2 a green pepper, de-seeded and finely sliced
1 small green or red chilli, de-seeded and finely chopped
1 clove of garlic, peeled and crushed
2 good dollops of ready-made mayonnaise
1/2 tsp mild chilli powder, paprika or pimenton
salt and pepper
2 small wraps or wheat tortillas

Remove the outer leaves and the hard central core of the cabbage and finely shred the remainder. Plunge in a bowl of ice cold water (add a few ice cubes). Prepare the other vegetables. Crush the garlic and add the mayo and chilli powder. Season to taste with salt and pepper. Drain the cabbage and mix with the other vegetables and refrigerate for an hour, ideally. Grill or fry the fish fingers. Wipe the pan and heat the tortillas through. Divide the fish fingers between the tortillas and top with the spicy slaw. Pull the sides of the wrap or tortilla towards the middle then roll into a cylinder. Eat immediately (and messily).

TOP STUDENT TIPS

I don't know anyone who doesn't like fish fingers. Anything so redolent of childhood is always going to be a hit, but with such high expectations it's important to get these right. Soggy fish fingers are an absolute no-no. My friend Leyla suggests baking them as normal and then grilling them for a minute or so on each side to really crisp them up. Making your own is pretty simple too. Plaice is a perfect fish for this: get some skinless plaice fillets and slice them into fingers. Toss them in flour with some salt and pepper and shake off the excess, then dip them into beaten egg before rolling them in breadcrumbs. Heat some oil in a non-stick pan and fry the goujons (as these posh ones are called) for a couple of minutes on each side until crisp and golden. Captain Birdseye eat your heart out. **JAMES**

The iconic fish finger – the ultimate comfort food

THAI GREEN FISH CURRY

SERVES 1

Thai curry devotees may regard this as a bit of a cop-out but it takes a fraction of the time of the authentic version and is surprisingly really tasty.

1 frozen skinless, boneless white fish fillet (about 110g–125g)
1 tbsp vegetable oil
half a bunch of spring onions, trimmed and sliced, or a small onion, peeled and roughly chopped
1 clove of garlic, peeled and crushed
2–3 tsp Thai green curry paste or Thai green curry powder
1/4–1/3 of a tin of coconut milk or 150ml coconut milk made from coconut powder
1 tbsp of plain yoghurt (optional but nice)
50g frozen peas
2 tsp lime or lemon juice, preferably freshly squeezed
1 heaped tbsp fresh chopped coriander (optional but good)

If you remember or have time, take the fish out of the freezer about 15 minutes before you start cooking so it's easier to cut. Heat the oil in a saucepan, add the spring onion and cook over a low heat for a couple of minutes until beginning to soften. Add the crushed garlic and stir in the curry paste or powder, then pour in the coconut milk and yoghurt and stir again. Heat through while you cut the fish into cubes (easiest with scissors) and add it and the peas to the coconut milk. Bring to the boil then turn the heat down and simmer until cooked (about 2–3 minutes). Stir in the lime or lemon juice and fresh coriander, cook for another minute then serve with rice.

VARIATIONS

For Four Increase quantities to 2 tablespoons of oil, 1 bunch of spring onions, 2 cloves of garlic, 2 tablespoons of Thai paste or curry powder, a whole tin of coconut milk, 500g of fish, a mug of frozen peas, 2 tablespoons of lime juice and 3 heaped tablespoons of coriander. Chuck in a few frozen prawns too. Instead of the fish you could make this with cooked chicken, cut into cubes.

TOP STUDENT TIPS

 The curry pastes you find nowadays in the bigger supermarkets really are pretty good, and a great quick fix when you're hungry and not particularly in the mood to start faffing around in the kitchen. But nothing compares with doing it from scratch. The two main issues are finding the ingredients and having the equipment to get a decent paste. A big pestle and mortar will do the job, if arduously, but a food processor like a Magimix will be much more efficient. While not cheap – and it's worth getting a good one that will last – you will use it again and again (though, quick caveat: NEVER attempt mashing potatoes in a Magimix, unless you're planning on re-grouting the bathroom). As far as shopping goes, a big supermarket should have all you need, otherwise an Asian food store will certainly come up trumps. It's worth sniffing one of these out anyway if you cook Asian food regularly. You'll find spices, rice, noodles, etc., at a fraction of the price they are in supermarkets. **JAMES**

SEARED TUNA WITH AVOCADO SALSA

SERVES 2

If you want a change from tinned tuna try buying it fresh – the nearest thing to a steak for someone who's not a meat-eater. It's best to buy it in small pre-cut portions (available from most large supermarkets) otherwise it can cost a bomb if cut to order.

For the tuna
a little olive oil
2 fresh (or thawed frozen) tuna steaks
salt and freshly ground black pepper

For the avocado salsa
5–6 cherry tomatoes, halved
$\frac{1}{2}$ a green or red pepper, pith removed and diced
$\frac{1}{4}$ cucumber, peeled, de-seeded and diced
1 shallot or half an onion, finely chopped or 1–2 spring onions, finely sliced
1 mild chilli or $\frac{1}{2}$ a larger one, de-seeded and finely chopped (optional)
1 avocado, peeled and chopped
$1\frac{1}{2}$ tbsp lemon or lime juice
3 tbsp olive oil
2 tbsp finely chopped parsley or coriander or a few torn basil leaves
salt and freshly ground black pepper

Simply put all the vegetables in a bowl, cutting the avocado up last so it doesn't discolour. Pour over the lemon juice and olive oil, season with salt and pepper and add the chopped herbs. Mix lightly but thoroughly.

Rub each side of the tuna steaks lightly with olive oil and season with salt and pepper. Heat a ridged grill pan or frying pan for a couple of minutes until really hot and sear the steaks for a minute to a minute and a half each side depending how thick they are and how well done you like them. Set aside and rest on a warm plate for 5 minutes. Serve the tuna with the salad, drizzling over a little extra olive oil.

VARIATIONS

You could also serve the tuna with a tomato and bean salad or with a stir-fry.

TOP STUDENT TIPS

 This salsa is delicious. I often dice up a ripe mango too as the sweetness of the juice contrasts well with the sharp lime flavour. Tuna can be expensive and is subject to rampant overfishing, so I often use mahi-mahi, which is usually available at the fish counter of the larger supermarkets. It has a meaty texture similar to that of tuna. **GUY**

THAI-STYLE SALMON WITH SUGAR SNAP PEAS

SERVES 1

Spoiling yourself doesn't necessarily mean stuffing yourself. Here's a healthy dish that'll make you feel fantastic.

For the dressing
juice of $^1/_2$ a lime (about 1$^1/_2$ tbsp)
1 tbsp fish sauce (nam pla)
1 tsp wine vinegar
1 tsp caster sugar
1 small clove of garlic, peeled and crushed
$^1/_4$ red pepper, de-seeded and finely chopped
1 small chilli, de-seeded and finely chopped (optional)
1 tbsp fresh coriander, roughly chopped

For the salmon and peas
1 tsp oil
1 salmon fillet, about 150g
100g sugar snap peas or mange-tout

First make the dressing: in a bowl mix together the lime juice, fish sauce, wine vinegar and 1 tablespoon of water. Stir in the sugar, garlic, red pepper and chilli, if using. Heat a non-stick frying pan, add the oil and place the salmon in the pan, skin side downwards. Cook for 3–4 minutes then flip it over and cook for another 1–2 minutes. Meanwhile, microwave or steam the mange-tout or sugar snap peas until just done (2–3 minutes). Remove the salmon from the pan and put on a plate. Drain the sugar snap peas, and spoon round the salmon. Pour the dressing into the pan and bubble up for 30 seconds, add the chopped coriander then pour over the salmon and peas.

The difference in the timing reflects the thickness of the salmon. Watch the salmon change colour from deep to pale pink as the heat penetrates it. Once the colour has changed half way through the fillet, flip it over.

TOP STUDENT TIPS

 One of the best ways to cook fish is with these zesty Thai ingredients, especially for those who are sceptical about fish or seafood in general. Try using the dressing for other oily fish such as mackerel, trout or sardines, and indeed white fish such as hake, haddock or pollack. I imagine mussels would work really well with the garlic, chilli, coriander flavours too. Think laterally with Thai flavours – they tend to go with most veggies, meat and fish. **SIG**

EASY CHICKEN KORMA

SERVES 2

There is a halfway house between buying a ready-made curry sauce (which are frequently foul) and cooking with dozens of individual spices - and that is a curry paste. You need to tweak the recipe with fresh ingredients such as lemon, yoghurt and coriander to make them taste homemade but they're a boon to have in the fridge as they last for weeks.

2–3 tbsp light cooking oil
2 skinless, boneless chicken thighs (about 300g in total) or 250–300g cooked chicken, cut into thick strips
$1/2$ a bunch of spring onions, trimmed and sliced into roughly 2cm lengths
1–2 cloves of garlic, crushed
1 tsp freshly grated ginger or ginger paste
$1/2$ tsp ground turmeric (optional)
2 tbsp korma paste or other mild curry paste
3 tbsp double cream or – even better if you have some – coconut cream
3 tbsp plain yoghurt or soy yoghurt
2 tbsp roughly chopped coriander
salt and lemon juice, to taste

Heat 2 tablespoons of the oil in a deep frying pan or wok and lightly brown the chicken strips (if uncooked). If the chicken is cooked, add it later. Add the spring onions, stir and cook for a minute then stir in the crushed garlic, ginger and turmeric, if using. Stir, then add the curry paste and 125ml of water then return the chicken to the pan. Spoon over the sauce, turn the heat down, cover the pan and simmer gently for about 15 minutes until the chicken is cooked (simmer the sauce for 10 minutes before adding the chicken if you're using cooked chicken, which only needs 4–5 minutes). Add the double cream or coconut cream and yoghurt, and heat through. Season to taste with salt and a squeeze of lemon and stir in the chopped coriander or parsley. Serve with boiled rice (page 100) or naan.

VARIATIONS

Add some leftover veg such as steamed broccoli or peas to the curry. If you have some cardamom pods you could add a few finely crushed cardamom seeds along with the garlic and ginger to make the curry more aromatic. You can also employ the same approach to a lamb or beef curry, using a Rogan Josh curry paste and some creamed tomatoes or passata.

TOP STUDENT TIPS

 Fiona is dead right in saying that most ready-made sauces are risibly bad: Chicken Tonight? Mmm, another time, perhaps. But if I may be permitted to suggest an even easier (for 'easier' here read 'lazier') chicken curry version, you can do as follows: take a couple of tablespoons of Madras curry paste and loosen it with a tablespoon of yoghurt and a squeeze of lime. Spread it on a couple of whole thigh and leg cuts of chicken – these are pretty easily found these days – and pop in the oven at 180C/350F/GAS 4, for about 45 minutes. Serve with rice, garnished with chopped coriander. **JAMES**

SPICY CHICKEN SALAD

SERVES 1-2

Also known as coronation chicken, invented to celebrate the Queen's coronation in 1953.

1 cooked chicken breast, skin removed and cut into strips
1/4 of a cucumber, peeled, deseeded and cut into strips
1/2 a carrot, peeled and cut into fine strips
2 spring onions, trimmed and finely shredded*
a few chopped cashew nuts or unsalted roasted peanuts (optional)
crisp lettuce leaves

For the dressing
1/4–1/2 tsp mild to medium hot curry paste or powder
1/2 tsp tomato ketchup
1 heaped tbsp mayonnaise
1 heaped tbsp plain yoghurt
1 heaped tbsp apricot jam
a little salt

First mix together the ingredients for the dressing thoroughly together in a bowl, adding a teaspoon of water. Pour over the prepared chicken and vegetables and toss together. Lay a few crisp iceberg or Little Gem lettuce leaves on a plate and spoon over the salad. Sprinkle over a few chopped nuts if you have some.

• To get fine shreds of spring onion for a salad or stir-fry, trim off the root and coarser ends of the green leaves and cut the onion into quarters lengthwise. Then cut across into short pieces.

BANG BANG CHICKEN

SERVES 1-2

The same basic ingredients as for Spicy Chicken Salad, but with an even punchier dressing.

1 cooked chicken breast
vegetables list from Spicy Chicken Salad, above
2 tbsp crunchy peanut butter
3–4 tbsp vegetable stock made with 1/4 tsp vegetable bouillon powder
1 tbsp fresh lime or lemon juice
1/2–1 tsp soy sauce
1 small clove of garlic, peeled and crushed
1–2 tsp sweet chilli sauce or a few drops of hot pepper sauce

Put the peanut butter in a bowl and work in 2–3 tablespoons of vegetable stock until you have a smooth sauce. Add the lime or lemon juice, soy sauce and crushed garlic and beat again.

Season to taste with sweet chilli sauce or a few drops of hot pepper sauce. Mix with the chicken and prepared vegetables.

TOP STUDENT TIPS

 A salad like this calls for super-fine slivers of carrot: you might find it easier to peel the carrot as normal, discarding trimmings, then continue to make shavings of carrot. Use the same technique for stir-fries and the like. Bang Bang dressing is a wonderfully flexible and adaptable condiment. The Indonesian parallel is Gado-Gado, which incorporates many of the same aspects – peanut, lime, chilli (something I don't think you should hold back on – the cucumber and lettuce will be soothing enough), but with the added bark of fragrant tamarind water and salty shrimp paste. **JAMES**

SWEET & SOUR CHICKEN (OR TURKEY)

SERVES 1-2

Sweet and sour sauce has a bad name but a good homemade version is surprisingly tasty.

2 tbsp soy sauce
1 chicken or turkey breast or fillet, cut into
    fine strips
2 tbsp oil
1 small carrot, peeled and cut into thin strips
1/2 a red or green pepper, de-seeded and cut
    into thin strips
1/2 a bunch of spring onions, trimmed and
    finely sliced or a small onion, peeled and
    finely sliced
1 clove of garlic, peeled and crushed
1/2 a small (227g) tin of pineapple pieces in
    natural juice
1 tbsp tomato ketchup
1 tsp lemon juice or vinegar, if needed

Put 1 tablespoons of the soy sauce in a bowl, add the chicken or turkey strips and mix together. Heat the oil in a frying pan or wok. Add the chicken, carrot and pepper and stir-fry for about 3 minutes. Add the spring onions and garlic and fry for another minute. Drain the pineapple, reserving the juice. Add half the pineapple and all the juice to the stir-fry, along with the ketchup and remaining soy sauce and cook for a couple of minutes. Taste and add the lemon juice or vinegar, if needed. Serve with rice or noodles.

LEFTOVERS

Eat the rest of the pineapple for breakfast with some low-fat fromage frais, yoghurt or add it to a fruit salad.

TOP STUDENT TIPS

 Kind of a Chinese restaurant cliché but when you make this from scratch it tastes really good. You also don't have to consume toxic levels of MSG (which although chock-full of umami deliciousness, is not so healthy). **GUY**

SOUTH AFRICAN-STYLE PORK CHOPS WITH APRICOTS

SERVES 1-2

South Africans are big on fruit and meat, particularly if it has a spicy twist. This is like a Cape Malay curry – mild and fruity.

1–2 tbsp vegetable or sunflower oil
1–2 pork chops or pork loin steaks
1 small onion, peeled and roughly chopped
1 stick of celery, trimmed and finely sliced or half a red pepper, de-seeded and finely sliced
1 tsp medium-hot curry paste
1 tbsp tomato ketchup
a small tin of apricots or ½ a 400g tin, drained and sliced
100ml chicken or vegetable stock made with ½ tsp vegetable bouillon powder

Heat a medium-sized frying pan and add the oil. When it's hot lay the pork chop in the pan. Brown for about 3 minutes on each side, then turn the heat down and cook for a further 2–3 minutes on each side depending how thick it is. Remove from the pan and set aside on a plate. Tip in the chopped onion and celery or pepper, adding a little bit more oil if needed. Fry over a moderate heat for about 5 minutes until they start to soften. Stir in the curry paste and tomato ketchup, add the sliced apricots then pour in the stock. Bring to the boil and simmer for 5 minutes then return the chop(s) to the pan and heat through. Serve with rice.

LEFTOVERS

Mix the leftover apricots with a few strawberries as I've done in the recipe on page 49 or simply serve them with yoghurt or fromage frais for a healthy breakfast

TOP STUDENT TIPS

Pork is often neglected, but it's a thrifty student's friend, as cheap as chicken and often tastier. The mix of fruit and spice is a great alternative to the traditional pork and apple combo (though that would be good too).You could use dried apricots instead of canned for an extra-apricotty flavour. Some need soaking first (if they're not marked ready-to-eat). **SIG**

THREE QUICK, EASY PUDS

Even if you're cooking for yourself, it's sometimes nice to have a pud – and pancakes are one of the great student staples.

PAN-FRIED APPLE WITH HONEY, LEMON & GINGER

SERVES 1

Obviously leave out the ginger if you don't like ginger. It still tastes good.

1 good quality crisp eating apple (such as Blenheim or Cox)
a small chunk of butter (about 15g)
a little grated fresh ginger or $1/4$ tsp ginger paste or $1/4$ tsp ground ginger
1 tbsp of runny honey
1 tbsp of lemon juice

Cut the apple into quarters, core and cut each quarter lenthways into three. Heat a small frying pan then add the butter. Just as it starts foaming throw in the apple pieces, coat them in butter then quickly lay them out in a single layer. Cook for about two minutes on each side until lightly browned then sprinkle over the ginger. Spoon over the honey and just as it starts to caramelise (about 30 seconds) add the lemon juice. Bubble up for a minute until the juices are reduced then tip the mixture into a bowl. Spoon over some plain or soy yoghurt and serve.

CRUNCHY LEMON PANCAKES

MAKES 6–8 LARGE PANCAKES

The classic Pancake Day pancake. 'Crunchy' should remind you to use granulated rather than caster sugar. Tastes much better.

110g plain flour
$1/4$ tsp salt
2 large fresh free-range eggs
275ml semi-skimmed milk
25g cooled melted butter plus another 25g melted butter for greasing the pan

For serving
2 lemons, cut into quarters
granulated sugar

Mix the flour and salt in a large bowl. Make a hollow in the centre. Beat the eggs lightly with the milk then add 25g cool melted butter. Gradually pour the mixture into the flour, stirring all the time, and beat well with a wooden spoon. Set the batter aside for $1/2$ an hour then beat again. Heat the pan until quite hot, then grease it with some scrunched-up kitchen towel dipped in the remaining butter. Add a small chunk of butter and rub it round the pan. Scoop out a small cup or $1/3$ of a mug of batter and tip it into the pan swirling it round quickly so the whole base of the pan is covered with batter. Cook for about 30 seconds till the edges begin to brown then flip over with a spatula and cook the other side. Serve up straight away as you make them, squeezing on lemon and sprinkling with about a teaspoon of granulated sugar, then rolling them up or folding them into four.

VARIATIONS

Other indulgent things you can put on a pancake:
- Golden syrup
- Shop-bought or homemade chocolate sauce
- Bananas cooked with butter and soft brown sugar
- Fruit compôte (see page 48) and cream
- Soft set cherry jam and vanilla ice cream

TOP STUDENT TIPS

 If you want to create a really spectacular dessert turn these pancakes into Crêpes Suzette, a dish lovingly detailed in the classic French film, *La Grande Bouffe* (in which four middle-aged men literally gorge themselves to death on a banquet of truly epic proportions). Mix grated orange zest into the pancake batter then make a sauce with orange juice, sugar, butter and Grand Marnier. Warm a ladleful of the sauce, carefully set it alight and pour over the crêpes. Just don't eat too many. **GUY**

SUGARED PLUM TOASTS

SERVES 1

Toast toppings don't have to be savoury – in fact this is a great way to serve the underripe fruit you so often find in supermarkets.

**2 plums
a small slice of butter (about 15g)
1 dessertspoon of caster sugar
¼ tsp cinnamon (optional)
2 thick slices of malt loaf**

Stone the plums by cutting round the stone and twisting the two halves of the fruit in opposite directions. (If the plums are not very ripe that may not work – you may just have to hack away the fruit from the stone.) Slice or chop into chunks. Heat a small frying pan, add the butter then when the sizzling dies down chuck in the plums. Stir-fry them for about a minute and a half then sprinkle over the sugar and cinnamon (if using) and fry for another minute. Toast the bread and pile the plums on top of the two slices. Top with a dollop of Greek yoghurt if you have some. Or, even better, some vanilla ice cream.

VARIATIONS

You could also make this with pears or peaches.

TOP STUDENT TIPS

 A brilliant riff on french toast – perfect for weekend breakfasts or brunches. Try stir-frying other kinds of under-ripe (or even ripe but bland) fruit such as strawberries, pears, apricots, nectarines or bananas for this dish. You can't beat cinnamon as a means of lifting the plums, but if you're in the mood for a change then give cardamom, nutmeg or star anise a go. A few drops of vanilla extract or essence is also great. You can also try other sweet breads such as cholla, briôche or panettone. **SIG**

CHEAP & TASTY MEALS TO SHARE FOR 3, 4 & MORE

If you're sharing a house where you take turns to cook it makes sense to make dishes that most of you will like. These can be family favourites like spaghetti Bolognese or macaroni cheese or simply recipes that you're happy to keep going back to because they're cheap and delicious.

GUY'S WINTER VEGETABLE SOUP

SERVES 8

 This soup is the perfect winter-warming meal. It's one of my cornerstone recipes and I cook it nearly every week in big batches which last our household for a good couple of days. Use whichever vegetables are in season at the time – you could switch to courgettes or broad beans in the summer. This soup is great left chunky but if your textural preference is for something smoother, you can blitz it with a handheld blender (though leave out the pasta if you're after a smooth version).

olive oil
1 leek, washed and chopped
2 medium red onions, chopped
8 carrots, chopped
6 sticks of celery, chopped
1¼kg Maris Piper potatoes, roughly chopped
1½ litres hot chicken stock
2 cans cannellini beans, drained and rinsed
salt and freshly ground black pepper
250g farfalle pasta
100g Parmesan

In a saucepan with a lid, heat the olive oil and add the leek and onion and cook for 10 minutes or so, until soft. Add in the carrots and celery, cook for a further 10 minuets and then add the potatoes. Keep adding a touch of olive oil to ensure that nothing sticks to the bottom of the pan.

Add the stock, beans and seasoning, and leave covered and simmering for an hour. After an hour, add the pasta and cook for another 20 minutes. Serve with a dash more olive oil and a generous sprinkling of Parmesan. Enjoy!

FIONA SAYS

 A bumper version of the Sad Unloved Vegetable Soup on page 73 though less random and accidental. (Speaking of which please read Guy's safety strictures on page 33 following a really terrible accident he had with hot stock when making this recipe.) The virtue of making a huge batch of soup like this is that you can either use it to feed a crowd or feed yourself cheaply for several days without having to keep cooking from scratch as Guy and his girlfriend Claire do.

'use whichever vegetables are in season at the time'

CHUNKY ITALIAN VEGETABLE SOUP

SERVES 6

Obviously it's the vegetables that are chunky not the Italians. This is a formula you can vary endlessly depending on what veg are cheap and in season. It also reheats well if you want to leave some for the next day.

3 tbsp olive oil
2 medium onions, peeled and chopped
2 large cloves of garlic, crushed
2 sticks of celery, trimmed and sliced or a
  large carrot, peeled and chopped
$1/2$ a 400g can chopped tomatoes
1 litre vegetable stock made with 1 tbsp
  Marigold vegetable bouillon powder
  or a vegetable stock cube
2 medium courgettes (about 225g), trimmed
  and sliced into rounds
A handful of fresh green beans (about 125g),
  trimmed and quartered
410g can cannellini or borlotti beans
$1/2$ small green cabbage, trimmed and finely
  shredded or $1/2$ bag of ready-sliced greens
  or 3 tbsp chopped fresh parsley
2 tbsp red pesto
salt and freshly ground black pepper
a little grated Parmesan

Heat the olive oil in a large saucepan or casserole and cook the onion and garlic over a low heat for about 5 minutes. Add the chopped celery or carrots, cook for a few minutes more then add the tomatoes and stock and bring to the boil. Lower the heat and simmer for about 15 minutes. Add the courgettes, green beans and cannellini beans and half the cabbage, if using, and cook for another 20 minutes or until all the vegetables are soft, adding the remaining cabbage or parsley and pesto about 10 minutes before the end of the cooking time. Season to taste with salt and pepper and serve with grated Parmesan.

VARIATIONS

This is a quick no-chopping version. Forget the onion and the other veg. Cook the garlic in the oil for a minute, add $1/2$ a can of tomatoes, smash them down a bit then add the stock and bring to the boil. Add a small packet (about 350g) of frozen vegetables, the cannellini beans and about 125g (a mugful) of small pasta shapes. Bring back to the boil and simmer for about 12–15 minutes till the vegetables are soft and the pasta is cooked. Add pesto and parsley as above.

TOP STUDENT TIPS

These kind of soups are just perfect for when you are short on time and money. An even simpler variation (if such a thing is possible) is to melt a little butter (or heat some oil) and add a tin of tomatoes. Season with salt, pepper and a little sugar and add a tin of drained butter beans. Simmer for 5 minutes and serve with chopped parsley and Parmesan. Easy as. In Fiona's soup you could expand on the Italian vibe and replace the beans with a handful of pasta – *conchiglie* ('shells') would be ideal. The soothing, soulfulness of soft pasta in a soup is hard to beat for those cold winter lunchtimes. **JAMES**

CLASSIC ITALIAN-STYLE BOLOGNESE

SERVES 4

Minced beef isn't the bargain it once was, particularly the 'extra-lean' type that can be quite pricey. If you're keeping the cost down the answer is to use less, or use another type of meat like pork or turkey – both good options. Apart from the Marmite this is a reasonably authentic Italian recipe – a modest quantity of meat, bulked out by a generous amount of veggies. The only downside is that it takes a long time to cook – but you can leave it simmering away just like a stew.

4 tbsp olive, sunflower or vegetable oil
250–300g minced beef
2–3 slices back or streaky bacon (about 75g), rind removed and very finely chopped (optional)
1 medium onion (about 125g), peeled and very finely chopped
1 clove of garlic, peeled and very finely chopped
1 medium carrot (about 75g), peeled and very finely chopped
1 stick of celery, very finely chopped (optional)
$\frac{1}{2}$ glass of white or red wine (optional)
$1\frac{1}{2}$ tbsp tomato paste
1 x 400g tin whole tomatoes
150ml stock made with $\frac{1}{2}$ tsp Marmite
salt and black pepper
400g spaghetti
Parmesan or Cheddar cheese, to serve

Heat a saucepan or casserole for 2–3 minutes until hot, add 1 tablespoon of the oil and fry the beef until lightly browned on all sides. Scoop the beef out of the pan with a large spoon, leaving the fat behind then discard the fat (see opposite). Add 3 more tablespoons of oil, heat through for a minute then add the bacon. Fry for a minute, then add the onion, stir and cook for 3–4 minutes over a low heat until the onion starts to soften.

Add the garlic, chopped carrot and celery, cover the pan and fry for another 5–6 minutes. Return the meat to the pan, fry for a couple of minutes then pour in the wine and bubble up for a minute or two until evaporated. Stir in the tomato paste and mix well with the meat and vegetables. Add the tinned tomatoes and break down with a wooden spoon. Pour in the stock, stir and bring to the boil. Turn the heat right down, partially cover the pan and leave the sauce to simmer for $1\frac{1}{2}$–2 hours, stirring the sauce occasionally. About 15 minutes before you want to eat put the spaghetti on to cook in a large pan of boiling, salted water, following the instructions on the pack. Spoon a little cooking water into the sauce. Drain the spaghetti. Check the seasoning for the sauce, adding salt and pepper if necessary. Divide the spaghetti between 4 plates, spoon the sauce on top and grate over a little Parmesan or Cheddar.

TOP STUDENT TIPS

If a recipe calls for wine to be added, and you haven't got any undrunk plonk hanging around the kitchen – a common occurrence in student accommodation, I find – you can substitute a spoonful or two of red or white wine vinegar.
JAMES

LIGHT, CREAMY BOLOGNESE

SERVES 4

An alternative Bolognese – lighter and creamier – based on turkey or pork mince both of which tend to be cheaper than beef mince.

2–3 tbsp vegetable oil
450g pork or turkey mince
a thin slice of butter (about 10–12g)
250g mushrooms, rinsed and very finely chopped
2 tbsp tomato paste
2 cloves of garlic, peeled and crushed
1/2 a 400g tin whole or chopped tomatoes or 150ml creamed tomatoes or passata
just over 100ml stock made with boiling water and 1/2 tsp Marmite
400g spaghetti
a small carton of whipping cream or double cream
salt, pepper and lemon juice or wine vinegar, to taste
2–3 tbsp finely chopped parsley, if you have some

Heat a frying pan and add 1 tablespoon of vegetable oil. Once the oil is hot, fry the mince until browned then remove it from the pan with a large spoon letting the fat drain away. Pour off the fat into a bowl. Add the remaining oil to the pan then add the butter. Tip in the mushrooms and stir-fry over a high heat for about 3–4 minutes until any moisture has evaporated. Turn the heat down and return the mince to the pan. Add the tomato paste and garlic and cook for a minute then add the tomatoes or passata. (If using whole tomatoes break them down with a wooden spoon or a fork.) Add the stock, stir and leave the sauce simmering over a low heat while you cook the spaghetti according to the pack instructions. Once the spaghetti has drained,

add about two thirds of the cream to the sauce and heat through gently. Season the sauce with salt, pepper and a few drops of lemon juice or wine vinegar. Stir in some chopped parsley if you have some. I don't think this needs cheese but feel free if you fancy it.

TOP STUDENT TIPS

If you are without a garlic crusher, fear not. Peel the garlic and sprinkle with salt, then crush with the back of a knife before scraping it until it becomes a paste – easy. For a milder garlic flavour you ought to slice the garlic – this releases less oil and makes for a mellower garlicky undertone. If you're concerned about your hands reeking of the stuff then wash them after handling the garlic, then rub them on a stainless steel tap. I've no idea why, but this gets the smell off – clever eh? Less successful, I find, is the chewing of parsley to rid your breath of garlic. **JAMES**

HOW TO MAKE A CHEESE SAUCE

Here are 3 different ways of making a cheese sauce. The classic method is the slowest but the best way of making a large amount, but do try the alternatives.

CLASSIC CHEESE SAUCE

SERVES 4

This requires your undivided attention for 5 minutes. Don't get distracted or lumps will ensue.

40g butter
3 tbsp (40g) plain flour
1 small 584 ml carton of semi-skimmed or
   ordinary milk (not skimmed)
75g strong or 100g medium Cheddar,
   coarsely grated
salt and pepper

Cut the butter into chunks and melt gently in a medium-sized non-stick saucepan. Take the pan off the heat and stir the flour into the butter with a wooden spoon until it is smooth. Put the pan back on a low heat for a few seconds to 'cook' the flour and butter mixture, stirring it all the time, then remove it from the heat again. Add the milk bit by bit stirring to amalgamate it completely before you add the next lot. (Don't worry if it suddenly goes very thick. Keep stirring and gradually adding the milk.) Leave about 100ml of the milk in the carton for the moment. Put the pan back on the hob, increase the heat slightly then bring the milk gradually to the boil, stirring all the time. You should end up with a satiny smooth sauce. Turn the heat right down again and leave the sauce to simmer for 5 minutes, stirring it occasionally. Add the grated cheese and stir till smooth again. Stir in a little extra milk if the sauce seems too thick (it should just coat the back of your spoon without running off it) and let it cook for a moment. Season to taste with salt and pepper. To make the sauce lighter, add a tablespoon or two of pasta or vegetable cooking water. To make it richer, add a couple of tablespoons of cream.

• If the sauce goes lumpy all is not lost. Force it through a fine sieve. You'll get slightly less sauce but it should still be edible.

THE ALL-IN-ONE METHOD

Quicker but scarier, this way the ingredients all go into the pan at once which obviously saves time. You need a small balloon whisk though. Put the butter, milk and flour (same quantities as the above recipe) in a pan and bring gradually to the boil, whisking energetically. Turn the heat down and simmer for 5 minutes then turn off the heat and add the cheese as described above.

A REALLY QUICK CHEESE SAUCE

Great if you just need a small quantity. Follow the method for Easiest Ever Cheese on Toast (page 52) or the Creamy Gorgonzola Sauce (page 200).

CLASSIC MACARONI CHEESE

SERVES 4

Although I call this macaroni cheese, it's actually better made with a thicker pasta like penne or rigatoni.

3 tbsp butter (40g) plus a bit for buttering the
   baking dish
3 tbsp (40g) plain flour
a small (584ml) carton of milk
150g strong Cheddar, coarsely grated
salt and freshly ground black pepper
350g penne or rigatoni
1 tsp Dijon mustard or ½ tsp English
   mustard (optional)

Make the base for the sauce as described opposite then leave it over a low heat without adding the cheese while you cook the pasta. Bring a large pan of water to the boil, add salt then tip in the pasta, stir and cook for the time recommended on the pack. Just before the pasta is ready, stir half the cheese into the sauce together with the mustard, if using, and season with salt and pepper. Drain the pasta thoroughly and pour into a lightly buttered shallow baking dish. Pour over the cheese sauce and mix it in well. Sprinkle over the remains of the grated cheese. Place the dish under a hot grill for about 5 minutes until the top is brown and crispy. If you don't have a grill, bake in a hot oven (200C/400F/Gas 6) for about 15–20 minutes until browned.

VARIATIONS

I'm a bit of a purist about macaroni cheese but you can of course add other things to it – ham, crisp-fried bacon bits, mushrooms, a layer of sliced tomatoes over the top, whatever. The best alternative version is to cook a couple of washed, sliced leeks in the butter before you add the flour then add the milk as usual (you may need slightly more). You can substitute other hard cheeses, but make sure they're medium or strong in flavour. Lancashire is good or Red Leicester.

CAULIFLOWER CHEESE

Basically you follow exactly the same method as macaroni cheese, cooking cauliflower instead of pasta. Take a medium to large cauliflower, cut off the base and remove the green outer leaves. Cut the white, creamy florets off the stalk and cut into even-sized pieces and either steam or cook them in boiling water until tender (about 6–8 minutes). Drain, put in an ovenproof dish, pour over the sauce, sprinkle with cheese and place under a hot grill until the top is brown and bubbling.

TOP STUDENT TIPS

 Mac 'n' cheese is a classic dish and deservedly so – perfect for entertaining a group of hungry mates. The trick to getting it right is adding punchy flavours like mustard, cayenne or even Marmite. Don't be afraid to season well with salt and pepper either. The cheese should be strong, as Fiona suggests, and if you're feeling adventurous try making this with several cheeses like blue, Cheddar and goat's. This is obviously less frugal but for a cheese-fiend it's total bliss. Definitely make sure to use at least semi-skimmed or whole milk for the sauce (it will be thin and runny if you use skimmed – this is not a dish to be worrying about your waistline!). A drizzle of slightly diluted Marmite over the top before grilling is *so* good. Also, resist incorporating too many veggies into the dish; instead, serve it with a salad, steamed broccoli or some green beans. You can expect to feel like a baby hippo if you eat mac 'n' cheese on its own – green veggies definitely help mitigate tummy bloatedness. **SIG**

ROAST VEGETABLE LASAGNE

SERVES 4-6

There are far easier ways of combining pasta and roast veggies (see opposite) but I know people are crazy about lasagne and it's cheap, so here we go. You can try making it without pre-cooking the lasagne but I always find it goes slightly cardboardy and makes the finished dish dry.

1 large aubergine (about 350g)
sea salt and freshly ground pepper
3 peppers (a mixture of red and green)
125ml olive oil
2 medium to large courgettes (about 300g)
2 cloves of garlic
2 x 400g cans of tomatoes
250g pack dried green lasagne
150g freshly grated Parmesan or 200g grated
   Cheddar

First prepare the vegetables. Rinse the aubergine, cut off the stalk and slice it into medium-thick slices (about the thickness of a pound coin). Lay them out on a chopping board or clean work surface, sprinkle them both sides with salt and leave them for 30 minutes to get rid of the bitter juices. Meanwhile set the oven to 200C/400F/Gas 6. Rinse the peppers, cut them into quarters and cut away the stalks, white pith and seeds.

Lay them out on a baking tray and trickle a little olive oil over both sides. Roast them for about 40 minutes or until just soft then cut each quarter into two. Once the aubergines have little beads of moisture all over them transfer them to a colander or sieve, rinse them thoroughly under the cold tap to get rid of the salt and pat them dry with kitchen towel. Lay them out on another baking sheet, trickle oil over both sides, rubbing it in well and roast them for about 25 minutes. (If you only have one baking sheet, cook the peppers first then cook the aubergines.) After roasting, lower the oven temperature to 190C/375F/Gas 5 ready to bake the lasagne.

Rinse the courgettes, cut off the stalks and cut them into diagonal slices about the same thickness as the aubergines. Heat about 3 tablespoons of olive oil in a frying pan and fry them quickly on both sides until they begin to brown. (You will need to do this in two or three batches.) Set aside the cooked courgettes on a plate, turn the heat down and add the crushed garlic to the pan. Stir for a few seconds then tip in the tinned tomatoes and break them up with a spatula or wooden spoon. Simmer for a few minutes then season with salt and pepper. Finally (told you this was time-consuming) bring a large pan of water to the boil. Add a little salt and a tablespoon of oil and drop in the lasagne sheets one by one. Cook for 4–8 minutes depending on how thick your lasagne is (cheap lasagne is usually thicker) until no longer hard, drain and rinse with cold water.

Now you can assemble the lasagne. You need a deep, ideally rectangular, dish slightly smaller than the average roasting tin. Grease it with a little olive oil then put a couple of spoonfuls of the tomato sauce over the bottom. Lay a layer of roast veggies over the top, season lightly with salt and pepper, spoon over some more sauce (about $1/4$ to a $1/3$ of what you have left in the pan) and sprinkle over about 2 heaped tablespoon of grated Parmesan or Cheddar. Lay over another layer of lasagne sheets, then another layer of vegetables, sauce and cheese, ending with a layer of lasagne. (Depending on the size of your dish you may be able to make a third layer but leave enough tomato sauce to top the lasagne.) Finally spoon the remaining sauce over the lasagne and top with a good layer of grated cheese. At this point you can refrigerate the lasagne and cook it later or even the following day, bringing it to room temperature again before you cook it. Trickle a little extra olive oil over the top of the lasagne and bake for about 40–45 minutes until nicely browned and bubbling. Serve with plenty of crusty bread and a big green salad.

ROAST VEGETABLE PASTA BAKE

This, I have to say, is a lot easier and quicker and you'll get just the same great flavours. Simply cut up all your veggies, put them in a roasting tin and roast for about 30 minutes. Pour over your tomatoes or passata and return to the oven while you cook about 250g of pasta shapes (I like penne for this). Drain the pasta, saving a little of the water and mix with the veggies, adding a little of the cooking water. Sprinkle with cheese and flash under the grill. Bingo!

TOP STUDENT TIPS

This is a great meal to cook for a group, as all the prep can be done beforehand it can be made in big quantities. There are so many different vegetables you can add to this depending on the season. I've used broccoli, cauliflower, carrots, mushrooms and spinach at different times. **GUY**

'a great meal to cook for a group'

GUY'S CHILLI CON CARNE

SERVES 6-8

A much-loved family recipe, this makes a big pot of chilli that will keep you going for a few days.

2 onions, peeled and chopped
3 cloves garlic, peeled and chopped
3 carrots, peeled and chopped
olive oil
4 tins of kidney beans, drained and rinsed
4 tins of chopped tomatoes
750g lean minced steak
2 tbsp ground cumin
2 tbsp paprika
2 tbsp mixed herbs
1 tsp piri piri pepper
salt and freshly ground black pepper
a small carton of yoghurt
crackers

Heat up the olive oil in a large pot and gently fry the onions, garlic and carrots. Add the lean minced steak and fry until brown. Add the drained and rinsed kidney beans and the chopped tomatoes. Add the cumin, paprika, herbs and piri piri pepper. Season with salt and freshly ground black pepper. Bring to the boil, then reduce to a bare simmer and leave to cook for 1–2 hours. Adjust seasoning and add more chilli if necessary.

Serve in bowls, topped with yoghurt and broken crackers. Enjoy with ice cold Sol, Coronas or Dos Equis Mexican beer.

FIONA SAYS

I love the addition of crumbled crackers at the end of the recipe which will give you a satisfying extra crunch. If you haven't got the individual spices Guy mentions you can use mild chilli powder and ratchet up the heat with a bit of cayenne pepper, paprika, chilli powder or hot sauce. (That said, I would always add cumin too if you've got it.) And as you're not frying off the meat for this recipe make sure you buy really lean mince. (For a nice quick version of chilli see page 80.)

TOP STUDENT TIPS

It's worth making chilli a day or two in advance of eating it as the flavour really improves if you refrigerate it overnight. It's also worth making a large batch and then freezing in smaller portions so you can take a portion out for lunch or a quick supper when you don't have the time or inclination to cook (e.g. during exams). A trick I learnt from Willie Harcourt-Cooze's Chocolate book is to add a teaspoonful of either cocoa powder (the type with no sugar) or some grated 'cacao' (looks like chocolate but again, has no sugar) to the sauce – adds an extra kick of flavour, and if you're a chocoholic like me, there's something really satisfying about adding 'chocolate' to savoury dishes! **SIG**

BLACK BEAN CHILLI

SERVES 4

I don't know why black beans make this look so much sexier but they do (though you can perfectly well use red kidney beans). If you're using dried beans remember to soak them a day ahead. This is a great everyday meal that can be turned into a feast by laying on all the suggested extras below.

250g dried black beans or, if you want to speed up the whole process, 2 x 400g cans black beans, borlotti beans or red kidney beans
1 green pepper (optional)
3 tbsp sunflower or olive oil
2 medium onions, peeled and thinly sliced
2 large cloves of garlic, peeled and roughly chopped
2 level tsp mild chilli powder
1/2 rounded tsp cumin powder (optional)
1 x 400g tin whole or chopped tomatoes
salt
3 heaped tbsp fresh coriander

Soak the beans overnight. Put them on to cook following the instructions on the pack. Meanwhile wash the pepper, cut into quarters, cut away the white pith and seeds and cut into chunks. Heat the oil in a large saucepan, add the onion and pepper and cook for about 7–8 minutes until beginning to soften. Add the chopped garlic, the chilli powder and cumin if using, stir, cook for a minute then add the tomatoes and stir again. Turn the heat down, cover and leave to simmer slowly while the beans carry on cooking (or for about 15 minutes if using canned beans). Drain the beans, add to the tomato mixture, stir, replace the lid and cook for another 10–15 minutes to let the flavours amalgamate. Just before serving check the seasoning, adding salt to taste and stir in the fresh coriander.

Serve with as many of the following as you have time to prepare or can afford. For a feast, lay each out in a bowl.

- A small carton of sour cream.
- 1–2 avocados, peeled, stoned and coarsely chopped.
- 1/2 small pack (about 125g) crumbled white cheese (such as Caerphilly, Cheshire or Wensleydale) or goat's cheese.
- A pack of tortilla chips.
- A medium-sized red onion, peeled and roughly chopped.
- Baked sweet potatoes (see page 164).

LEFTOVERS

Any cold leftover beans are really good as a filing for a pitta bread or a wrap.

TOP STUDENT TIPS

 What a cracking party recipe. There's nothing better than a dish like this that you can do well in advance (indeed, it will taste better if you do) and can then stick in the middle of the table and just let everyone pile in, adorning their own bowls to their personal preference. Stick a few sweet potatoes in the oven an hour before eating and you've got yourself a hell of a feast. Chuck a big bowl of guacamole (page 179) into the mix, singing with lime, coriander and chilli, and you're getting pretty close to perfection.
JAMES

FAKE DONER KEBABS

SERVES 4–8

This dish could serve 8, but I've seen 4 make short work of them! These are not really kebabs – more like flat kebab–flavoured hamburgers – but they are good. You could make them all beef or all lamb rather than a mix of the two. These would also go great on the barbecue.

1 small to medium sized onion peeled, quartered and roughly chopped
500g extra-lean minced beef
500g minced lamb
2 large cloves of garlic
1 level tsp ground coriander
1 level tsp ground cumin
3 tbsp fresh coriander leaves, finely chopped
3 tbsp fresh parsley, finely chopped
the leaves from 3–4 sprigs of mint, finely chopped (optional)
salt and pepper
$3/4$ tbsp light olive oil
a little flour for dusting

To serve
2 packs of pitta breads
some shredded iceberg lettuce, washed and ready to eat
homemade or shop bought hummus (see page 178) mixed with a couple of spoonfuls of yoghurt and a squeeze of lemon
2 lemons, cut into quarters
1 mild onion, finely sliced

Place the onion in the bowl of a food processor and pulse until finely chopped. Add the minced beef and lamb, the garlic, ground coriander, cumin, fresh herbs and salt and pepper and process until the mixture is almost like a paste in texture. Leave for at least half an hour for the flavours to amalgamate. Divide the meat mixture into 16 portions. With lightly floured hands, roll each into a ball then with the heel of your hand press it down firmly so that you have a flat disc. Heat a ridged grill pan or non stick frying pan for about $3/4$ minutes until really hot then brush the patties lightly in oil and fry them in batches, pressing them down firmly with a wooden spatula as you cook them, until they're well browned each side and thoroughly cooked through (about 3 minutes each side). Set aside and keep warm. Warm the pitta breads through briefly in a toaster or under a low grill, keeping them covered on a plate with a tea towel so they keep warm and don't go hard. Put the salad leaves in a bowl, lay out the lemon wedges, sliced onion and hummus. Split the pitta breads and fill each one with one or two patties plus whatever other ingredients each person wants – for the full monty you'd go for a dollop of dip, a few slices of onion, a squeeze of lemon juice, and a few lettuce leaves. Wheel out the ketchup only if you have to.

TOP STUDENT TIPS

Kebabs have a reputation for being typical late night student nosh but actuallly they're quite a healthy option. A quicker way to make them is simply to take some diced lamb or chicken and marinate it in a mixture of oil and lemon juice with a bit of garlic and dried oregano then thread the pieces on a skewer with slices of onion and pepper in between. Brush the marinade over the kebabs then cook in a foil lined grill pan or on a barbecue **GUY**

EASY MEATBALLS

SERVES 4-6

A really easy way of making meatballs using sausages instead of breadcrumbs (you can use breadcrumbs too which will make them stretch even further).

400–450g premium range sausages
400–500g minced beef
2 cloves of garlic, peeled and crushed
3 heaped tbsp finely chopped fresh parsley,
  plus extra for sauce
plain flour, for rolling the meatballs
5–6 tbsp sunflower or vegetable oil
2 x 400g tins of tomatoes
salt and ground black pepper
a little sugar for seasoning
grated Parmesan for serving

Cut through the skin of each sausage and pull it off. Put the sausage meat into a large bowl with the mince. Add the crushed garlic, spring onions and parsley and mix well together with a fork, wooden spoon or your hands. Sprinkle a chopping board with flour. Scoop out dessertspoons of the mix, dip them in the flour and roll them between your palms. Heat 3 tablespoons of the oil in a large frying pan or wok and fry the meatballs in batches, browning them on all sides. Set aside on a plate. When you've fried all the meatballs, pour away any excess fat and rinse and dry the pan. Pour in the remaining oil, heat for a minute then add the remaining garlic and fry for a few seconds. Tip in the tomatoes and break them down with a fork or wooden spoon. Cook over a moderately high heat for 5 minutes until jammy and season to taste with salt, pepper and a little sugar. Tip in the meatballs, and turn them over in the sauce, ensuring they're well covered. Cover the pan and cook the meatballs over a low heat for about half an hour, spooning over the sauce occasionally and adding a little extra water if it's becoming too dry. After 15 minutes, cook some spaghetti or rice to go with the meatballs (see page 80 or 100). To serve, stir in some more parsley and spoon the meatballs and sauce over the spaghetti or rice. Sprinkle with grated Parmesan.

VARIATIONS

If you want to spice up the recipe, use spicy sausages or add a teaspoon of paprika to the meat mix. Add $\frac{1}{2}$ a teaspoon of paprika to the tomato sauce too. Or give them a Middle-Eastern flavour by mixing the sausage meat with lamb mince (or beef mince with lamb sausages, whichever is cheapest). Season with 1 tablespoon of Moroccan Spice Mix (page 107) and replace some or all of the parsley with chopped fresh coriander and a little chopped mint if you have some and serve with pitta bread, cucumber and yoghurt.

TOP STUDENT TIPS

Meatballs are great fun to make, production line style. One person can roll them, while another person cooks them in batches. I like to put capers in my mixture, which adds a salty tang. Try baking instead of frying the meatballs to make them healthier. If you have any leftover, cook them in a barbeque sauce (a gloopy mixture of onion, garlic, ketchup, honey, Worcestershire sauce) and serve with rice the following day. **GUY**

GREEK(ISH) SHEPHERD'S PIE

SERVES 4

If you can't decide between shepherd's pie and moussaka this is the perfect solution – a shepherd's pie with a moussaka-ish taste.

3 tbsp olive or other oil
450–500g minced lamb
1 onion, peeled and finely chopped
1 carrot, peeled and very finely chopped (optional)
1 large clove of garlic, crushed
1/2 tsp oregano or marjoram (optional)
1/4 tsp ground cinnamon
1 tbsp tomato purée or sundried tomato purée
1/2 x 400g tin of tomatoes (save the rest for a pasta sauce) or 200ml passata
a small glass (about 125ml) red wine
about 3 tbsp chicken or vegetable stock (if you have some handy)
2 tbsp chopped fresh parsley (optional)
salt and freshly ground black pepper

For the topping
700–750g boiling potatoes, peeled and cut into even sized pieces
a heaped tbsp of soy or Greek yoghurt
2–3 tbsp extra virgin olive oil

Heat a frying pan, add 1 tablespoon of the oil and fry half the mince until lightly browned. Remove with a slotted spoon and drain off the excess fat/liquid. Without adding more oil, repeat with the remaining meat. Put some fresh oil in the pan and fry the chopped onion and carrot over a low heat until soft. Add the crushed garlic, cook for a minute then stir in the oregano and cinnamon, then the tomato purée, tomatoes or passata and red wine. Season lightly with salt and pepper, bring up to boiling point then reduce the heat to low and leave to simmer while you boil the potatoes.

Once the potatoes are cooked, drain them, cut them up roughly and mash them with a potato masher or fork. Add the yoghurt and olive oil, beat well then season to taste. Add a little extra stock, water or wine to the lamb filling if it has got a bit dry, stir in the parsley and check the seasoning.

Preheat the grill*. Transfer the meat to a shallow dish and top with the mash, spreading it evenly over the meat. Place under the grill until the top is nicely browned.

* If you're making this ahead you'll need to reheat the pie in a moderately hot oven (190°C/375°F/Gas 5) for about 30–40 minutes depending whether or not you've taken it out of the fridge.

TOP STUDENT TIPS

 If you don't have potatoes to hand, try making a yoghurt (dairy or non-dairy) topping by whisking two eggs, adding about 150–200ml of plain or soy yoghurt and seasoning with salt and pepper and, if you're not dairy-intolerant, some grated or crumbled cheese: Parmesan, feta or Cheddar all work well. SIG

MITZIE'S ENCHILADAS

SERVES 4

A great student recipe from fellow cookery writer Mitzie Wilson, author of *Mince! 100 Fabulously Frugal Recipes* (also published by my illustrious publisher).

500g minced beef
1 onion, finely chopped
1 clove garlic, crushed
1 x 400g can chopped tomatoes
3 tablespoons tomato purée
$1/2$ tsp dried oregano
$1/2$ tsp ground cumin
$1/2$ tsp chilli powder or to taste
8 flour tortillas
150g Cheddar, grated
$1/2$ small red chilli, sliced
1 tablespoons chopped fresh parsley
avocado salsa or Guacamole (see page XX),
    sour cream, shredded lettuce and lime
    wedges to serve

Dry-fry the minced beef and onion in a medium pan for about 5 minutes until browned. Add the garlic and fry for 1 minute then add the tomatoes, tomato purée, oregano, cumin, chilli powder and a little salt. Bring to the boil then cover and simmer for 15 minutes.

Set the grill to hot.

Warm the flour tortillas in a frying pan. Spread a little mince over half of each tortilla, roll up each one and place together in a 2-litre baking dish. Top with grated cheese, chilli and parsley and grill until golden. Serve with avocado salsa or guacamole, sour cream, shredded lettuce and lime wedges.

FIONA SAYS

In my view, you can never have too many mince recipes. Or too much Tex Mex. If you can make chilli con carne you can easily make this which is basically a chilli mince mixture without the beans. If you've time it's worth making some fresh tomato salsa (page 110) or guacamole (page 179) to go with them too.

'some like it hot'

COTTAGE PIE WITH GUINNESS

SERVES 4

Adding stout or porter to a cottage pie makes a fantastically rich, savoury filling.

3 tbsp olive or sunflower oil
450g minced beef
1 medium to large onion (about 150g), peeled and finely chopped
2 carrots (about 150g), peeled and finely chopped
1/2 tsp dried thyme
1 level tbsp plain flour
225ml beef stock or stock made with 1 level tsp Bovril or half a beef stock cube
175ml Guinness or other stout
2–3 tsp Worcestershire sauce
1 tbsp tomato ketchup (optional)
salt and freshly ground black pepper

For the potato topping
800g potatoes, peeled and quartered
25g butter
50–75ml warm milk
salt and freshly ground black pepper

Heat a large frying pan, add 1 tablespoon of the oil and fry half the mince until lightly browned. Remove the meat with a slotted spoon, letting the fat run back into the pan then discard the fat. Add the remaining mince to the pan, brown it and drain off the fat in a similar way. Add the remaining oil and fry the chopped onion and carrot over a low heat for about 5 minutes until soft. Stir in the dried thyme and flour and cook for a few seconds then add the beef stock and Guinness or other stout. Bring to the boil and simmer until the gravy thickens. Tip the mince back in the pan, bring back to simmering point then add the Worcestershire sauce and a little ketchup for sweetness if it needs it. Turn the heat right down and leave on a low heat for about 30 minutes. Meanwhile put the potatoes in a saucepan, cover with cold water and bring to the boil. Cook for about 20 minutes until you can stick the point of a knife in them easily. Drain the potatoes, return them to the pan and cut them up roughly with a knife. Mash them thoroughly with a potato masher or fork. Beat in the butter and warm milk. Season with salt and pepper. Preheat the grill. Tip the mince into a pie dish and spread the potato evenly over the top, roughing up the surface with the prongs of a fork. Place the pie on a baking tray and grill for 5–10 minutes until the potato is nicely browned.

• You can assemble the pie ahead, refrigerate it then bake it in a hot oven (200C/400F/Gas 6) for about 35–40 minutes.

TOP STUDENT TIPS

As a student it's likely you'll find yourself chucking an unhealthy amount of bad beer down your gullet. Without naming any names, there are a lot of beers out there that taste of little, and whose only attributes are the fact that they get you stonkingly drunk and facilitate a pretty impressive belchy chorus in the queue for the club. Stick to drinking those beers if you enjoy them, but for cooking it's essential that you use decent, flavoursome ales, bitters, stouts and porters. They're the ones with the deep, complex flavours, beers that have the clout to stand up to a rich stew or pie, or that stirred into melted cheese give an extraordinary earthiness to a cheese on toast (like the one on page 52).
JAMES

MEXICAN SALSA CHICKEN

SERVES 4–6

There's a long, involved explanation as to how this recipe came about (check out the Frugal Cook blog, 26th May 2008) but suffice it to say it was originally designed to be made with tomatillos but works equally well with ripe summer tomatoes.

1kg chicken thighs or thighs and drumsticks
750g ripe tomatoes, skinned and chopped
1–2 mild onions (about 200g in total) peeled
   and roughly chopped
3–4 cloves of garlic, peeled and chopped
1–2 chillies, de-seeded and roughly chopped
rind and juice of 2 limes (preferably unwaxed)
a good handful of coriander, well washed and
   trimmed
3–4 tbsp olive oil
1–1¹/₂ tsp salt
2 spring onions, trimmed and very finely
   shredded (optional)

**you will need a large casserole or deep
   frying pan**

Remove the skin from the chicken thighs and drumsticks. Skin the tomatoes by making a cut in the skin, pouring the boiling water over them, leaving them for a minute then plunging them into cold water. Put the peeled chopped tomatoes, onions, garlic, chillies and rind and juice of the limes in a blender. Cut the stalks off the coriander, chop roughly and add them to the blender goblet then whizz together until you have a liquid but still rough-textured sauce. Heat 2 tablespoons of oil in the casserole or frying pan and tip in the salsa. Add 1 teaspoon of salt and the skinned chicken, turning it in the sauce. Bring to the boil then turn the heat down low and simmer for about 45–50 minutes until the chicken is cooked and the salsa reduced and thick. Roughly chop half of the remaining coriander leaves and add them to the pan. Stir and cook for 3–4 minutes. Serve the chicken with warm tortillas or with brown rice, scattering over some more chopped fresh coriander and some finely shredded spring onions, if you have some.

VARIATIONS

You could add a bit of smoked chilli or pimenton to the salsa for a slightly smokier flavour.

LEFTOVERS

To die for. If there's any chicken, wrap it and the leftover sauce in a tortilla with some crumbly white cheese and extra spring onion and coriander as above. The sauce on its own would turn fried eggs into huevos rancheros, the classic Mexican breakfast dish.

TOP STUDENT TIPS

 Peeling tomatoes might seem like a bit of a faff, but for the vast majority of recipes it really is worth doing. The skins add little flavour and are stringy and not particularly toothsome. A tomato salad is improved immeasurably by having skinless tomatoes, as they are much more receptive to any dressing and seasoning you add, the flesh soaking up the flavours with much greater readiness than when shrouded in its red cagoule. Tomatoes also respond very well to sugar, its addition really emphasising their sweetness. **JAMES**

NO-CARVE ROAST CHICKEN

SERVES 4-6

This is exactly the same as roasting a whole chicken other than the fact that you don't have to carve it. If you only have one roasting dish, serve boiled potatoes instead.

1¼kg potatoes
salt and freshly ground black pepper
6 tbsp olive oil or vegetable/sunflower/
   rapeseed and olive oil mixed
1kg chicken thighs and drumsticks or
   chicken legs, free-range if possible
½ tsp dried oregano or thyme (optional)
8 streaky bacon rashers
4 cloves of garlic (optional)
400–454g pack of good-quality sausages

Preheat the oven to 200C/400F/Gas 6. Peel the potatoes, halve or quarter depending how big they are and place in a large saucepan. Cover with cold water and bring to the boil (about 5 minutes). Add a little salt and boil for 5 minutes, then strain the potatoes in a colander or sieve, saving 450ml of the cooking water for the gravy.

Put 4 tablespoons of oil into a roasting tin and tip in the potatoes, turning them in the oil. Pour the remaining oil into another tin then put in the chicken pieces. Turn them in the oil and season with salt, pepper and a little thyme. Put both the tins in the oven and cook for 30 minutes. Cut the rind off the bacon rashers if necessary then stretch each rasher by running the blunt edge of the knife along the rasher. When 30 minutes is up take out the tin with the chicken, turn over the chicken pieces and season them on the other side.

Add the garlic cloves, sausages and arrange the bacon rashers over the top. Replace the tin in the oven, take out the potato tin and turn the

potatoes too. Put them back in the oven and continue to cook while you make the gravy following the recipe for Amazing Marmite Gravy (below), using the reserved potato water to dissolve the Marmite. Leave it to cook over a very low heat. After another 15 minutes turn over the sausages, turn the heat up to 220C/425F/Gas 7 and continue to cook until the potatoes, chicken and bacon are crisp (about another 15 minutes). Cook whatever veg you're serving in the meantime (frozen peas would be fine).

AMAZING MARMITE GRAVY

This may sound wildly unlikely but believe me it works. And it's so much better than gravy granules. Measure out 450ml (2 mugfuls' worth) of boiling water (or potato stock) and dissolve 2 teaspoons of Marmite in it. Set aside. Melt 2 tablespoons of soft butter (about 30g) gently in a saucepan and then stir in 2 tablespoons of plain flour. Cook over a low heat for a minute then add the Marmite stock, stirring continously. Bring back to the boil and simmer till ready to use.

TOP STUDENT TIPS

 Roast chicken replete with sausages, bacon and roasties? My idea of a perfect Sunday lunch. You could make this for an impromptu dinner party as all it requires is chucking everything in a pan, letting the bird and various accoutrements do their thing in the oven whilst you chill with your mates. You could tuck loads of garlic cloves around the roasting tin too. And if you just want to make it an all-chicken dish, lemon also lends itself particularly well to chicken, so try zesting one into a marinade with plenty of herbs and slathering the pieces with that. **SIG**

BAKED CHICKEN
WITH GARLIC & LOVELY LEMONY POTATOES

SERVES 4

Good enough for a feast. Irresistible enough to want to make most weeks. But use free-range chicken if you can possibly afford it.

4 medium to large potatoes (about 600–700g)
2–3 tbsp olive oil plus a little soft butter
salt and freshly ground black pepper
1 large lemon, preferably unwaxed
2–3 cloves of garlic
2–3 sprigs of fresh rosemary or thyme or 1
   tsp dried oregano
4 chicken quarters (about 1 kg in total) or 1kg
   chicken thighs and drumsticks

Heat the oven to 200C/400F/Gas 6. Peel and cut the potatoes into thick slices (slightly thicker than a pound coin). Generously smear a roasting tin with soft butter or olive oil and lay the potato slices in a single layer over the base. Season with salt and pepper. Cut half the lemon into thin slices, halve them and lay the pieces over the potatoes. Peel and finely slice the garlic and strip the leaves from the rosemary and scatter them both over the top. Pour over a couple of tablespoons of water.

Cut any loose bits of skin off the chicken pieces and lay them skin side down over the potatoes. Squeeze the juice from the remaining half of the lemon over the chicken, drizzle over a tablespoon of olive oil and season with salt and pepper. Bake in the oven for half an hour then turn the chicken pieces over, spoon the pan juices over them and season again with salt and pepper. Turn the oven down to 190C/375F/ Gas 5 and continue to cook for about 25–30 minutes until the chicken is well browned and the potato cooked through. (Spoon off a couple of tablespoons of the cooking juices about 10 minutes before the chicken is ready, to crisp the potatoes up.) Fish out the lemon slices when you serve up. This tastes good with any green vegetable, especially broccoli, spinach and beans or with a salad.

TOP STUDENT TIPS

As student kitchens are about as likely to include a dishwasher as a Turkish bath, one pot cooking is the best way to avoid prune fingers from spending too much time in a filthy sink. Chicken skin can go soggy when cooked this way, so remove it first if you prefer. Watch closely, and if the pan looks a little dry, pour over some stock. **GUY**

ROAST CHICKEN WITH HERBS

One recipe you just have to master – unless you're a veggie, obviously.... Please buy a free-range bird.

a medium-sized chicken (about 1½ kg)
a whole lemon or a handful of parsley
olive oil or sunflower oil
salt and freshly ground black pepper

Preheat the oven to 200C/400F/Gas 6. Remove any giblets from inside the bird (usually tucked in a plastic bag) and stuff it with a lemon or a handful of parsley. Smear the chicken with oil, season with salt and pepper and place it in a roasting tin, breast side upwards. Roast for 20–25 minutes until the breast begins to brown then turn it on one side and roast for another 20 minutes. Holding the chicken, carefully pour or spoon out most of the fat that has accumulated in the pan, then turn the chicken on its other side and cook for another 20 minutes. If it seems to be cooking too quickly turn down the oven a setting and cover it loosely with a sheet of foil. Finally turn it breast side upwards again and give it a final 20 minutes. To test if it's cooked, stick a sharp knife into the thickest part of the chicken leg. When you withdraw it any juices that emerge should run clear. Take the chicken out of the oven and let it stand, lightly covered with foil for 10 minutes, before you carve it. Meanwhile make the gravy and finish cooking the veg.

• If you've got more than four to feed it's actually easier to cook two smaller chickens side by side than one really big one.

HOW TO CARVE A CHICKEN

This is a much easier method than attempting to cut neat slices. Cut down either side of the bird and remove the two legs then cut each leg into two pieces – the thigh and drumstick. Run your knife along the left-hand side of the breastbone and loosen the chicken breast away from the carcass. Cut it away in one piece then cut it in half. Repeat with the right hand breast. Cut off the two chicken wings. That's it.

HOW TO MAKE GRAVY?

Depending on your bird and the temperature of your oven you may or may not have some sticky caramelised juices around the sides of the roasting tin on which to base a gravy. If you have, pour off most of the fat, sprinkle in a little flour, work it into the fat and pan juices, then pour in some chicken stock and bring to the boil until thickened. Adjust the seasoning and add a little diluted Marmite or soy to taste. Otherwise, make the Amazing Marmite Gravy on p149.

TOP STUDENT TIPS

 For a recent Sunday lunch, I attempted an unusual variation of the standard roast chicken. By placing the chicken on top of spring onions and basting it with a mixture of soy sauce, honey, fresh ginger and fresh garlic you can have a really easy but substantial Asian roast dinner. It turned out incredibly juicy and quite sweet. Serve with boiled udon noodles and steamed mange-tout. **GUY**

SUPER-CRISPY ROAST POTATOES

SERVES 4-6

If you want proper old-fashioned crusty roast potatoes you have to cook them in a separate tin and finish them once you've taken everything else out of the oven. You also need to use old potatoes (i.e. ones that are suitable for roasting, not ones you've had hanging around in a cupboard for several weeks).

1¼kg roasting potatoes
4–5 tbsp rapeseed or vegetable oil

Preheat the oven to 200C/400F/Gas 6. Peel the potatoes, halve or quarter them depending on how big they are and place them in a large saucepan. Cover with cold water and bring to the boil. Add a little salt, boil for 5 minutes then strain off the water. Put 4 tablespoons of oil into a roasting tin and tip in the potatoes, turning them in the oil. Roast the potatoes for 45 minutes turning them half way through. Turn the heat up to 220C/425F/Gas 7 and continue to cook until the potatoes are crisp (about another 15 minutes).

TOP STUDENT TIPS

 A trick I learnt at Leith's is to do exactly as this recipe suggests, except place the oiled roasting tin in a hot oven for 10–15 minutes before you toss the parboiled potatoes in the oil. Doing this really seals the outside of the potatoes and adds extra crispiness when they're roasting. Make sure the potatoes sizzle when they hit the oil to seal the exterior. You can, of course, jazz up roasties with garlic, rosemary, Marmite, chilli, fennel seeds, coriander, etc., for extra pizzazz. If the occasion calls for extra decadence – say at Christmas – try roasting potatoes with goose or duck fat. **SIG**

HOW TO MAKE PERFECT MASH

SERVES 4

Even though you can use packet mash (see below) and now chilled and frozen mash, nothing is as good (or as cheap) as the real thing.

1kg King Edward or other good boiling potatoes (now marked on supermarket packs)
a good slice (25g) of butter
50–75ml warm milk
salt and freshly ground black pepper

Peel the potatoes and halve or quarter them so you have even-sized pieces. Put them in a saucepan of cold water and bring them to the boil (about 5 minutes.) Skim off any froth, season them with salt then cook them for 20–25 minutes until you can put the tip of a knife into them without any resistance. Drain the potatoes thoroughly in a colander then return them to the pan and put it back over the heat for a few seconds to dry up any excess moisture.

Take the pan off the heat, chop the potatoes up roughly with a knife then mash them with a potato masher or a fork until they are smooth and lump-free. Beat in the remaining butter and enough milk to make a soft but not sloppy consistency (unless, like the French, you like your mash sloppy). Season with salt and freshly ground black pepper plus any of the seasonings that follow.

WHAT YOU CAN ADD TO MASH

• A teaspoon or two of Dijon mustard, creamed horseradish, pesto or wasabi.
• A tablespoon of Parmesan or 2 tablespoons other hard grated cheese.
• A couple of spoonfuls of double cream or crème fraîche instead of some of the milk.
• Add a couple of cloves to the water when you cook the potatoes then mash them with the potatoes for garlic mash.
• Some lightly cooked chopped greens or shredded cabbage, tossed in a little butter (called colcannon in Ireland).
• 1–2 leeks, cleaned, sliced and cooked in a little butter.

HOW TO TART UP PACKET MASH

It may lack the irresistibly fluffy texture of the real thing but packet mash can be made to taste almost as good. Choose the French kind which is made from flakes rather than Smash-type granules and make it slightly sloppier than you would home made mash. Be generous with the butter and other seasonings.

ROOT VEG MASH

Root veg like carrots, parsnips, celeriac and swede also make good mash though carrots and celeriac are best combined with another mashed vegetable like swedes (good with carrots) or potato (with celeriac). Unlike potatoes you can whizz these in a food processor (potatoes go gluey). Add a slosh of cream to parsnip mash for a really decadent purée.

TOP STUDENT TIPS

I cannot recommend buying a potato ricer strongly enough. They are a bit of an extravagance, clocking in around the twenty quid mark, but a sturdy one will last you a lifetime, and a lifetime of perfect mash at that. The problem with using a conventional masher, as Jeffrey Steingarten points out in the brilliant *The Man Who Ate Everything*, is that you end up pounding bits of spud that you've already mashed, essentially breaking down molecules that are already broken, and you run the risk of an over-worked, gluey mashed potato. A potato ricer, a sort of giant garlic crusher, eliminates this risk, as each piece of potato only gets the one mashing. Then all you have to do is beat in the warmed milk and a generous amount of butter. Once you've made mash this way, you will not look back. **JAMES**

'it doesn't take much effort to get perfect mash'

SALMON & LEEK HASH

SERVES 3-4

If you like salmon fishcakes you'll like this hash which is actually quite a bit easier.

450–500g uncooked – or cooked – new
   potatoes
250g–300g cooked or uncooked boneless,
   skinless salmon fillet or a pack of smoked
   trout
2 medium leeks, cleaned and chopped
1 tbsp olive oil
a slice of butter (about 25g)
1/2 small packet of fresh dill or 3 tbsp
   chopped fresh parsley
about 1 tbsp lemon juice
salt and freshly ground black pepper
a small carton of sour cream (optional)

Boil the potatoes, if uncooked in salted boiling water until just tender (about 12–15 minutes). Drain and set aside until cool enough to handle. Meanwhile microwave or steam the salmon and break it into chunks with a fork. Clean and slice the leeks. Heat a large frying pan or wok over a moderate heat then add the oil and the butter. Gently cook the sliced leeks for about 5 minutes until they are beginning to soften but still green. Slice the potatoes thickly and add to the pan. Crush them roughly with a fork and fry with the leeks for about 5 minutes until beginning to brown.

Add the salmon and heat through, turning the mixture carefully with a fork so as not to break it up too much. Strip the dill leaves from the stalks and chop them or snip them finely with scissors. Sprinkle half the dill over the hash and season it with lemon juice, salt and black pepper. Divide the hash onto plates, spooning a little sour cream over the top of each serving and sprinkle with the remaining dill.

LEFTOVERS

Any leftover dill would be great with a cucumber salad or mixed with sour cream for a smoked salmon bagel if you feel like having a splash-out brunch.

TOP STUDENT TIPS

 This is a great meal to make out of fishy leftovers. Perfect as a simple supper or even better as a Sunday brunch. Put in any back-of-the fridge vegetables that you're having trouble finding a use for. **GUY**

CHILLI BEEF HASH

SERVES 4

This is a zipped-up version of that great American store cupboard standby – corned beef hash. If you haven't got any cooked potatoes, boil some first.

2 tbsp oil
1 large onion, peeled and roughly chopped or a bunch of spring onions, trimmed and sliced into thin rings
2 cloves of garlic, peeled and crushed
1 tsp smoked pimenton (Spanish paprika), paprika or mild chilli powder
1 tin of corned beef, cut into large cubes
3 medium to large cooked potatoes (about 600g), roughly chopped
3 heaped tbsp chopped fresh parsley
salt

Heat the oil in a large frying pan or wok. Cook the onion over a moderate heat until beginning to brown (about 6–7 minutes). Add the garlic and 1–2 teaspoons of pimenton or paprika (depending how hot it is) and cook for another minute then add the corned beef and potatoes. Break them up roughly with a spatula then turn the heat up and cook, turning the mixture over occasionally until it begins to form a crust (about 5–8 minutes). Add the chopped parsley and season with salt and a little extra pimenton if you think it needs it. Serve on its own with ketchup or with a fried egg on top.

TOP STUDENT TIPS

Fiona, Sig, and Guy are all aware of my notorious beetroot fetish, and so will smirk when they see that I suggest beetroot would make a fine addition to this dish. The ready-cooked version is fairly adequate (though avoid the stuff that has been cooked in vinegar), but they're easy to roast or boil. Then just chop them up and add them to this mixture. They add a lovely earthy undertone with a sweet edge that goes extremely well with smoked paprika. **JAMES**

'beetroot... a fine addition'

SAUSAGE & MASH WITH ONION GRAVY

SERVES 4

Having written a book titled *Sausage and Mash* (Absolute Press) I feel I could do a PhD on the subject. Here's a good simple version. Personally I prefer frying them, but shoving them in the oven is undoubtedly less messy and leaves you more room on the top of the stove. I've given both options.

2 x packs of decent quality sausages (such as Cumberland)
3 tbsp oil

For the mash
4–5 large potatoes, about 900g in total
A good slice of butter (about 40g)
50–75ml warm milk
sea salt and freshly ground black pepper

If you're baking the sausages, heat the oven to 200C/400F/Gas 6. While it's heating put the potatoes on to boil following the recipe on page 154. Meanwhile put 2 tablespoons of the oil in a roasting tin and heat it in the oven for about 4–5 minutes. Cut the links between the sausages and tip them into the pan, turning them so they are evenly covered with oil. Return to the oven and cook for about 20 minutes, turning them occasionally. If you're frying the sausage, heat the oil in a pan over a moderate heat, add the sausages, turn the heat down slightly and cook for 20 minutes, turning occasionally. Pour off any excess fat if they seem to be stewing rather than frying. While the sausages and spuds are cooking make the gravy (see opposite). Once the potatoes are cooked pour off the water (or drain them in a colander and return them to the pan). Mash the potatoes following the method on page 154. Once cooked they'll keep warm for about 20 minutes with the pan lid on. Serve the sausages with a good dollop of mash and gravy spooned over.

FOR THE ONION GRAVY

3 medium onions (about 300–350g), peeled and sliced
1 tbsp cooking oil
a lump of butter (about 20g)
1 tbsp plain flour
350ml of stock made with boiling water and 1½ tsp Marmite or Bovril
black pepper
soy sauce or brown sauce to taste (optional)

Heat a heavy saucepan or small frying pan over a moderate heat, add the oil then a few seconds later, the butter. Tip in the onions, stir well and cook over a medium heat for 10–15 minutes until soft and beginning to brown. Stir in the flour and gradually add the hot stock, stirring well as you go. Bring to the boil then turn the heat right down and simmer for 5 minutes, or until ready to use it. Season with pepper and a few drops of soy sauce or brown sauce if you have some.

TOP STUDENT TIPS

 Sausages are my nemesis. Invariably I under or overcook them – once after incinerating sausages under the grill I spent an entire day questioning the meaning of life. Call it sausage trauma. Mash, however is less problematic. The trick is not to over beat mash when mixing in the milk, and if you want to show off to your mates, add some horseradish to the mash. Wasabi also does the trick. For the less daring, simply embellish your mash with garlic, parsley and/or mustard. **SIG**

JAMES' SAUSAGE CASSEROLE

SERVES 4

 Simple, nourishing, and super-frugal, this dish is wonderful served with a baked potato and some broccoli.

1 red onion, peeled and roughly chopped
8 sausages
1 tin butter beans, drained and rinsed
1 tin flageolet beans, drained and rinsed
1 tin chopped tomatoes
100ml red wine
100ml hot vegetable stock
1 teaspoon smoked paprika
salt and pepper
olive oil

In a casserole with a lid, sweat the onion over a low heat in a little olive oil. Increase the heat and add the sausages. Stir for a couple of minutes and add the beans, tomatoes, wine, stock and paprika. Season with salt and pepper. Bring to the boil, cover and then simmer over a gentle heat for an hour. This is one of those dishes that are excellent done ahead and reheated.

FIONA SAYS

 I have to admit I'm not a big fan of sausage casseroles but know I'm in a minority here. And James' version which includes red wine (good move) is a particularly tasty one. Canned beans are a godsend for all sorts of impromptu meals. They're quick to cook and add easily stretch a meal for a crowd. See more ideas on page 73 and 138.

TOAD-IN-THE-HOLE

SERVES 4

No apologies for repeating this sausage classic from my book *Sausage & Mash* (Absolute Press). I can't resist the combination of porky sausages and puffy batter.

110g plain flour
1/2 level tsp salt
2 medium eggs, lightly beaten
175ml semi-skimmed milk mixed with 125ml water
8 herby pork sausages, e.g. Lincolnshire (about 450g–500g)
4 tbsp of grapeseed or rapeseed oil or 1 tbsp oil and 25g of lard or vegetable shortening, diced

you will need a deep rectangular roasting tin about 22 x 28cm

Sift the flour into a large bowl and sprinkle over the salt. Make a hollow in the centre and add the egg and about a quarter of the milk and water mix. Work the flour into the egg with a wooden spoon until it is all incorporated, beating it briskly until smooth. Gradually add the rest of the milk, beating well between each addition. (Or, easier still, simply bung all the ingredients in the bowl of a food processor and whizz until smooth.) Pour the batter into a jug and leave in the fridge for at least 30 minutes. When the batter is rested heat the oven to 225C/425F/Gas 7. Pour 3 tablespoons of the oil or the diced fat in a large roasting tin and heat till the oil is smoking hot (about 7–8 minutes).

Meanwhile heat a frying pan, add the remaining oil and brown the sausages lightly on all sides. Take the roasting tin out of the oven, give the batter a final stir or whisk, then pour it into the tin (it should immediately start to bubble up and sizzle). Drop in the sausages one by one with a pair of tongs. Put the pan back in the oven and cook for about 35–40 minutes until the toad is well browned and puffed up. Serve with onion gravy on page 159.

TOP STUDENT TIPS

 The most important thing to remember when making toad, or Yorkshire puddings for that matter, is that your oil needs to be absolutely stinking hot before you add the batter. You'd jump if you were poured into boiling hot oil, wouldn't you? Well that's exactly what you want the batter to do – to rise, creating a light, airy and crisp pudding. Don't worry if you prefer the 'soggy' part of a toad – you'll still have that at the bottom – but surely you want the dish that you bring out of the oven with a flourish to tower impressively, eliciting such responses from your friends as, 'crikey, what a whopper!' or' 'gadzooks! ne'er have I seen such a gargantuan toad-in-the-hole in all my life!' **JAMES**

NICE FLUFFY BAKED POTATOES

SERVES 4–6

The mistake most people make when cooking baked potatoes is to buy absolutely gigantic ones that take an age to cook and end up like a soggy football. If you're cooking several at once they also need to be even-sized so you don't end up with a mix of over- and under-cooked potatoes.

4–6 large but not ridiculously large potatoes
    (about 250–300g each)
a little sunflower or vegetable oil

Preheat the oven to 200C/400F/Gas 6. Give the potatoes a good scrub if dirty and dry well with kitchen towel. Prick the skin with a fork in several places to ensure the potatoes don't burst (not necessary if you have a spike – see below). Pour a little oil into your palms and rub it over the potatoes (this makes the skin nice and crisp). Put the potatoes on a baking tray or in a roasting tin for about an hour to an hour and a quarter, turning them half way through. Cut a cross in the centre of each baked potato as you take it out of the oven then, protecting your hands with oven gloves, squeeze the sides of the potato so it opens up at the top. This lets the steam escape and makes the potato fluffier.

• To speed up the cooking time impale the potatoes on a baked potato spike. You can buy them in department stores, kitchen shops or those weird catalogues full of gadgets nobody really needs. Except the potato spikes, obviously!
• You can also roast sweet potatoes the same way. They tend to be smaller so will take slightly less time – about 45–50 minutes. They go really well with chilli and spiced vegetable stews.

SOME GOOD TOPPINGS

• **Cottage cheese tzatziki**
For 4–6 mix a 227g carton of cottage cheese, with a crushed clove of garlic, about a tablespoon of finely chopped onion or spring onion and 2 tablespoons of plain yoghurt. Peel and coarsely grate a third of a cucumber, squeeze out the excess moisture and add to the cottage cheese along with 5–6 finely chopped mint leaves or some chopped fresh parsley. Season with salt and pepper.
• **Prawns and mayo**
Mix 200g fresh or thawed, frozen prawns with 3 tablespoons of mayo mixed with 3 tablespoons of plain yoghurt. Add a little finely chopped spring onion or some snipped chives if you have some.

• **Bolognese sauce or chilli con carne**
• **Sour cream and chives**
• **Baked beans with chilli or barbecue sauce**
• **Blue cheese, sour cream and bacon**
• **Soft garlic and herb 'roulé' cheese (supermarket own brands are cheapest)**
• **Roast peppers (can be cooked at the same time as the potatoes) and goat's cheese**

TOP STUDENT TIPS

 Jacket potatoes are the easiest base for whatever is hiding in the back of your fridge – tail ends of cheese (cut away the mould first!), odd tubs of tuna, sweetcorn or baked beans, leftover chilli con carne... whatever. Use up your left-overs and be creative! Ensure that the potato skin is really crispy by rubbing it with a little oil before you bake it. It's by far the best bit. **GUY**

CHEESE, ONION & BACON STUFFED BAKED POTATOES

Life, you might think, is too short to stuff a potato but you get the best of all worlds – crispy baked potato skin, mashed potato filling and crispy cheesy crust. Mmmmm.

4 x medium to large potatoes, about 250g–300g each
3 tbsp vegetable or sunflower oil
1 medium onion, peeled and finely chopped
4 back bacon rashers or 8 streaky rashers (about 125g in total), finely chopped
a good slice (25g) butter
4–5 tbsp milk or a mixture of milk and cream, sour cream or fromage frais
125g mature Cheddar, grated

Preheat the oven to 200C/400F/Gas 6. Scrub the potatoes clean, dry them, prick them with a fork and rub them lightly with oil. Bake them for an hour to an hour and a quarter, turning them half way through. (You can go off and do something else at this point.) Take the potatoes out of the oven and leave to cool slightly while you heat the remaining oil and fry the chopped onion and bacon until crisp. Cut the potatoes in half and carefully scoop out the centre without breaking the skin. Mash until smooth then add the butter and milk or milk and cream and mash again. Add the fried onion and bacon and a third of the cheese, mix well together and season with salt and pepper. Pile the filling back into the potatoes, top with the remaining grated cheese. Turn the oven up to 220C/425F/Gas 7 and cook the potatoes until the topping is nice and crispy. Good with salad or lightly cooked broccoli or spring greens.

VARIATIONS

You could replace the Cheddar with other hard cheeses such as Lancashire or Red Leicester, a crumbly blue cheese like Stilton or a soft herb and garlic-flavoured cheese.

'the crisp potato skin is by far the best bit'

SPICED SWEET POTATO, PEPPER & AUBERGINE BAKE

SERVES 4–6

A veggie main that meat-eaters will definitely want to share. You can of course vary the veg depending on what's available though I like this combination.

2 medium to large onions (about 350g)
6 tbsp olive or sunflower oil
2–3 sweet potatoes (about 450g), peeled and cut into large cubes
1 medium to large aubergine (about 350g), cut into large cubes
1 large red or green pepper (about 175g), cut into large chunks
250g okra (optional), washed and stalks trimmed
2 large cloves of garlic
1 tbsp Moroccan Spice Mix (see page 107)
400g can of chopped tomatoes
250ml stock made with 1 tsp Marigold vegetable bouillon powder
salt, sugar and Tabasco or hot pepper sauce, to taste
400g can of chickpeas, drained and rinsed
3 heaped tbsp fresh coriander leaves, roughly chopped
1 small carton of sour cream

Preheat the oven to 200C/400F/Gas 6. Peel one of the onions and cut into eight. Pour 4 tablespoons of the oil in a large roasting tin. Add the onion, cubed sweet potatoes, aubergine and pepper, mix well with the oil and bake in the oven for 30 minutes, turning them half way through. Meanwhile peel and roughly chop the other onion and prepare the okra, if using. Heat the remaining 2 tablespoons of the oil in a large frying pan and fry the onion and okra gently for about 10 minutes. Add the garlic and spices and stir well. Add the chopped tomatoes and cook

for about 5 minutes. Stir in the stock then check the seasoning adding salt and a pinch of sugar to taste. Add a dash of chilli sauce or Tabasco if you don't think it's hot enough. Lastly add the chickpeas. When the vegetables in the oven have been cooking for 30 minutes pour over the spiced tomato mixture and stir in well. Turn the oven temperature down to 190C/375F/Gas 5 and cook for another 20–30 minutes until the vegetables are well cooked, turning them half way through. Just before serving add the chopped coriander. Serve each portion with a dollop of sour cream.

TOP STUDENT TIPS

This is the kind of veggie dish I could easily convert to vegetarianism for. I'm not, but if you're omnivorous and want a tasty recipe for upping your daily veg count, then give this a go, it's the kind of dish that will render veggie sceptics speechless, and is redolent of somewhere farflung and exotic. A great dish any time of the year, but especially during the dark days of winter when all those spices will bring a smile to your face.Try other veg such as butternut squash, cauliflower, spinach, carrots, parsnips – whatever's in season and takes your fancy. Any leftovers are just as tasty next day. **SIG**

BAKED SWEET POTATO FALAFEL

MAKES ABOUT 18 FALAFEL, ENOUGH FOR 4-6.

A great recipe from chef and writer Allegra McEvedy's *Leon: Ingredients and Recipes* (Conran Octopus). Falafel, which are generally deep-fried, are a pain to make so this baked version is really clever. Tasty too.

2 medium sweet potatoes (orange inside), around 700g or 1¹/₂ pounds in total
1¹/₂ teaspoons ground cumin
2 small cloves of garlic, chopped
1¹/₂ teaspoons ground coriander
2 big handfuls of fresh cilantro/coriander, chopped
juice of ¹/₂ a lemon
a scant cup (120g) gram /chickpea flour
a splash of olive oil
a sprinkling of sesame seeds
salt and pepper

Preheat the oven to 220C/425F/Gas 7 and roast the sweet potatoes whole until just tender – between 45 minutes and 1 hour. Turn off the oven, leave the potatoes to cool, then peel.

Put the sweet potatoes, cumin, garlic, ground and fresh coriander, lemon juice and gram/chickpea flour into a large bowl. Season well, and mash until smooth with no large chunks. Stick in the fridge to firm up for an hour, or the freezer for 20–30 minutes. When you take it out, your mix should be sticky rather than really wet. You can add a tablespoon or so more of chickpea flour if necessary (the water content of sweet potatoes varies enormously).

Reheat the oven to 400F/200C/GAS 6. Using a couple of soup spoons (put a well-heaped spoonful of mix in one spoon and use the concave side of the other to shape the sides) or a falafel scoop if you have one, make the mixture into falafelly looking things and put them on an oiled tray. Sprinkle sesame seeds on top and bake in the oven for around 15 minutes, until the bases are golden brown.

TOP STUDENT TIPS

 Fragrant and moist, these vegan and gluten-free falafel are utterly moreish – even if you don't have a sweet potato fetish like me, I bet you'll find it hard to resist tucking into a handful. In contrast to regular falafel this sweet potato version isn't as dry, nor are they deep-fried but rather baked in the oven. Make in a big batch and eat with abandon as a midnight snack or wow your mates by bringing them to picnics and BBQs in the summertime. SIG

BIG VEGGIE CURRY

SERVES 4–6

A totally flexible recipe you can adapt depending on what's available. You just need to make sure all the veg are cooked properly – some take longer than others. If you want to reduce the quantity to serve one or two, it's easiest to base it on one of those mixed bags of microwaveable vegetables you can often find reduced.

about 1kg mixed veg which could include:
  1 medium onion, peeled and roughly chopped, 1 large carrot, peeled and sliced, $^1/_2$ a medium cauliflower, cut into florets, 1 small to medium-sized aubergine, cut into cubes, $^1/_3$ to a $^1/_2$ butternut squash, peeled, de-seeded and cut into chunks, a handful of green beans, a courgette, trimmed and cut into rounds
4 tbsp vegetable oil
2–3 cloves of garlic, peeled and crushed
2–3 tbsp curry paste, depending how strong the paste is and how hot you want the curry
$^1/_2$ –1 x 400g tin of tomatoes, roughly chopped
up to 600ml vegetable stock made with a vegetable stock cube or 1 tbsp vegetable bouillon powder
1 x 400g tin chickpeas (leave out if you're serving a dal alongside)
3 tbsp chopped fresh coriander – optional but good
salt and lemon juice, to taste
plain yoghurt, to serve

Put the root veg in a saucepan and cover with boiling water. Bring to the boil and cook for about 10 minutes (adding the cauliflower and beans, if using, half way through). Meanwhile, heat the oil in a wok and stir-fry the aubergine and squash for 3–4 minutes. Add the chopped onion and courgette, turn down the heat a bit and keep frying until the vegetables are soft (about another 5 minutes). Stir in the curry paste and tomatoes then pour in the boiled veg and their cooking water and enough extra stock to cover all the vegetables. Bring to the boil, cover the wok and simmer until the vegetables are tender (about another 10–15 minutes). Add the chickpeas, and coriander if using, and heat through. Check the seasoning, adding salt and lemon juice to taste. Serve with rice, naan or pitta bread and onion raita (page 171) or a dollop of plain or soy yoghurt.

TOP STUDENT TIPS

 I would gingerly suggest that aubergine is a pretty essential vegetable to be included in the medley here. Texturally, it is a good replacement for meat, being chunky, rich and substantial, while its flavour marries incredibly well with spices. It's a woefully underrated vegetable in this country. Try getting hold of pea aubergines, which can be found in ethnic food stores, and added whole to a curry – they look beautiful and taste even better. If you're using large aubergines it's often prudent to remove the seeds, which can have a bitter edge. It's a simple operation – cut the aubergines in half vertically and just scoop out the seeds with a large spoon. **JAMES**

TARKA DHAL WITH CRISPY ONIONS

SERVES 4–6

Grinding your own spices might seem a slog but really does give a better flavour. If you haven't got a pestle and mortar, place them on a piece of foil on a chopping board and crush them with the side of a tin.

250g red lentils
1 tsp turmeric
a small chunk (about 2cm square) fresh ginger, peeled and coarsely grated
4 tbsp sunflower or grapeseed oil
1 medium onion, peeled and finely sliced
1 tbsp coriander seeds or 2 tsp ground coriander
2 large cloves of garlic, peeled and finely chopped
1 tbsp cumin seeds or 2 tsp ground cumin
a pinch (about 1/4 tsp) chilli powder or cayenne pepper
1/2–1 tsp salt
2 heaped tbsp finely chopped fresh coriander

Put the lentils in a pan with the turmeric, grated ginger and 850ml cold water. Bring to the boil and carefully spoon off any froth on the top. Part-cover the pan and simmer for about 25–30 minutes or until the water is absorbed (you want it sloppy rather than stiff). Meanwhile, fry the onion in 2 tablespoons of the oil over a medium heat turning regularly until the edges of the slices have turned dark brown (about 10 minutes). Remove from the pan. Crush the coriander seeds. Heat the remaining oil, fry the garlic for a minute then add the crushed coriander, cumin seeds and chilli powder. Cook for another minute then return the onions to the pan and heat through. Season the dhal with salt to taste and stir in the fresh coriander. Tip into a bowl and top with the crispy spiced onions. Very good with any kind of Indian bread or even warm pitta bread.

VARIATIONS

You could also add a handful of chopped fresh spinach leaves towards the end of the cooking time.

TOP STUDENT TIPS

 This recipe doesn't have to be part of an Indian meal. Add in some garlicky Toulouse sausage as they are so well suited to lentils. Bring the cooking pot to the table and let a big group of friends fight over the ladle. **GUY**

FRESH CORIANDER CHUTNEY

SERVES 4-6

If you make nothing else to go with your curry, make this.

a large pack or small bunch of coriander
4–5 sprigs of mint
a small carton of plain, unsweetened low-fat yoghurt
1 clove of garlic, peeled and crushed with a little salt
1 chilli, de-seeded and finely chopped
1 tbsp fresh lemon juice
$\frac{1}{4}$ tsp ground cumin
salt to taste

Wash the coriander thoroughly, shake dry then chop off the thicker stalks. Chop the leaves as finely as possible. Wash the mint, strip the leaves from the stalks and chop very finely too. Put the yoghurt in a bowl and mix in the mint, coriander, crushed garlic and chilli. Season to taste with salt, lemon juice and a little cumin if using. Cover and leave in the fridge for half an hour to let the flavours infuse. Eat within 2 hours of making it (which shouldn't be difficult).

• If you have a food processor or blender you can simply bung this all in together but don't overprocess it or you'll get something that resembles a pale green soup rather than a relish. Alternatively you can give it a bit of a whizz with a hand-held blender.
• To de-seed a chilli, cut it in half lengthways and scoop out the seeds with the tip of a teaspoon. Take care not to let your hands touch your face and wash them immediately afterwards to avoid chilli burn.

ONION & CUCUMBER RAITA

SERVES 4-6

Most Indian restaurants offer either onion or cucumber raita. I like both but feel free to leave out the cucumber.

1 small onion, peeled and very finely sliced
$\frac{1}{4}$ cucumber, seeded and finely diced
300ml low-fat yoghurt
$\frac{1}{4}$ tsp ground cumin
a pinch of chilli powder or cayenne pepper
1 tbsp lemon juice
salt and extra cayenne pepper

Combine the onion, cucumber and yoghurt in a bowl. Mix well. Season with cumin, chilli powder or cayenne pepper, lemon juice and salt. Cover and set aside for 30 minutes for the flavours to infuse. Stir again and sprinkle lightly with chilli powder or cayenne pepper before serving.

TOP STUDENT TIPS

The storing of coriander is a dilemma that I have wrestled with since forever. It is heart breaking to reach for the bag of coriander you bought a week ago, only to find it rancid and brown. Buying the potted stuff from a supermarket is a complete waste of rations. There's enough on them for, oh, a couple of handfuls. Much better, as the esteemed maestro of this weighty tome, Fiona Beckett, taught me, is to buy the stuff by the bunch with the roots still intact. Pop the roots into an old jam jar of cold water, cover the leaves with a plastic bag and secure with a rubber band round the lip of the jar. Kept in the fridge, the coriander should keep for almost a week, if you change the water every day or two. Always wash the coriander before use. **JAMES**

BIG VEGGIE COUSCOUS

SERVES 8

This really is a great recipe – easy, tasty, cheap and filling. It takes a bit of time though so I'd make it at a weekend or on a day when you're not in a rush. Some elements – the onions, carrots and spices – are constant, others can be substituted depending on what's in season. You need about a kilo to a kilo and a half of veg in total.

3 tbsp olive, sunflower or vegetable oil
2 medium onions, peeled and sliced
2 level tbsp Moroccan spice mix (see page 107) or 2 tsp ground cumin, 2 tsp ground coriander, 1 tsp turmeric and 1/2 tsp chilli powder
1 level tbsp plain flour
1 1/2 litres of weak vegetable stock made with 1 rounded tbsp Marigold vegetable or vegan bouillon powder or a vegetable stock cube
3 medium or 2 large carrots, peeled and cut into even-sized chunks
2 medium or 1 large parsnip, peeled and cut into even-sized chunks
a small swede or 1/2 a medium sized swede
a small cauliflower, trimmed and cut into florets
1 x 200g tin or 1/2 a 400g tin of tomatoes or 3 fresh tomatoes, skinned and chopped or 3 tbsp passata or creamed tomatoes
1 x 400g tin of chickpeas, drained and rinsed
4 heaped tbsp chopped fresh coriander or coriander and parsley
salt and lemon juice, to taste
500g instant couscous
hot sauce (or harissa, for authenticity), to serve (optional)

First get all your veg ready and chopped into even-sized chunks. Put them in piles depending on how long they will take to cook (root veg take longer than other veg). Heat the oil in a large saucepan or casserole and add the onions. Cook over a moderate heat for about 5 minutes then stir in the spices. Cook for a minute then add the flour, stir then gradually add the stock. Bring to the boil, add the carrots, parsnip and swede, bring back to the boil and simmer for about 7–8 minutes. Add the cauliflower bring back to the boil and cook for another 10 minutes or so until the cauliflower is cooked. Spoon off about 300ml of the cooking liquid with a ladle or mug, pour it into a bowl and add enough boiling water to bring it up to the amount you need for cooking the couscous (check the packet). Sprinkle the couscous over the hot stock, stir, cover and leave to absorb the stock. Meanwhile add the tomatoes or passata, chickpeas and coriander to the couscous, heat through and leave to simmer for about 5 minutes. Check the seasoning, adding salt and fresh lemon juice to taste. Fork through the couscous to fluff it up then serve in bowls with the vegetables spooned over the top. Offer hot sauce or harissa for those who like it hotter

VARIATIONS

This is mainly based on winter vegetables. You could also use squash, or sweet potatoes. In the summer you could substitute turnips, courgettes, fennel, aubergines, peppers or green beans.

TOP STUDENT TIPS

 Mmm, these are great ingredients: Moroccan spice mix, veggies, tomatoes, chickpeas. Perfect for a veggie fiesta or if you want to cook something for the week ahead. Instead of couscous you could use quinoa. I like the idea of adding sweet potato too. Though I like sweet potato with pretty much everything. **SIG**

CHARRED AUBERGINE & TOMATO SALAD

SERVES 4-6

There's a hugely popular Greek dip which involves charring or roasting an aubergine then gouging out the flesh and making a dip. I've never been really grabbed by it because a) it takes ages to make b) turns a dirty beige colour and c) you discard the skin which is the best bit. Here's the solution – a salad which includes all those lovely smoky flavours. A good homemade addition to a selection of mezze like taramasalata, hummus, etc., or with feta cheese and olives. With other mezze, this should serve 4 to 6 – less, obviously, if you eat it on its own.

2 medium or 1 large aubergine (about 500g)
4 tbsp olive oil
1 medium onion (about 100g), peeled and roughly chopped
1 clove of garlic, peeled and crushed
2 medium tomatoes, skinned, de-seeded and diced (see page 77)
2 tbsp roughly chopped parsley and 1 tbsp chopped mint leaves
1–1½ tbsp lemon juice
1 tsp ground cumin
salt and freshly ground black pepper

Cut the stalks off each aubergine, cut in half lengthways then cut into cubes. Heat a wok for about 2 minutes over a high heat, add the oil, heat for a few seconds then tip in the aubergine cubes. Stir-fry over a moderate heat for about 5 minutes until lightly browned then turn the heat down low, add the onion and garlic, stir, cover the pan and cook gently for a further 15 minutes, stirring from time to time. Tip the aubergine into a shallow dish while you prepare the other ingredients. When the aubergine is cool (about 20 minutes), cut it up roughly with a knife and fork, then mix in the chopped tomato, parsley and mint. Season with the lemon juice, cumin and salt and pepper. Serve with pitta bread.

TOP STUDENT TIPS

 Charring gives vegetables a deep, smoky flavour. I would also recommend cooking red peppers in this way. Mezze is great for convivial eating with a bunch of friends. You could also put out a couple of bowls of hummus and some vine leaves stuffed with feta. **GUY**

COURGETTE & PRAWN COUSCOUS SALAD

SERVES 4-6

Couscous is actually simpler to cook than potatoes, pasta or rice. You simply pour over hot water (or, better still, veggie stock), add a little oil, let it absorb the liquid then fluff it up with a fork. You can either use it as an accompaniment for spicy bean and vegetable stews or a base for an easy salad like this one.

250g instant couscous
4 tbsp olive oil
1 bunch of spring onions, trimmed and finely sliced
3 medium courgettes, trimmed and coarsely grated
200g fresh or thawed frozen prawns (the tiny North Atlantic ones)
1 tbsp lemon juice
2 heaped tbsp finely chopped parsley or coriander and a little finely chopped mint if you have some
salt and freshly ground black pepper

Make up the couscous following the instructions on the pack, adding 1 tablespoon of olive oil to the water. Leave it to cool in a large bowl, forking it through to break up any lumps.

Heat a frying pan, add the oil, heat for a few seconds then chuck in the spring onions and grated courgette and fry over a high heat for about 2 minutes. Tip the vegetables into the cooked couscous along with the prawns and fork through along with the lemon juice. Season to taste with salt, pepper and more lemon, if you think it needs it. Stir in some chopped herbs – whatever you've got to hand.

VARIATIONS

You can also make a good couscous salad with leftover roast veggies like onions, red peppers and butternut squash (good with feta or other white crumbly cheese) or with some leftover grilled chicken, cucumber, tomato and lime. Add a bit of pesto to the dressing for extra zip.

TOP STUDENT TIPS

Couscous makes for an excellent base for so many ingredients. It is so neutral in flavour that it can be paired with most things, particularly dishes that are Middle Eastern or Mediterranean. Try slinging in some caramelised red onion and sun-dried tomatoes, or peas, mint and feta cheese. The Italian equivalent, polenta, is another cracking accompaniment to rich dishes. The quick-cook variety that you can find easily is great: pour into boiling water, stirring as you go, and after a couple of minutes you have the starch element of your dish. Add Parmesan and butter and you have something really rather special. **JAMES**

THE ULTIMATE POTATO SALAD

SERVES 8

All-time family favourite from an original German recipe. In a totally different class from the potato salads you buy in cartons or even from delis. Awesome!

1kg new potatoes
4 tbsp light salad dressing made from 1 tbsp wine vinegar whisked with 3 tbsp sunflower oil or light olive oil, seasoned with a little salt and pepper
5–6 spring onions, trimmed and finely sliced or 1 small red onion, peeled and finely chopped
1 large or 2 medium pickled sweet-sour cucumbers
3 large hard boiled eggs (optional)
2 heaped tbsp low-fat mayonnaise
1 heaped tbsp low-fat crème fraîche
2 tbsp each finely chopped dill and flat-leaf parsley or 4 tbsp finely chopped parsley
salt and freshly ground black pepper

'an all-time family favourite... awesome!'

Cut the potatoes into even-sized pieces leaving the smaller potatoes whole and put into a saucepan. Cover them with boiling water, bring them to the boil, add a little salt and simmer for 15 minutes until just cooked. Drain them in a colander, spreading them out so they cool quickly. As soon as they are cool enough to handle (about 8–10 minutes) cut each piece into 2–3 pieces. Transfer to a mixing bowl and pour over the salad dressing and the chopped spring onions. Turn the potatoes in the dressing taking care not to break them up. Meanwhile finely chop the pickled cucumbers, hard boiled eggs and herbs. Spoon the mayonnaise and crème fraîche into a small bowl, mix well, thin with 3–4 teaspoons of liquid from the pickled cucumber jar and season with pepper. Once the potatoes are cool add the rest of the ingredients holding back about a third of the egg and the herbs. Mix together lightly but thoroughly. Check the seasoning adding more pepper and a little salt if you think it needs it. Transfer to a clean serving bowl (if you have one) and sprinkle the remaining egg and chopped herbs over the surface. Serve with anything you fancy (or even on its own) but great with frankfurters, ham and other Germanic-style meats. And cold roast chicken.

TOP STUDENT TIPS

The tag of 'ultimate' fits this potato salad. Pickled cucumbers (otherwise known as gherkins or cornichons) add crunchiness and an extra hit of umami. I also love Fiona's suggestion of using dill – a fabled herb in Scandinavia, where we use it in everything from curing salmon (*gravadlax*) to prawn sandwiches. Much as I love parsley, I'd go with just dill for this dish. The eggs are also a fabulous ingredient to make this stretch further, adding more protein and nutrients so that you can afford to be a little parsimonious with meat if you're preparing a big feast like a barbecue. **SIG**

HOMEMADE HUMMUS

SERVES 6–8

You might think it crazy to make your own hummus when it's so easily available readymade but if you're feeding a crowd or want to make enough to last a week, making it yourself is much, much cheaper. You'll need to soak the chickpeas a day ahead, and you'll need a handheld blender or a food processor. This recipe comes from my book, *The Healthy Lunchbox* (Grub Street).

125g dried chickpeas
2–3 large cloves of garlic, peeled
3 tbsp tahini paste (stir well before you measure it out)
2 tbsp plain or soy yoghurt (optional)
3–4 tbsp lemon juice
1/2 tsp ground cumin
1/2 tsp salt

Put the chickpeas in a bowl, cover with cold water and leave them to soak for at least 12 hours. The next day discard the water and rinse the chickpeas then put them in a saucepan of fresh cold water. Bring them to the boil, skim off any froth, add 2 cloves of garlic (but no salt) and boil them for about 1^1/$_2$–2 hours, topping up the water as necessary, until the skins begin to come away and they are soft enough to squish between your fingers. Turn off the heat and leave them to cool in the pan. Once they are cold, drain the chickpeas, reserving the cooking water and put them in a food processor (you might have to do this in two batches) or blender (or return them to the saucepan if you have a handheld blender). Start to process them, adding enough of the cooking liquid to keep the mixture moving until you have a thick paste. Add the tahini paste, yoghurt, if using, 3 tablespoons of lemon juice, cumin and salt and whizz together until smooth. (If you want it more

garlicky just add one more crushed clove.) Check the seasoning, adding more lemon juice if you think it needs it and some chopped coriander if you like and are eating it straight away.

CHEAT'S HUMMUS

If you have a blender or food processor you can also make an easy economical hummus with a can of chickpeas. Drain and rinse the chickpeas and whizz them with a couple of tablespoons of water in a blender till you have a thick paste. Add a clove of crushed garlic, 1^1/$_2$ tablespoons of tahini, 1 tablespoons of yoghurt, 1^1/$_2$ tablespoons of lemon juice and ^{1}/$_4$ teaspoon each of ground cumin and salt, and whizz again. Adjust the seasoning, adding a little extra water if it seems too stiff.

TOP STUDENT TIPS

 The lemon juice is essential in this recipe, giving the hummus a lovely acidic edge but also preventing the hummus from going brown. For added pizzazz you could add some chopped coriander, or spicy smoked paprika. Try serving with pitta crisps – cut the pittas into rough triangles, drizzle with oil and sea salt, and pop under grill for a couple of minutes. **JAMES**

AUTHENTIC ROUGH-CRUSHED GUACAMOLE

SERVES 6–8

This is not only easier than having to put everything in a blender – it's the way they do it in Mexico. And it's a lot nicer too.

3 ripe medium-sized avocados
juice of a lime (2 tbsp)
1/2 white or red onion (about 75g) finely chopped
1 small green chilli, de-seeded and finely chopped
1 large clove of garlic, peeled and crushed with 1/4 tsp salt
1 tbsp olive oil
2 tomatoes, skinned, seeded and finely chopped
3 tbsp finely chopped fresh coriander

Peel the avocados and scoop their flesh into a large bowl, removing any black bits. Mash with a fork until you have a chunky paste. Pour over the lime juice then add the finely chopped onion, chilli, crushed garlic and olive oil and mix in well. Season with black pepper and extra salt if you think it needs it. Stir in the chopped tomatoes and fresh coriander. Cover and refrigerate until ready to serve (don't make it more than an hour in advance). Good with Fresh Tomato Salsa (see page 110) and tortilla chips.

TOP STUDENT TIPS

Totally agree that guacamole should be chunky, not smooth. Add a splash of Worcestershire sauce to add extra umami – trust me, it works, though watch out when serving to your veggie friends, I once was upbraided by a highly principled veggie for adding Worcestershire sauce. Apparently it contains anchovies! **SIG**

Leaving the stone in your guac' helps to keep the colour longer. No... I've no idea why. **JAMES**

FLASHY, SHOW-OFF RECIPES

Once you've mastered the art of stir-frying and spag Bol' you may want to flex your culinary muscles and try something a little more challenging. Or showy. There's nothing quite as cool as being able to cook someone you fancy a cheffy-looking meal. Works every time...

PRAWN & AVOCADO MARTINIS

SERVES 2

AKA prawn cocktail. Martinis sounds much cooler, though.

125g small North Atlantic prawns, fresh or thawed frozen
1 ripe avocado
1 tbsp lemon juice
a handful of finely shredded iceberg or little gem lettuce

for the dressing
2 tbsp mayonnaise
2 tbsp low-fat yoghurt
1–1$\frac{1}{2}$ tsp tomato ketchup – depending how pink you want it
1 small clove of garlic, peeled and crushed or, 1 spring onion, trimmed and finely sliced (optional)
$\frac{1}{2}$ tsp Thai fish sauce (optional but adds an edge)
salt, pepper and hot pepper sauce if you have some
1 tbsp finely chopped parsley, or fresh coriander plus a little extra for decoration

you'll need two large martini glasses or other stemmed glasses

First make the dressing. Mix together the mayo, yoghurt, ketchup and garlic or onion. Add the Thai fish sauce, if using, and season with salt, pepper and a few drops of hot pepper sauce if you like. You could add a squeeze of lemon too but the avocado will taste quite lemony. Drain any liquid off the prawns, mix them with the dressing and stir in the parsley or coriander. Put the lemon juice in a bowl. Quarter and peel the avocado*, cut into small cubes and mix with the lemon juice. Put a little shredded lettuce in the bottom of each glass, spoon over half the cubed avocado and top with half the prawns. Decorate with a little extra parsley or coriander and serve straightaway with triangles of brown bread and butter (very retro!).

• When you're buying avocados check that they're ripe by squeezing the top gently by the stalk (it should give slightly and not be rock-hard). If you buy unripe ones leave them in a paper bag to ripen, not in the fridge. To cut open, run your knife round the length of the avocado then twist to pull the two halves apart.

TOP STUDENT TIPS

This gloriously kitsch '70s classic is infinitely sexier in a martini glass. It also looks pretty in shot glasses and espresso cups. Make this with sweet North Sea or North Atlantic prawns as Fiona suggests, rather than bland king or 'tiger' prawns which are often tasteless and much more expensive. Look for the Atlantic ones in the freezer section, and keep them on hand for curries, seafood risottos, pasta sauces and sandwiches. Instead of mayo try using salad cream in the dressing – this adds a certain something that mayo fails to deliver (ahem, namely, flavour!). If you'd prefer a less creamy dressing simply omit the mayo/salad cream and season with lots of lemon juice and chopped herbs. SIG

OTHER SEXY STARTERS OR INDULGENT SNACKS

PATE AND TOAST

French food isn't that fashionable currently so pâté is cheap. Serve with toast, a few cornichons (small pickled cucumbers) or onion marmalade and maybe a few lightly dressed salad leaves if you're feeling flashy.

FISH PATE AND TOAST

Smoked mackerel, smoked salmon and crab pâté are all bargain buys. Scoop out of their unglamorous plastic containers and serve with wholemeal toast, a few salad leaves and a wedge of lemon.

READY-MADE FRESH SOUPS

Again, it's just a question of tarting them up. A squeeze of lemon, a swirl of cream or yoghurt and a sprinkling of fresh herbs can work wonders. Everybody does it, darling.

FRESH ASPARAGUS

A fantastic treat when in season (May to June). Cut the spears about two thirds of the way down from the tip and rinse with cold water. Put them in a steamer or microwaveable dish with 3 tablespoons of water, cover with a damp sheet of kitchen towel and cook for about 3–4 minutes until just tender. Serve hot, dunked into a hot lemon butter dip (50g of melted butter with 2 tablespoons of lemon juice) or, after cooking, refresh with cold water to preserve the colour, pat dry and serve with a drizzle of vinaigrette and a little crumbled goat's cheese. (Don't chuck away the ends of the spears, save them for a soup or stock. Cut off the woody end first.)

GOOD ITALIAN DRIED EGG PASTA

Cook following the instructions on the packet and serve with loads of butter and freshly grated Parmesan cheese. Allow about 75g a head for a starter or snack.

BAKED CAMEMBERT

Cheat's fondue! Buy a Camembert in a wooden box, remove any plastic wrapping and replace it in its box. Rub a halved clove of garlic over the surface of the cheese and trickle over a spoonful of oil. Replace the lid of the box and bake in a hot oven (200 C/400 F/Gas 6) for about 15 minutes. Serve with crusty bread or breadsticks to dunk in the gooey cheese. Enough for 2.

TOP STUDENT TIPS

Baked Camembert is one of the most joyfully indulgent starters there is. And so simple! The only problem with it that I have encountered is that the box often has a tendency to split. Not a disaster, but be sure to place it in an oven proof serving dish before baking, just in case. A small sprinkle of white wine on top works well too, as does tucking a sprig of thyme in before cooking.
JAMES

SPRING VEGETABLE & GOAT'S CHEESE RISOTTO

Just one of the many number of risottos you can make with quite humble ingredients. Once you've got the knack they're really easy to rustle up. The key things to remember are to cook the rice before you add any liquid and make sure your stock is at simmering point when you add it.

SERVES 6 AS A STARTER, 3 AS A MAIN COURSE

a small bunch of asparagus
4 tbsp olive oil
1 medium-sized onion, peeled and finely chopped
250g risotto rice (e.g. arborio or carnaroli)
a small (125ml) glass of dry white wine
1 litre hot vegetable stock made with
   1 rounded tbsp Marigold Bouillon Powder or an organic vegetable stock cube
1/2 a fennel bulb, trimmed and finely sliced (optional)
125g podded fresh or frozen broad beans
100g podded fresh or frozen peas
150g fresh young goat's cheese
3 heaped tbsp chopped fresh dill or fennel fronds, or parsley plus a little tarragon if you have some
salt, pepper and lemon juice, to taste

Break the tips off the asparagus spears about one third of the way down the stalk and set aside. Cut off any woody bits at the lower end of the stalk and chop the rest into small pieces. Heat 3 tablespoons of the olive oil in a medium-sized saucepan or sauté pan and add the chopped onion. Stir and cook over a moderate heat for about 3 minutes then tip in the rice and stir. Let it cook for about 2 minutes without colouring, stirring occasionally so it doesn't catch on the pan. Meanwhile heat the stock in another saucepan till it's almost boiling and leave on a low heat. Pour the wine into the rice – it will sizzle and evaporate almost immediately. Add the chopped asparagus stalks and fennel, if using, then start to add the stock bit by bit, about half a mugful at a time, stirring the risotto in between and cooking it until the liquid has almost been absorbed. Then add the next lot of stock and repeat until all the stock is used up and the rice is creamy but still has a little 'bite' to it (i.e. you don't want it soft and mushy). This will take about 20 minutes. While you're stirring away lightly cook the broad beans, peas and asparagus tips for about 3 minutes in the hot stock then scoop them out and set them aside on a plate or a saucer. Add the broad beans* and peas to the risotto a few minutes before adding the last of the liquid. Once the risotto is cooked stir in the goat's cheese and let it melt then stir in the herbs and season with salt, pepper and a good squeeze of lemon juice (about 2–3 teaspoons). Gently reheat the asparagus tips in the remaining oil. Serve the risotto in small bowls with one or two asparagus tips on top.

* You can remove their skins before you do this by simply pinching them with your fingers and popping out the bright green bean inside.

TOP STUDENT TIPS

 Risotto is a dish that should always be made with what's in season. This version takes advantage of the fantastic asparagus that is available in springtime. A winter risotto could use the same basic ingredients but with butternut squash, mushrooms or beetroot instead of asparagus. Think of risotto as a starting technique and use your imagination. I'll reinforce Fiona's assertion that the rice must be toasted and the stock must be really hot so as not to stall the cooking process. **GUY**

JAMES' PEARL BARLEY RISOTTO
WITH SAUSAGE, SPINACH & GORGONZOLA

SERVES 4

This is a lovely twist on a classic Italian risotto – as comforting as the real thing, but without the hassle of having to be constantly stirring it.

1 onion, peeled and finely chopped
1 clove garlic, crushed
4 large sausages
400g pearl barley
150ml red wine
1½ litres hot chicken stock
100g Gorgonzola
100g washed spinach
salt and pepper
olive oil

Heat the olive oil in a large saucepan and add the onions and garlic. Cook covered over a gentle heat for 5–10 minutes until softened. Meanwhile, slit the skin of the sausages and remove the meat, discarding the skin afterwards. Increase the heat and add the sausages, breaking up with a fork. Stir for a minute or two, getting a little colour on the meat, then stir in the pearl barley and red wine. Simmer until the wine has reduced and add the stock. Season well, cover and cook for 45 minutes over a medium-low flame, stirring occasionally. Remove the lid and stir in the Gorgonzola and spinach. Taste for seasoning and adjust if necessary (both sausages and Gorgonzola tend to be quite salty so there shouldn't be any need for salt). Serve in warmed bowls with a little drizzle of olive oil.

FIONA SAYS

This is a really great combination of flavours – nirvana for cheese and sausage lovers. One tip: try and find either fresh Italian sausages (which you should be able to track down in an Italian deli) or other sausages with an all-meat content. You want a sausage that will crumble for this recipe rather than a traditional British sausage which has a high proportion of rusk and is therefore softer. Pearl barley can be substituted for Italian rice in other risottos.

JAMES' CHICKEN, LENTIL & BUTTERNUT SQUASH KORMA

SERVES 6

This is a little hotter than your average korma. De-seed the chillies if you want it milder, but don't then rub your eyes.

5 large chicken breasts
20g fresh coriander
2 fresh red chillies
1 plump clove of garlic, peeled
½ teaspoon ground cumin
juice of half a lemon
a good slug of olive oil
a large onion, peeled and sliced
10 cardamom pods
2 cloves
2 teaspoons coriander seeds
1 teaspoon cumin seed
2 teaspoons ground turmeric
1 teaspoon hot chilli powder
½ teaspoon ground ginger
½ teaspoon ground cinnamon
1 tin coconut milk
2 tbsp tomato purée
300 ml chicken stock
100g lentils
a small butternut squash, peeled, de-seeded and chopped into chunks

Chop the chicken into large chunks and place in a bowl. Put the coriander, chillies, garlic, lemon juice, cumin, olive oil and a little salt in a food processor. Blend thoroughly. Add to the chicken, stir well to coat the meat, cover and leave in a fridge for a couple of hours, or preferably overnight.

Preheat the oven to 210C. Sweat the onion in olive oil in a large pan. Meanwhile, remove the seeds from the cardamom and discard the pods, or save to boil with the rice. Grind with the cloves, coriander and cumin seeds, and add the turmeric, chilli powder, ginger and cinnamon. Increase the heat in the saucepan, stir the onions for 2 minutes then add the spices. Stir for a further minute then add the coconut milk, tomato purée and stock. Bring to the boil and stir in the lentils and squash. Season with salt and pepper, cover and simmer over a low heat for 45 minutes, stirring occasionally. After 20 minutes, tip the chicken and marinade into an oven proof dish and bake for 25 minutes. Check the consistency of the squash and lentil component and simmer uncovered until reduced, if necessary. Add the chicken, stir through and serve with basmati rice and a glass of cold beer or a punchy red wine (Shiraz would be good).

FIONA SAYS

This may seem a long list of ingredients (let's face it, it is) but if you're into curries there comes a moment when it's worth making them from scratch with individual spices. The initial outlay is expensive – though can be mitigated by buying them from Indian shops rather than supermarkets – but once you have them you can then rustle up a curry or spice other dishes whenever the mood takes you. And the taste is incomparably better.

KERALAN-STYLE PRAWN CURRY
WITH MUSSELS, COCONUT & CORIANDER

SERVES 6

A really easy but great-looking – and tasting – recipe that gives an exotic south Indian spin to a pack of frozen prawns and garlic mussels. One of my most popular recipes ever.

- 1 large onion (about 200g), peeled and finely chopped
- 3 tbsp sunflower or light olive oil
- 2 cloves of garlic
- a chunk of fresh ginger about 2 cm square or 1 tsp ginger paste
- 2 fresh green chillies
- 1 tbsp ground coriander
- 1 tsp turmeric
- a pinch of chilli powder or cayenne pepper
- salt to taste
- 2 ripe tomatoes (about 175g) skinned and cut into small dice (optional)
- 400ml can coconut milk
- 400g pack of frozen prawns or fresh prawns
- 400g pack chilled or frozen mussels in garlic butter sauce
- 2–3 tsp lemon juice
- 4 heaped tbsp of finely chopped fresh coriander

Finely chop the onion. Heat the oil in a wok or large saucepan and fry the onion until well browned (about 10 minutes). Peel and finely chop the garlic and ginger and de-seed and finely chop the chillies. Add to the onion and cook, stirring, for a couple more minutes then add the ground coriander, turmeric, chilli powder and a pinch of salt and cook for a minute more. Add the diced tomatoes and coconut milk, bring to the boil and simmer for 10 minutes until the sauce has thickened slightly. Add the prawns to the curry and heat through for about 10 minutes (5 minutes if they're fresh or have thawed). Microwave or boil the mussels in their bag,

following the instructions on the pack, and add to the curry once the prawns are ready. Check the seasoning adding a little more salt if necessary, some lemon juice and half the chopped coriander.

Ladle into soup plates, sprinkle over the remaining coriander. This goes well with fluffy rice and/or garlic and coriander naan warmed under the grill or in a toaster.

TOP STUDENT TIPS

 Almost any ready-made Indian curry or sauce can be improved by a squeeze of lemon, a dollop of plain yoghurt and some chopped fresh coriander or – in the case of Thai curries – coriander, 3–4 finely sliced lime leaves and a squeeze of lime. Garlic lovers like me may want to add extra garlic too. In this recipe try adding a pinch of ground cardamom – you'll find it works really well with the tomato, coconut and chilli flavours. If you're not a fan of seafood, convert the recipe to a vegetarian curry with lots of aubergines, peppers and potatoes. Or replace the mussels and prawns with chicken, veal or pork. **SIG**

SEARED SALMON WITH LEEKS AND CHIVES

SERVES 2

So long as you buy it on special offer (there are frequently good deals on frozen fillets) salmon's quite affordable these days and being farmed it's not endangered. An elegant main course for a special – or not so special – occasion

1 tbsp olive oil
2 evenly sized boneless salmon fillets (about 150–175g) with their skin left on

for the leeks
1 tbsp olive oil
25g butter
2–3 leeks (about 350g) trimmed, washed and finely sliced
1 heaped tbsp crème fraîche
1 heaped tbsp finely chopped chives plus a few snipped chives, for decoration
salt, pepper and a squeeze of lemon juice

Start the leeks first. Heat a frying pan, add the olive oil, then add the butter. Tip in the leeks and stir-fry over a low heat until soft (about 5 minutes) then take the pan off the heat. Season the salmon with salt and freshly ground black pepper. Heat another frying pan until quite hot. Add a tablespoon of olive oil and place the fillets in the pan skin side down. Fry for 4–5 minutes until you see the salmon flesh change colour half way up the fillet then turn over the fillets and cook for a further minute the other side. Turn off the heat and leave for a further couple of minutes. Put the pan of leeks back over a low heat and add the chives and crème fraîche. Heat through without boiling then season with salt, pepper and lemon juice to taste. Serve the salmon on warm plates with the creamed leeks alongside. Scatter over a few more chives.

TOP STUDENT TIPS

 In an effort to create tea-smoked salmon without a level of smoke that would set off our fire alarm I recently cooked some salmon fillets in foil with a couple of wet Lapsang Souchong teabags. The bits of the fish that had been in contact with the teabags had a really good smoky flavour but the rest wasn't hugely smoky, if at all. I still reckon it's probably inventive and interesting enough to give it a crack, upping the number of teabags. For 4 salmon fillets you need 4 lapsang souchong teabags. Pour 2 tablespoons of boiling water over each teabag, wrap the fish in foil with the teabags and bake for 20–25 minutes at 180C until cooked. **JAMES**

SIG'S UMAMI SALMON

SERVES 4

 A slightly crazy recipe I adapted from an old Leith's recipe called 'sweet and hot salmon' but have re-named it 'umami salmon' due to the generous addition of nam pla, or Thai fish sauce (see below).

4 large fillets of salmon
3 heaped tbsp of good grainy mustard (Pommery or Dijon work well)
1 heaped tbsp of hot horseradish sauce
1 tbsp nam pla (Thai fish sauce)
1 tsp dry English mustard
1 tsp Demerara sugar
zest and juice of 1 lemon
½ tsp cayenne pepper
1 tsp ground fennel seed (coriander would also work well)
generous sprinkling of salt and pepper

Preheated the oven to 200C/400F/Gas 6. Take the salmon fillets and place in a roasting tin. Mix together all the other ingredients in a bowl. Slather the mixture over the salmon, making sure you cover it completely. Place in the oven for 12–15 minutes (depending on whether your salmon is fridge-cold or not) then place under a hot grill for 3–5 minutes to get a bit of caramelisation on top of the fish. Serve with some freshly cooked new potatoes, some greens or a salad. If you're cooking to impress a date, then this might just do the trick. Did I mention the aphrodisiacal qualities of umami, as yet unproven by science, but definitely something to bear in mind....

WHAT IS UMAMI?

Without getting too technical, umami is the fifth taste after sweet, salt, sour and bitter. Translating from the Japanese as a taste akin to 'savouriness' or 'deliciousness' umami is found in a variety of foods across the globe, both in their natural state or in matured/fermented form. Some sceptics believe umami's a gimmick, but I intuitively trust the Japanese on this matter – they don't have an awesome food culture for nothing. Basically, the taste of umami is comprised of amino acids called glutamates, inosinates and guanylates which act synergistically and are each found at different levels in ingredients such as Kombu (a type of seaweed) Parmesan cheese, ketchup (tomatoes, and especially the seeds are very high in umami), Marmite, Vegemite and Bovril, Worcestershire sauce, preserved anchovies, nam pla (Thai fish sauce) and all fermented fish sauces for that matter, soy sauce, mirin, miso, chicken stock and roast chicken skin, dried mushrooms such as shiitake, porcini and morels, cured meat such as chorizo, pepperoni and proscuitto and cured fish such as smoked salmon.

Pairing umami-rich ingredients in a dish is a genius way to cook in a more freestyle, off-piste manner and if you've ever wondered why Italian food is so moreish, take a look at their umami-rich ingredients: tomatoes, Parmesan, anchovies – all dominant ingredients. That's not to say other European cuisines suffer from a paucity of umami-rich food. Think of Dutch *Maatje* herrings, German *sauerkraut* and Scandinavian cured fish in general. OK, that might not appeal to everyone, but for the dedicated fermento-philes, these foods are manna from heaven. A little practice makes perfect, so try pairing umami ingredients next time you're making a dish. Throw in some anchovies to your bolognese, dried mushrooms in a plain risotto, or a bit of Marmite to your roasties or Macaroni Cheese (see page 133). Be adventurous: you'd be surprised how umami ingredients lift a humble dish to something memorable. **SIG**

SALMON BURGERS
WITH GOAT'S CHEESE & SUNDRIED TOMATOES

SERVES 3–6
(depending how hungry you are)

Salmon burgers make a great alternative to ordinary hamburgers for a barbecue for those who prefer fish to meat.

450g skinless filleted salmon, cut into chunks
80g goat's cheese
4 spring onions, trimmed and finely chopped
80g slow-roasted or sundried tomatoes in oil, finely chopped
a handful of fresh basil leaves
40g natural dried breadcrumbs
salt, freshly ground black pepper and a pinch of paprika
oil for frying or coating the burgers

Chop the salmon finely or pulse 4 or 5 times in a food processor. Break up the goat's cheese with a fork and add it to the salmon along with the chopped spring onions and tomatoes. Mix well or pulse again (keeping some texture – you don't want to reduce the mixture to a paste). Finely chop the basil and add along with the breadcrumbs. Season with salt, pepper and a pinch of paprika, mix again and set the mixture aside for half an hour for the breadcrumbs to soften and absorb the moisture. Divide and pat out into six burgers. Fry in a little oil or rub both sides with oil and fry or barbecue over an indirect heat for about 6–7 minutes turning once or twice during the cooking process. I quite like them on their own with salad and a salsa but you could put them in a bap or bun with lime-flavoured mayo, sliced cucumber and shredded lettuce.

TOP STUDENT TIPS

Fish has, all of a sudden, turned into something of a minefield. Farmed or wild? Line-caught? What on earth does the disconcertingly vague 'Responsibly Sourced' tag even mean? When it comes to salmon, it's worth looking closely at what you're buying. While Alaskan salmon might seem an un-green ingredient, this wild version is sustainable and ultimately better for the environment than farmed Atlantic salmon, which is widely held to have had a devastating effect on marine ecology. Many fish are routinely fed antibiotics and food-colorants, so don't be hoodwinked by their colour – it's highly unlikely that it is natural.

CHICKEN POT PIE

SERVES 6

This is a really fantastic way of making a homemade pie. You bake the lids separately then pop them on top of a ready-made filling. Looks dead impressive and also has the virtue of keeping the pastry beautifully crisp. You could make a special Valentine's version with heart-shaped lids, cutting down the amount of filling, obviously (unless your loved one can put away a lot of chicken).

1 pack ready-rolled puff pastry
1 egg, beaten
1 tbsp light olive or sunflower oil
50g butter
4 skinless, boneless chicken breasts (about 550–600g) cut into chunky slices
175ml chardonnay or other full-bodied dry white wine
2 tbsp finely chopped fresh tarragon
2 level tbsp plain flour
1 large leek (about 250g) washed, trimmed and finely sliced
300ml whole (as opposed to semi-skimmed) organic milk
a small pack of asparagus tips
200g frozen peas
2 tbsp crème fraîche or double cream (optional)
sea salt and freshly ground pepper

Pre heat the oven to 200C/400F/Gas 6. Unroll the pastry and cut into 6 rectangles. Lay on a lightly greased baking sheet, brush with beaten egg and prick with a fork. Bake for 15 minutes then turn the heat down to 180C/350F/Gas 4 and continue to cook for another 5–10 minutes until well browned (or follow the timings and temperatures on the pack). Meanwhile heat the oil and half the butter in a large frying pan and fry the chicken until lightly coloured. (You may need to do this in two batches). Pour over the wine and cook over a moderate heat until the liquid has reduced by two thirds (about 5–7 minutes). Stir in the fresh tarragon. Melt the remaining butter in a non-stick, lidded saucepan, add the sliced leek, stir, cover and cook gently for about 5 minutes until it is soft. Stir in the flour and cook for a few seconds. Add the milk gradually, stirring continuously and cook over a low heat until the sauce has thickened (about 5 minutes). Tip the chicken and reduced wine, asparagus and frozen peas into the sauce, stir and simmer over a low heat for about 10 minutes. Check the seasoning of the pie 'filling', adding salt and pepper to taste. Stir in a spoonful or two of crème fraîche or double cream if you feel specially indulgent. Divide the chicken between six plates and arrange a slice of pastry over the top of each.

TOP STUDENT TIPS

 Akin to a de-constructed pie, this is totally foolproof and such an easy way to serve pie without the pastry going soggy. Definitely buy the puff pastry, life is too short to start rolling and folding puff (but then anyone who knows me will tell you pastry's my nemesis so I'm biased). You could convert the filling to a fish pie, or use other ingredients – herbs such as chives or parsley would make decent substitutes for the tarragon, and mushrooms would also make a tasty addition to the chicken. Make sure the sauce thickens – you don't want a thin chicken soup on your plate. Great comfort food for cooler autumn evenings or, indeed, when winter's chill really starts to bite. **SIG**

POSH FISH PIE

SERVES 4-5

Fish pie may sound a homely sort of dish rather than a flashy one but it never fails to impress, in a way that shepherd's pie just doesn't quite pull off. You can dress it up all kinds of ways, depending on what seafood you spot on special offer – just double the recipe for a crowd.

500g skinless white fish fillets (could be frozen)
200g cooked, peeled prawns (choose the
    small North Atlantic ones)
150g queen scallops
600ml semi-skimmed milk
40g butter
40g plain flour
2 tbsp double cream (optional)
2 tbsp chopped parsley
salt, ground black pepper and a good
    squeeze/squirt of lemon juice

For the potato topping
750g potatoes, cut into even-sized pieces
15g butter
50–60ml warm milk
salt and frshly ground black pepper

Cut the fillets into pieces that will fit into a medium to large saucepan (if frozen rock-hard, leave for 15 minutes or so before you attempt this). Lay them in the pan skin side up (if they still have a skin). Pour over the milk, bring slowly to the boil and then turn the heat right down and simmer for 3–5 minutes (depending on the thickness of the fillets). Remove the fish with a fish slice and strain the milk into a measuring jug.

Melt the butter in a non-stick saucepan, stir in the flour and cook for a few seconds. Take the pan off the heat and tip about two thirds of the hot strained milk into the flour, all in one go, whisking continually. Bring to the boil, turn the heat down and leave to simmer, adding a little more of the reserved milk if the sauce seems too thick. Season with pepper and a little salt.

Remove any skin from the fish and flake it into largeish chunks, carefully removing any bones. Tip the fish, prawns and scallops into the sauce and fold in the parsley. Check the seasoning, adding lemon juice and extra salt and pepper to taste and tip into a shallow pie dish or baking dish.

While you're assembling the pie put the potatoes in a saucepan, cover with cold water and bring to the boil. Cook for about 20 minutes until you can stick the point of a knife in them easily. Drain the potatoes, return them to the pan and cut them up roughly with a knife. Mash them thoroughly with a potato masher or fork. Beat in the butter and warm milk. Season with salt and pepper. Spread the potato evenly over the top of the fish roughing up the surface with the prongs of a fork. Bake in a hot oven (200C/ 400F/Gas 6) for about 20–25 minutes until the base is bubbling and the top is nicely browned.

VARIATIONS

Substitute smoked haddock for half the white fish. You could also add some quartered hard boiled eggs or skinned, seeded, diced tomato and/or top the potato with a layer of grated cheese.

TOP STUDENT TIPS

Try adding a smidgeon of nutmeg to the potato topping. My granny used to make a gratin like this with macaroni (the squidgy macaroni tastes really good with fish and creamy sauce). Also, try sprinkling breadcrumbs on top of the pie and dotting with little pieces of butter for a crispy topping when cooking in the oven. **SIG**

RED ONION, CHICORY & GORGONZOLA TART

SERVES 4-6

As well as making easy pastry lids you can use ready-rolled pastry to make a seriously impressive cheffy looking tart that's perfect for veggie friends.

2 tbsp olive oil
40g butter
4 red onions (about 100g each) peeled and finely sliced
1 tsp balsamic vinegar
6 medium-sized heads of chicory (2 x 200g packs)
juice of ½ lemon
1 tbsp caster sugar
1 x 375g pack fresh ready rolled puff pastry
1 medium egg yolk
175g Gorgonzola

Heat a large deep frying pan, add the oil and fry the onions over a moderate heat for about 15 minutes until soft. Add 15g of the butter and continue to fry, stirring, until deep brown (about another 10 minutes or so) then season with the balsamic vinegar, salt and pepper. Tip the onions onto a plate to cool and wipe the pan. Trim the bottom off each head of chicory and cut it in half lengthways. Put the lemon juice and 4 tablespoons of water in the frying pan along with the remaining butter and sugar. Heat gently until the sugar has dissolved then bring to the boil. Carefully place the chicory pieces in the pan, turning them in the lemon and butter mixture so they don't discolour. Cover the pan and cook them cut side upwards for 5 minutes then turn them over and cook for another 5 minutes. Take the lid off the pan, turn the heat up slightly and cook until most of the liquid has dissolved and caramelised (about another 5 minutes).

Meanwhile preheat the oven to 220C/425F/Gas 7. Lay the pastry on a lightly greased rectangular baking tray, trimming the pastry if necessary to fit. With a sharp knife score a line a round the edge of the pastry about 1½ cm from the edge to create a rim. Brush the edge and the base of the tart with lightly beaten egg yolk taking care not to brush over the cut you've made. Spread the caramelised onions over the base then carefully line up the chicory down the tart alternating from side to side so that the tips meet in the centre. Pour over the remaining pan juices, season with a little salt and pepper and crumble the cheese over the top. Bake in the pre-heated oven for 10 minutes then reduce the heat and bake for a further 15–20 minutes until the tart is well puffed up and the top nice and brown. You could serve this with a watercress, spinach and rocket salad.

TOP STUDENT TIPS

Don't be tempted to add sugar to nudge the caramelisation process along. Onions, and particularly red onions, are full of sugar, which will gradually find its way out as you gently cook them. It's all about patience! If the pan is too hot you run the risk of burning, not caramelising the onion (though, for future reference, when you do burn something just tell your guests that it's 'caramelised' – works every time). To achieve the real depth of flavour and texture that you are looking for, keep the pan on a medium heat and stir the onions every now and then, until they are rich and slippery. When combined with the heavenly Gorgonzola, crisp chicory and flaky pastry, you will realise that it was worth the effort. JAMES

HOW TO COOK A STEAK

You might think steak has no place in a student cookbook but I'd respectfully suggest that you'd be wrong. It's one of the things that's most often discounted so it's perfectly possible to pick one up at a knockdown price. You also don't need as much as you might think (or want, of course) – 150g, which is a pretty titchy steak, is the recommended portion size for the average adult. Still, you want to treat it with respect so here are some tips to help you get the best out of it.

• The best bargains tend to be on rump or sirloin. Try and pick one without too much fat to cut off.
• Start with your steak at room temperature. If it's straight from the fridge you may find the outside's well done while the centre is still cold.
• Trim off any visible fat. Most steaks are cooked too quickly to cook the fat through and you'll probably want to cut it off anyway once it's on your plate.
• Pat the meat dry with kitchen towel so it will brown, particularly if it has been vacuum packed or stored in a plastic bag. Even if you marinade the steak beforehand, dry it before you cook it or it will simmer rather than sizzle.
• If you're frying steak get the pan hot before you start. Very hot in the case of a ridged grill, not quite so hot if you're frying in oil and butter or cooking steak coated in peppercorns or a spicy rub which might catch and burn if the temperature is too high. If you're using a ridged grill or barbecue, oil the steak rather than the grill.
• Do rest your steak, lightly covered, on a warm plate for at least 3 minutes. I can't stress how important this is. It results in a much more tender, juicier steak.

HOW LONG SHOULD YOU COOK A STEAK?

It depends how thick the steak is and how well cooked you like it. The timings below will give you a rare or medium rare steak but If you prefer yours better done simply add a minute or two to the cooking times in the recipes.

A THIN STEAK
0.5–0.75cm thick: 1 minute per side

A THICKER STEAK SUCH AS RUMP, SIRLOIN OR RIB-EYE
1–1.5cm thick: 2 minutes a side

A THICK STEAK SUCH AS FILLET
1.5–2.5cm thick: 3–4 minutes per side.

'rare steak with creamy gorgonzola sauce'

FAJITAS AND OTHER THINGS TO DO WITH STEAK

FAJITAS

One of the best ways to stretch steak is to cut it into strips once you've rested it. If you add some fried onions and peppers and some tortillas or wraps (and some sour cream if you fancy it) you can then make fajitas. Simply spoon the steak and veg down the middle and roll up. Steak also lends itself well to Thai seasoning. Make the dressing for the Thai salmon recipe on page 115, cut the steak into strips as above and chuck in a few cherry tomatoes and fresh herbs like coriander, mint and torn basil leaves (Thai basil, if you can get hold of it) and serve with a rocket salad.

RED WINE SAUCE

A slightly cheffy sauce but easy once you've mastered it – and really delicious. Enough for 4 steaks.

1 tbsp olive oil
10g butter
110g shallots, peeled and roughly sliced
125ml red wine
1 tbsp balsamic vinegar
150ml beef stock made with ⅓ of an organic beef stock cube
1 tsp butter paste*
salt, pepper and a little Worcestershire sauce

Heat the oil in a pan then add the butter. Once it has melted add the shallots, stir and cook for about 10 minutes until lightly browned, stirring occasionally. Add the red wine and balsamic vinegar, bring to the boil, turn the heat down and simmer for about 10 minutes, stirring occasionally until the liquid has reduced by about three-quarters. Add the stock and simmer for another 5 minutes. Strain, return to the pan and whisk in the butter paste with a wire whisk. Bring back to the boil and simmer until thickened. Season to taste with salt, pepper and a few drops of Worcestershire sauce.

* To make butter paste, mash together equal quantities of soft butter and plain flour with a fork (on a saucer) until you have a smooth paste.

CREAMY GORGONZOLA SAUCE
SERVES 4

Another really good steak sauce. Also delicious over portabella mushrooms.

150g mild (dolce) Gorgonzola cheese (sometimes called Dolcelatte) or similar creamy blue cheese
5–6 tbsp whipping cream
freshly ground black pepper and lemon juice, to taste
finely chopped parsley, to garnish

Cut the Gorgonzola into cubes, put it in a bowl and mash it with 2 tablespoons of the cream. Tip the mixture into a small saucepan and heat gently, stirring occasionally till the cheese has melted. Add another 3–4 tablespoons of cream until it achieves a sauce-like consistency. Check seasoning, adding black pepper and – if you think it needs it – a little lemon juice to taste. Pour the sauce over the steaks and sprinkle over a little chopped parsley.

HAIR-DRIED DUCK

SERVES 4

Yes, you did read that right! This recipe involves a hair-dryer. I got the idea from Kevin Gould's book, *Dishy* (Hodder & Stoughton), which suggests it as an alternative to the Chinese way of hanging duck in the open air to get a super-crisp skin. There are, admittedly, simpler ways to roast a duck but none that are quite as much fun.

1 Gressingham duck, about 2kg in weight, with its giblets

2½ litres of hot chicken stock (about 3 stock cubes) mixed with 1 tbsp Chinese five-spice seasoning

sea salt, soy sauce and Marmite, to season

you will need a very large saucepan or deep casserole to fit the duck

Take the duck out of the fridge at least an hour before you plan to cook it. Remove the giblets (innards) and any large chunks of fat inside the carcass. Put the duck in the saucepan, breast side downwards and pour over enough boiling stock to cover it. Partially cover the pan, bring back to the boil then turn the heat down and simmer for 40 minutes, turning the duck half way through. Remove the duck from the pan, and set aside till cool enough to handle (about 10 minutes). Pat it dry with kitchen towel and place on a rack in a roasting tin, making sure the tin is well away from any water. Plug in the hairdryer (without a diffuser or nozzle) and turn up to the highest setting. Dry the duck all over for about 15 minutes (you should see the fat running off it). Pat dry again with kitchen towel and set the duck aside until ready to cook. (You can cool it completely and refrigerate it at this stage.) Pour off the fat from the tin and save it for roasting potatoes.

When ready to finish the duck, preheat the oven to 200C/400F/Gas 6. Lay the duck, breast side upwards, rub the skin with sea salt and roast for 45 minutes to an hour. Pour off the fat every 15 minutes or so. When cooked (any juices that run out when you pierce the skin should be completely clear) set aside and keep warm.

Pour off any excess fat from the pan, pour in the remaining chicken stock and work it round the pan, loosening the sticky residues. Bubble up and boil fiercely for 5 minutes until reduced. Season to taste – you may want to add a little soy sauce or ½ teaspoon of Marmite dissolved in 2 tablespoons of hot water – and strain into a warm jug. Serve with rice or mashed potatoes and peas.

• If you want to use the giblets, set aside the liver and put the rest in a saucepan with a quartered onion and a chopped carrot. Cover with cold water, bring to the boil, spoon off any froth and simmer for about 45 minutes. Strain and use instead of stock to make the gravy. You can fry the duck liver in a little olive oil and butter and serve with the duck.

TOP STUDENT TIPS

 Though this recipe makes excellent use of the rendered duck fat, often you will find that after cooking duck you are left with an alarming amount of fat and nothing to do with it. Don't even think of throwing it away. Store in a bowl or jar in the fridge and use it for roasting potatoes. You won't believe the improvement in flavour to your roasties. Once you've parboiled the spuds, get a couple of tablespoons of duck fat hot in a roasting tray. When the spuds are dry (too wet and the fat will spit horribly) add them to the pan and coat with the duck fat. Season with salt and pepper and roast. Sundays will never be the same again. **JAMES**

HONEY ROAST DUCK WITH STIR-FRIED GREENS

SERVES 2

Duck is the new chicken. Well maybe not quite yet but it's suddenly become much more affordable. Added to which people obviously don't quite know what to do with it so you often find it knocked down in price at the end of the day. A really easy, swanky recipe to make for a romantic dinner.

1 tbsp clear honey
2 tbsp soy sauce
2 duck breasts
1 head of spring greens or, 1/2 a small green cabbage or a head of broccoli
1 clove of garlic, peeled and crushed
1 tbsp wine vinegar
3–4 tbsp chicken or light vegetable stock made with 1/4 tsp vegetable bouillon powder
salt

Preheat the oven to 200C/400F/Gas 6. Spoon the honey into a bowl and add 1 tablespoon of boiling water, 2 tablespoons of soy sauce and a few drops of hot pepper sauce, if you have some. Using a sharp knife, trim any excess fat from around the edges of the duck breasts. Score diagonally across the fat with a sharp knife. Put a small frying pan on the hob without any oil and heat for 2–3 minutes until hot. Place the duck breasts, skin side down and fry for 5 minutes, pressing down with a spatula to make sure the skin browns evenly. Turn the breasts over and brown the other side for 30 seconds. Place the duck, skin side up, in a small roasting tin and smear over the honey and soy marinade. Roast for 10 minutes (rare) 15 minutes (medium rare) or 20 minutes (well done). Meanwhile, pour off all except 1 tablespoon of the duck fat that has accumulated in the frying pan, put back on the heat, add a crushed clove of garlic, stir and add the greens or cabbage. Stir-fry for 2–3 minutes

until tender, adding the remaining soy sauce. When the duck has cooked transfer it to a warm plate and cover lightly with foil. Pour off the excess fat from the roasting dish and add the vinegar, bubble up for a minute. Pour in the stock and simmer for 5 minutes, then pour in any juices that have accumulated under the duck breasts. Slice the duck breasts thickly and serve with the stir-fried greens and the pan juices. Mashed sweet potato – or ordinary mash – would also go well with this (see page 154).

TOP STUDENT TIPS

 Duck's one of my favourite ingredients. I'd probably use legs for this recipe as their texture really goes well with the Asian flavours of the soy and honey (and they are much cheaper than breast!). Don't cook them rare, otherwise you won't get that lovely fall-off-the-bone effect. You need to turn the heat down a bit (190C/375F/Gas 5) and give them another 20 minutes or so – round about 40 minutes in total. **GUY**

SLOW ROAST LAMB

SERVES 4–6

Slow roasting is a fantastic technique for cooking meat. Basically you bung the meat in a hot oven to get it going then turn it right down low and leave it for several hours. When you come back the meat is meltingly tender. It's particularly well suited to fattier meats like shoulder of lamb and pork.

2 tsp herbes de Provençe
1 tsp coarse sea salt
1 tsp cumin seeds
1 tsp peppercorns
2kg lamb shoulder
2 large cloves of garlic, peeled
   and finely sliced
olive oil
175ml red or white wine
175ml light stock

Pre-heat the oven to 180C/350F/Gas 4. Put the herbs, sea salt, peppercorns and cumin seeds in a mortar* and grind together with a pestle until roughly ground. Trim off any extra thick patches of fat off the lamb shoulder with a sharp knife (but not all of it – you need to leave a thin layer over the joint). Make some small incisions all over the meat and stuff the garlic into the slits. Put the lamb in a roasting pan and rub all over with olive oil. Sprinkle half the herbs over the lamb and rub in well too. Put the lamb in the oven and roast for 20 minutes then turn the heat down to 140/275F/Gas 1 and cook for another 4–4½ hours. Ovens vary so you'll have to keep an eye on it. If it seems to be cooking too fast – unlikely, but ovens are odd – the heat down. Basically the fat and juices should be gently bubbling away and you should be able to smell the meat cooking. Baste the meat occasionally and pour off (and keep) any surplus fat that accumulates but don't open the oven door too

often as it reduces the heat. Once you appear to have got rid of most of the fat (after 2½–3 hours or once it stops accumulating in the pan) baste the meat again, sprinkle a little more herbs over the meat and add the wine to the pan. Keep checking to ensure the pan juices are not burning, which will spoil your sauce. (Add more wine or a little water if they look like getting dry.) When the meat is cooked and falling away from the bone, put it on a carving plate and leave it in a warm place. Add about 150ml of stock and work off the stuck on juices in the roasting pan. Skim or spoon off the lamb fat you have set aside and you should find some jellied meat juices. Add those too. Check the seasoning, adding a little salt and pepper to taste, then strain the gravy into a small saucepan. If you have time, leave it to cool a little, then you can skim the sauce again. Cut the meat into large chunks and serve on a large platter. Reheat the meat juices and serve in a warm jug.

• If you haven't got a pestle and mortar you can use a mixing bowl and the end of a rolling pin to crush the herbs and spices. And if you've got a Greek deli nearby pick up some of their dried herbs like oregano, rosemary and thyme which are usually sold in bunches. They have a fantastic flavour.

TOP STUDENT TIPS

 Slow roasting is a great way to cook as there are no worries about timings. It gives a fantastic flavour and it should result in meat that is fall-apart tender. It's particularly good if you cook the garlic in its skin, then squeeze it out when cooked and mix it in with gravy. It really intensifies the flavour. **GUY**

SPRING LAMB STEW WITH HERBS & LEMON

SERVES 4

Stews are normally quite wintry but this is really quite light and fresh – perfect for beginning of spring/Easter eating. Look out for special offers on boned lamb or lamb steaks – it can be quite good value.

450g lean lamb steaks, cubed
3 tbsp light olive or sunflower oil
1 medium onion, peeled and roughly chopped
2 medium carrots, peeled and thinly sliced
grated rind of $\frac{1}{2}$ lemon
1 rounded tbsp plain flour
350ml chicken stock or stock made with $\frac{1}{2}$
   an organic chicken stock cube
125g (podded weight) small fresh
   or frozen broad beans
75g fresh or frozen peas
1 heaped tbsp finely chopped fresh dill
1 heaped tbsp finely chopped fresh parsley
2 tbsp crème fraîche or double cream
salt, freshly ground black pepper and lemon
   juice, to season

Trim any excess fat off the lamb. Heat a frying pan over a high heat for 2–3 minutes, add 1 tablespoon of the oil and fry the meat quickly on all sides until lightly browned. Transfer to a casserole or saucepan. Turn the heat down, add the remaining oil and tip in the chopped onion and carrot and cook gently for about 5 minutes until beginning to soften. Add the lemon rind and flour, stir for a minute then add the stock and bring to the boil. Pour the stock and vegetables over the meat, cover and simmer over a low heat for about 45 minutes until the meat is just tender. Add the broad beans and peas, bring back to simmering point and continue to cook for about

15 minutes until the vegetables are ready. Turn off the heat and stir in the dill, parsley and crème fraîche or cream. Season with salt, pepper and a good squeeze of lemon.

TOP STUDENT TIPS

 Ever wondered why you sear meat before adding it to a stew? The act of searing results in a 'Maillard reaction' which produces complex, meaty flavours due to the interaction between carbohydrates and amino acids. According to food scientist Harold McGee, other examples include bread crusts, chocolate, coffee beans, dark beers (think Guinness) and, of course, roasted meat. By adding liquid such as wine or stock to the pan after searing the meat and bringing this to the boil you lift the leftover meaty Maillard flavours from the pan. Known as 'de-glazing' it's worth doing this when making stews so no flavour goes to waste, but only add the *déglaçage* after tasting it. If there's a bitter residue from searing meat this will make the stew taste bitter. **SIG**

PORK, PEPPER AND POTATO GOULASH

SERVES 6–8

If you've several friends round and don't want too much last-minute hassle this favourite is the perfect all-in-one dish. It's also economical. I invented it for a Red Nose Day feast.

1.5kg pork shoulder steaks
4 tbsp sunflower oil or other light cooking oil
500g onions, peeled and finely sliced
2 large cloves of garlic, peeled and finely chopped
3–4 tsp paprika or, better still, Spanish pimenton
1 tbsp tomato paste
2 level tbsp plain flour
1 tsp of dried oregano or herbes de Provence
500ml passata
250ml light chicken or vegetable stock made with 1½ tsp vegetable bouillon powder
2 large or 3 medium red peppers
1kg new potatoes
salt and ground black pepper

to serve
284ml carton of sour cream
6–8 sweet and sour pickled cucumbers, finely sliced (optional but good)

you will also need a large heavy saucepan or casserole

Trim the pork steaks of excess fat (but don't worry about leaving a bit – it will help the texture of the goulash) and cut into large cubes. Heat a large casserole or frying pan, add 1 tablespoon of the oil, heat through again then add enough pork pieces to cover the pan in a single layer. Brown on both sides, remove with a slotted spoon and set the meat aside. Continue browning the remaining meat, adding a little extra oil with each batch. Once you've fried all the meat add another 2 tablespoons of oil to the pan and tip in the onions. Stir and fry them for about 5–6 minutes until beginning to soften. Add the garlic, paprika and tomato paste, stir well then return the meat to the pan. Stir to ensure the meat is thoroughly coated and then add the flour, oregano or herbes de Provence, passata and stock. Bring to the boil then cover the pan, turn the heat right down to a bare simmer, or transfer the pot to a low oven (150C/300F/Gas 2). Cook for 2 hours, checking from time to time that the meat is not cooking too fast. After an hour, cut up, de-seed and slice the peppers, removing any white pith, add them to the pot, stir and replace the lid. Cut the potatoes into even-sized pieces and cook in boiling water for 10 minutes. Drain and add them to the pan half an hour before the end of the cooking time, carefully mixing them into the sauce. Check the seasoning, adding salt and pepper to taste. Stir the sour cream and spoon a little over each portion as you serve up. Offer the pickled cucumbers to accompany.

VARIATIONS

You can make this with beef, though may have to increase the cooking time slightly. If you don't eat meat, substitute 1kg of mushrooms for the pork. You can also leave out the new potatoes and serve it with baked potatoes, if you prefer.

TOP STUDENT TIPS

 While trimming the pork of excess fat is important – you don't want a goulash swimming in the stuff – it is equally important that you do leave some fat on the pork, as it both imparts a lot of flavour and helps to keep the meat juicy. This is why many stews and casseroles call for bacon – not only does it enhance the flavour of a dish, but the fat ensures that the meat isn't dry and stringy. **JAMES**

GORGEOUS GOOEY CHEESE FONDUE

SERVES 2–4

Fondue is a bit like riding a bicycle. You think you're never going to be able to do it then suddenly you get the hang of it. The trick is to get the liquid (usually wine though you could use dry cider) hot but not boiling then add the cheese bit by bit so it doesn't ball up into an indigestible lump. And to stir with a figure of eight movement rather than round and round. Ideally you need a fondue set – a cast-iron one rather than the metal one – but you could make it in a cast-iron Le Creuset-type saucepan or casserole, keep it over a very low heat and just stand round the cooker while you eat it.

Use the best cheese you can afford – preferably from a good cheese shop. The traditional cheeses to use are Gruyère and Emmental but you could chuck in a bit of Cheddar.

about 425g coarsely grated cheese – at least half of which should be Gruyère and the rest Emmental and/or another strong hard cheese like Cheddar.
2 tsp cornflour
1 clove of garlic, halved
a large glass (about 175ml) very dry white wine (e.g. Muscadet or Picpoul de Pinet)
1–2 tbsp kirsch (optional)
freshly ground black pepper
pain de campagne or other dense rustic bread or ciabatta, to serve

Toss the sliced or grated cheese in a bowl with the cornflour. Let it come to room temperature. Rub the inside of the pan you're using (see above) with the cut garlic. Pour in the wine and heat until almost boiling. Remove the pan from the heat and tip in about a third of the cheese.

Keep breaking up the cheese with a wooden spoon using a zig-zag motion. (Stirring it round and round as you do with a sauce makes it more likely that the cheese will separate from the liquid).

Once the cheese has begun to melt, return it over a very low heat, stirring continuously. Gradually add the remaining cheese until you have a smooth, thick mass (this takes about 10 minutes, less with practice). If it seems too thick, add some more hot wine. Add the kirsch if using (try 1 tablespoon to start with) and season with pepper. Place the pot over your fondue burner (or pour the cheese into a warmed fondue dish) and serve with bite-size chunks of sourdough or other country bread. Use long fondue forks to dip the bread in, stirring the fondue as you do so to prevent it solidifying.

TOP STUDENT TIPS

 Gooey cheese fondue always reminds me of the cheese orgy scene in *Asterix in Switzerland*, a great read even if you're not into comics. As Fiona mentions above, it's important to follow a certain order in making fondue, and it's this ritual aspect in preparing, then sharing the fondue – along with the hilarity of the orgy scene in Asterix – that makes cheese fondue so memorable. Make sure to have an extra glass of wine, a shot of schnapps or a hot tea to wash down with the cheese to aid digestion. Cool liquid will solidify the cheese into a big lump in your stomach, and believe me you won't feel like any sort of orgy, let alone a cheese one, if this occurs.

SIG'S EASY BREAD ROLLS

MAKES 12 ROLLS

This recipe is from the *Leiths Baking Bible* (Bloomsbury), a fabulous compendium of recipes for baking enthusiasts and amateurs alike. If you want to learn all there is to know about baking, then this really should be your bible.

170g strong white flour
170g wholemeal flour (doesn't matter so much if it's strong or plain)
1 tsp salt
290ml milk with a squirt of lemon in it (this curdles the milk, don't worry, it's meant to!)
45g melted butter
7g sachet quick-action bread yeast
1 tsp treacle or clear honey

1 egg yolk for glazing
topping ingredients (such as seeds or spices)

you will also need a lightly oiled 12-hole muffin tin

Sift the flours and salt into a large bowl.

In a small saucepan, bring the milk and butter to just below boiling point and allow to cool to blood temperature (not more than 50°C, to be finickety about it) before adding the yeast. (The yeast will die if hotter). Finally, in a small cup, place the yeast with the treacle and add a little of the warm milk, stirring to dissolve the treacle.

Make a well in the middle of the flours in your big bowl, and add the yeast and warmed milk/butter mix. Use a large spoon, to stir the dough and give it a good thrashing for 5 minutes. This is mess-free kneading. Think of it as therapeutic kneading – a break from the books! Portion out scoops of dough into the muffin tin, and gently

place a lightly oiled sheet of clingfilm over the top of the muffin tin, allowing the buns to double in size – this will take about 1 hour. If you want to assist the rising process, put the tin in a warm place. If you want to bake these the next day, place in the fridge overnight....

Preheat the oven to 200C/400F/Gas 6. After an hour, give one of the buns a gentle nudge with your little finger. They have risen enough if the indentation left by your finger stays – in other words, the dough doesn't 'spring back'. When the rolls have risen, remove the Clingfilm, and brush the buns with a bit of egg yolk – make sure you don't poke the buns too much with the brush otherwise they'll deflate! Then sprinkle the rolls with whatever toppings you have. Favourites for me are seeds such as sunflower, pumpkin and sesame. Try something like fennel, or coriander seeds – a bit of aromatic oomph never goes amiss! Bake the rolls on the top shelf of the oven for 15–20 mins (25–30 if you like them very toasty). How do you check if they're done? They should be a golden-brown colour, and if you tap on a roll, it should produce a hollow sound. Also, the rolls should feel lighter than when they went in the oven... if that makes sense.

FIONA SAYS

It really is worth making your own bread, particularly these days when bread is so expensive. If you feel a bit nervous about the whole exercise twist someone's arm to give you a bread machine – you can buy them quite inexpensively – but really, once you get started it's not difficult. And very soothing and therapeutic. The only downside is that homemade bread tastes so much better than shop-bought that you'll probably eat twice as much.

IRISH SODA BREAD

SERVES 4-6

If you've never made bread in your life you could make Irish soda bread. It requires no kneading or rising time – you can make it from start to finish inside an hour. Everyone's version differs slightly. This is based on the recipe that baker Dan Lepard gives in *Baking with Passion* (Quadrille).

284ml carton buttermilk or very low-fat bio yoghurt
1 level tbsp black treacle
225g self-raising flour
225g plain wholemeal flour (not bread flour) plus extra for dusting
1 tbsp wheatgerm
1/2 level tsp cream of tartar
1 level tsp bicarbonate of soda
1 rounded tsp fine sea salt

Preheat the oven to 190C/375F/Gas 5. Warm the buttermilk very gently in a pan with the treacle until the treacle melts, stir well then take it off the heat. Combine the dry ingredients in a large mixing bowl. Pour over the milk and treacle mixture and mix with a wooden spoon then pull the mixture together with your hands, trickling in a little water as needed. The dough should be soft but not sticky. Shape the dough into a ball about 18cm wide and place on a floured baking tray. Cut a deep cross in the centre of the loaf, dust with a little more flour and bake for about 35–40 minutes until the bread is well browned and the bottom of the loaf sounds hollow when you tap it. Transfer onto a wire rack, cover with a clean tea-towel to stop the crust getting too hard, and cool for about 20–30 minutes. Serve while still warm.

TOP STUDENT TIPS

The fantastic thing about soda 'farls' is that they can be made without baking. Just cut the dough into quarters and fry in a little butter for 5 minutes on each side. My girlfriend Claire has Irish-potato-farming heritage and loves to make this. As buttermilk is pretty hard to get hold of, you can make your own substitute from regular milk with a teaspoon of vinegar or a squeeze of lemon juice. Traditionally, it would be served with thick lashings of butter and potato and turnip broth (or 'skink' to the Irish!). **GUY**

JAMES' GUIDE TO MAKING YOUR OWN PIZZAS

 Making your own pizzas is a cracking way to enjoy good fast(ish) food without spending a ridiculous amount of money for a greasy pizza drenched in MSG. It is also an excellent way to feed guests as, once you have your dough made and toppings prepared, you can get them to cook their own supper.

Organisation is the key. The whole process can turn into a bit of a nightmare unless you keep on top of things. First thing I'd recommend is giving the kitchen a decent clean, clearing as many work surfaces as possible. Ideally, you want enough space for one person to roll out the dough while the next adorns their pizza with goodies, so a cluttered kitchen is going to make your life tricky.

Get each of your guests to bring a topping, that way you're not spending a fortune buying all of them, and can concentrate on just the dough, plus the tomato sauce and a couple of your favourite things to scatter on the pizza. Don't get carried away when building your pizza. I reckon three or four toppings max – you can always make smaller pizzas and have a couple of different ones.

Make sure your oven is really hot before cooking, and open it for as little time as possible. Not only is leaving the oven open while it's on a terrible waste of energy, but you will also end up with soggy pizza.

Before you go about making the dough, it's worth knocking up a decent tomato sauce. Take a couple of jars of passata and add some chopped marjoram or oregano – dried is fine if you can't find fresh. Season with salt, pepper and sugar, and put over a medium heat. Simmer for half an hour, or until it has thickened considerably. Leave to cool then refrigerate.

This recipe serves about four people. If you're cranking up numbers, I'd recommend making the dough in batches of this quantity, unless you are an experienced baker.

500g strong white bread flour
1 teaspoon salt
a 7g sachet of dried yeast
2 teaspoons caster sugar
350ml lukewarm water

An hour before you are ready to eat: In a large bowl mix the flour, salt, yeast and sugar. Make a well in the centre and pour in the water. Using a fork or your (clean) hands, mix the ingredients together until they form a loose dough. Turn the mix onto a clean, floured surface, and knead for 10 minutes by pushing the dough away from you with your right hand while pulling it back with your left. Bring the mix back together, turn 90° and repeat. You will notice the dough gaining strength as you go on. By the end it should be smooth and elastic. Form the dough into a ball, dust with flour, and cover with cling film. Leave to rest for 15 minutes.

WHEN YOU'RE READY TO COOK

Get the oven as hot as you can. Pull off a piece of dough the size of a fist and roll out on a floured surface. Don't worry about getting a perfect circle – it looks much more authentic if it's a bit rustic. Transfer it onto a floured sheet of baking parchment and spread a little of your tomato sauce on top, going almost to the edges, but not too thickly. Now you can add your toppings, of which you will know many and, being the creative student that you are, have lots of good ideas, but these are a few of our favourites:

POSSIBLE PIZZA TOPPINGS

- Mozzarella (clearly the Daddy of pizza toppings)
- finely chopped red chilli
- artichoke hearts
- rocket leaves (to be scattered on after cooking)
- chorizo
- roasted red peppers and goat's cheese – an epic combo!
- pilchards (...he-he, just kidding)

When you have fashioned such a thing of beauty as you are happy to hoi it in the oven, do just that, gently placing it directly on the bars of the oven (still on the baking parchment, that is) for 5–7 minutes, till it is starting to brown at the edges and smells better than a Neapolitan trattoria. Try not to burn your mouth as you wolf it down with a bottle of Peroni or glass of Chianti. **JAMES**

FIONA SAYS

 James is right – making your own pizza should be seen as entertainment rather than a chore. Once you get the hang of making the dough (to which I would add a couple of tablespoons of olive oil) it's a doddle. I'm not sure I'm with James on Mozzarella being the Daddy of pizza toppings though – it's a bit bland for me unless you have access to authentic buffalo mozzarella but there's another Italian cheese, Taleggio, which has a fantastic flavour and melts equally well. You can also use blue cheese very effectively.

'roasted peppers – team them up with goat's cheese'

SMOKED SALMON PIZZA

This pizza is a total cheat, using a ready-made pizza base. Buy the ones in the chill counter rather than the ones in foil packs in the grocery section, as they're lighter and less cardboardy.

1½ tbsp olive oil
1 ready-to-cook thin, plain pizza base
125g cream cheese
1½ tbsp milk
2 tsp onion, very finely chopped (optional but good)
a small (125g) pack of wafer-thin smoked salmon or, ordinary sliced smoked salmon
a quarter of a lemon or about 2 tsp lemon juice
½ a small bag of rocket
ground black pepper

Lightly brush or smear the top of the pizza base with oil. Cook for about a minute each side under a moderate grill until crisp but still soft. Set aside on a rack and cool for 15 minutes. Turn the cream cheese into a bowl and mash up with the milk so you get a soft, spreading consistency. Add the chopped onion, if using, and season with ground pepper (you shouldn't need salt because the salmon will be salty). When the base has cooled down, spread it with the cream cheese mixture then drape the smoked salmon pieces artistically over the top. Squeeze over a little lemon juice and season with black pepper. Scatter a small handful of rocket leaves over the salmon and drizzle over a little extra oil.

TOP STUDENT TIPS

Smoked salmon also makes a great pasta sauce. Mix 1 small pot crème fraîche or sour cream with a generous grating of Parmesan, some chopped parsley and the juice and zest of 1 lemon. Season with black pepper (and maybe salt, depending on how much Parmesan you use) then add this to cooked spaghetti, stir through and then sprinkle some strips of smoked salmon on top along with some more parsley. This will definitely woo any prospective love interest. **SIG**

'a total cheat pizza'

HOW TO BARBECUE

It might seem odd putting a section on barbecues in a student cookbook but if there's any space to set one up at the back of your house, chances are you're going to be out there lighting up. Even if you haven't one, these recipes are great for summer eating.

WHICH BARBIE TO BUY?

You can buy a disposable barbecue for as little as £4 though obviously it won't cook that much food and you'll only be able to use it once. A better bet is to buy one of the foldaway barbecues or a small bucket or beach barbecue you can move about (a tenner or so in supermarkets). If you're cooking a barbie for friends, several small barbecues will do the work of one bigger, more expensive one. The downside is that they only work on charcoal, which is messier and harder to light than gas, so you may feel it's worth paying extra for a gas one (£50 upwards: look for summer sales bargains).

WHICH CHARCOAL?

You can either buy lumpwood (which looks like small pieces of coal) or briquettes. Lumpwood burns quicker, briquettes last a bit longer. Unless they're already impregnated with fuel you'll also need some kind of firelighters or lighting fluid (use ones that are designed for barbecues not for ordinary fires).

HOW TO LIGHT UP

Tip a good layer of charcoal (about 3–4 cm deep) in the base of the barbecue tray then pile it up into a pyramid. Tuck pieces of firelighter around the pile or pour over firelighter fluid following the instructions on the bottle. Light (preferably with a long match) and wait until you can see the coals starting to glow (about 15 minutes). Spread them out and leave them to get really hot (another 30 minutes). Once there are no more flames and the coals are covered with a fine layer of white ash you're ready to cook. (You should be able to hold your hand about 15cm away from the coals for 3–4 seconds.) Brush the cooking rack lightly with oil before you start. Obviously the nearer the rack is to the coals the hotter it will be and the centre of the barbecue will also be hotter than the sides. If it doesn't seem hot enough, open any vents in the base of the barbecue, knock some of the ash off the coals and push them closer together. To reduce the heat, close the vents and push the coals apart. You should get about 30–45 minutes cooking time from the original fire. Push some extra coals around the edge of the barbecue to heat up if you want to extend that.

SAFETY TIPS

• NEVER pour lighting fluid on a barbecue once it's alight or use anything other than a product designed for barbecues. Don't use aerosol oil sprays on food either once it's cooking.
• Make sure the barbecue is stable. Put it on an even surface away from overhanging branches, fences or anything else that could catch fire.
• Don't cook with floppy sleeves. Use long handled cooking tools (again, quite cheap to buy).
• Don't barbecue if it's windy.
• Once the barbecue is alight someone should stay with it. Don't attempt to move it. Make sure it's completely out before you leave it.
• Don't use portable barbecues indoors.
• Have a spray bottle of water handy to dampen down any flare-ups.
• Don't leave raw meat lying around in the hot sun.

WHAT TO COOK

On an inexpensive barbecue, stick to food that is going to cook easily – such as burgers, sausages or kebabs. They should be at room temperature before you start. If you want to cook chicken, part-cook it first – either in a conventional oven, microwave or grill – then finish it off on the barbecue. Vegetables like aubergines, peppers and courgettes also barbecue well but don't cut them too small or they'll fall through the grill. All food needs to be brushed lightly with oil so it doesn't scorch or stick; that is unless it has been marinated (in which case shake off the marinade before cooking or your food will catch fire). You'll also need to turn it at least once during the cooking time, brushing on a little more oil or marinade.

HOW LONG IT TAKES...

• Burgers: roughly 3–4 minutes each side. Very thin ones might take a bit less.
• Sausages: Frankfurters (a good option for barbies) take 3–4 minutes. Fatter sausages should be part-cooked like chicken then finished off for 5–6 minutes on the barbecue.
• Chicken: use thighs and drumsticks. If you part-cook them for about 10 minutes in a hot oven or under a grill they should only take another 10–15 minutes to cook.
• Aubergines, peppers and courgettes: about 3–4 minutes each side.
• Flat mushrooms: about 7–8 minutes (cook with the underside upwards and don't turn them or you'll lose the delicious juices).
• Halloumi cheese (a good option for vegetarians): about 3 minutes each side.

HOW TO CLEAN UP AFTERWARDS

Once you've finished cooking, douse the coals with cold water or simply leave the barbecue to die out if there aren't many coals left. Once completely cold, tip out the ash and clean any burnt food off the rack with a wire brush, crumpled piece of newspaper or foil. Wipe the rack lightly with oil.

OIL AND LEMON MARINADE FOR CHICKEN THIGHS & DRUMSTICKS

This is a great marinade that goes exquisitely with chicken. This makes enough for 1kg of thighs and drumsticks.

juice of 2 lemons (about 5–6 tbsp)
4 tbsp olive oil
2 cloves of garlic, crushed
a couple of sprigs of fresh thyme or rosemary or $1/2$ tsp dried oregano, thyme or herbes de Provence

1kg of chicken thighs and drumsticks

Whisk the oil and lemon juice together in a shallow ovenproof dish with 2 tablespoons of water, the garlic and herbs. Stab the fleshy parts of the meat a few times, to help the marinade penetrate, then lay the pieces in a single layer in the marinade. Turn so both sides are coated, cover with Clingfilm and leave in a cool place for 1–2 hours. Either heat the grill or a moderate oven (190C/375F/Gas 5) and cook the chicken pieces for about 10–15 minutes, turning them once. Transfer them to the barbecue, shaking off any excess marinade (which would make the coals flare up) and cook for another 10–15 minutes or until any juices run clear when you stick a sharp knife in them. (If you haven't a barbecue you can finish the cooking under the grill or in the oven.)

TOP STUDENT TIPS

 Lemons have a magical ability to transform something unremarkable into something really quite special. Most sauces are improved with a squeeze of lemon (or a dash of vinegar, if you find yourself lemonless). JAMES

BEER-CAN CHICKEN

SERVES 4–6

Unlikely though it might sound this has to be the best ever way of cooking a bird – a cross between roasting and barbecuing. Basically what you're doing is forcing beer flavoured steam up the inside of the chicken while the fat from the skin runs down the body, constantly basting it and giving it a super-crisp, spicy skin. The only downside is that you ideally need a barbecue with a high-domed lid but you can improvise with a loose foil 'tent' draped over your bird – or even cook it in the oven.

1 small to medium-sized chicken – about 1.3–
    1.5kg (3lb–3lb 5 oz)
about 1 tbsp jerk seasoning or other spicy
    rub
a little oil
a 330ml can of lager

Rinse the chicken inside and out and dry thoroughly with kitchen towel. Remove any surplus fat from the carcass and sprinkle the inside of the chicken with about 1 teaspoon of the rub, rubbing it in well. Rub a little of the oil into the chicken skin, sprinkle the remaining rub over the rest of the chicken and rub it in. Fire up the barbecue. Pour half the contents of the beer can into a glass. Lightly oil the can and lower the chicken onto the can so that it stands upright propped up by its legs (yes, it does look ludicrous...). Stand the can and chicken carefully on the barbecue rack then cover and cook over an indirect heat for about 50 minutes to an hour until the juices run clear when you pierce the leg with a skewer. Holding the can with a pair of tongs very carefully remove chicken from the can and transfer to a carving tray (this is ideally a two-person operation). Rest for 5–10 minutes then carve and serve with a barbecue sauce or a salsa.

VARIATIONS

You could use other types of dry rub – or none at all and simply season your bird with salt and pepper. It'll still taste good.

HOMEMADE BARBECUE SAUCE

Heat 2 tablespoons of oil in a small saucepan, add a small, finely chopped onion and cook for about 5–6 minutes until beginning to soften. Add a crushed clove of garlic and a teaspoon of the spice rub you used for the chicken, cook for a minute then stir in 1 tablespoon of soft brown sugar. Add 4 tablespoons of tomato ketchup, 2 tablespoons of cider or malt vinegar, 1–2 teaspoons of Worcestershire sauce and the juice of half an orange, stir then pour in about half a mug (100ml) of brown ale or water. Bring to the boil, turn the heat down and simmer for about half an hour, adding more beer or water if it gets too thick. Check seasoning adding more ketchup, vinegar or Worcestershire sauce if you think it needs it, sieve and serve.

TOP STUDENT TIPS

 Make sure you take a big slug out of the can of beer before you push it up the chicken's butt. If it is too full it will overflow. You need to be careful that the chicken stays vertical. We cooked it in the wood oven and it was a brilliant, incredibly moist chicken with crispy almost burnt skin. Fantastic. Cooking with a beer can like this is always a good conversation topic. **GUY**

HOW TO COOK TURKEY & OTHER CHRISTMAS TIPS

Why anyone should want to eat more than one Christmas dinner beats me but I know there are plenty who do. Here's how to do it for 6–8 people.

THE TURKEY

There's nothing particularly tricky about cooking a turkey. It's just like roasting a chicken except it takes about four times longer. The important thing is to get it cooked right through. There's nothing nastier (or more dangerous) than a turkey with a nicely browned skin and raw meat inside, so make sure it's fully defrosted – if frozen allow 24 hours.

The best way is to start it off with a good blast of heat – 20 minutes at 220C/425F/Gas 7. Then turn the heat down to 190C/375F/Gas 5 and continue to cook it for about 20 minutes per 500g. A 4.5–5kg bird (enough to feed 6–8 generously) will take about 4 hours in total, maybe more. At some stage you'll need to stop it browning too much (especially the legs and wings) by wrapping them in foil. Spoon off some of the fat that accumulates in the pan otherwise it'll make it hard to crisp your potatoes. If you don't have room to cook potatoes anyway, boil them for 10 minutes, then leave them till you take the turkey out. Turn the oven back up to 220C again, then roast them for 20–25 minutes. The turkey will be fine if you cover it loosely with foil. Check the turkey carefully before you take it out of the oven. Stick a knife in the thickest part of the leg and see if the juices run clear. If in doubt give it another 10–15 minutes.

A REALLY GOOD STUFFING (AS IT WERE)

Stuffing the bird itself is not a great idea a) because it absorbs all the fat b) makes it harder to ensure the turkey is properly cooked c) is a pain to do anyway. I would either buy a ready-made (chilled not packet) stuffing and bake it separately or fry up a pan of some of those Christmassy sausages you can buy in most supermarkets. However, if stuffing is the only point of Christmas dinner so far as you're concerned this is a classic.

a 454g pack of sausage meat or traditional English sausages (e.g. Cumberland)
about 3–4 tbsp dried natural breadcrumbs (not the bright orange ones)
1 large egg, beaten
1/2 small onion (50g) peeled and finely chopped
1 small flavourful apple (e.g. Blenheim or Cox), peeled, quartered, cored and finely chopped
100g ready-to-eat prunes, finely chopped (easiest with scissors)
1 tsp ground mixed spice
salt and pepper
1 tsp oil

Put the sausage meat in a bowl with the breadcrumbs and the beaten egg and mix thoroughly together (if you're using sausages, slit the skins and pull them off). Leave while you prepare the rest of the ingredients then mix them in too. Heat the oil in a small to medium size non-stick frying pan and tip in the stuffing. Pat it down with a wooden spoon or fork until it resembles a cake then let it cook for about 5 minutes, covered with a lid or foil. Turn the stuffing over. (Don't worry if it breaks up, just mash it together again.) Continue cooking for another 5–6 minutes till the stuffing is cooked.

THE GRAVY

The good news about all that long slow cooking is that you get some really dark, sticky, meaty juices in the pan which should make loads of gravy. Carefully pour off most of the fat from the roasting tin into a bowl, leaving the juices behind then stir in 2–3 tablespoons of flour (enough to make a thickish paste). Cook for a minute then gradually stir in about 500ml of the water you've cooked the potatoes in, or stock made with Vegetable Bouillon Powder, bring to the boil and simmer for 5 minutes. Adjust the seasoning, adding salt and pepper and strain.

THE VEG

Roast potatoes, obviously (see page 152) and sprouts. Here's how to tart up frozen ones.

HOT BUTTERED SPROUTS WITH ALMONDS

Take about 700g of frozen sprouts and plunge them into a large saucepan of boiling, salted water. Cook for about 2 minutes less than they recommend on the pack (as soon as you can stick a sharp knife right through them they're done). Drain them thoroughly in a colander. Meanwhile rinse and dry the pan and add a good lump (25g) of butter. Melt it over a moderate heat then tip in about a quarter of a small pack (about 25g) of flaked almonds. Stir them around then, when they start to brown, return the sprouts to the pan and toss with the butter and almonds. Season generously with freshly ground pepper.

CHEAT'S CHRISTMAS PUDDING
SERVES 8

Unbelievably easy, and a bit lighter on the stomach than the traditional pud.

2 tubs of good quality vanilla ice-cream
a 400g jar of mincemeat
a 5cl miniature of brandy or whisky or a good
  slosh of sherry

Scoop the mincemeat into a small saucepan and add the brandy, whisky or sherry. Heat slowly, stirring, and pour over the ice-cream.

TOP STUDENT TIPS

 I have never been brave enough to attempt cooking a turkey in a student kitchen. It's bad enough at home with a temperamental Aga, so having a crack at it with a shoddy student oven takes a bold cook. But I'm sure you're up to it. In all likelihood you'll be using a frozen turkey, so make sure it is fully defrosted before you cook it. You ought also to be careful not to open the oven too much, losing heat and prolonging the cooking time. When you take the bird out to baste it (something you should do every three quarters of an hour or so) don't leave the oven door open while you do it. When the bird is done, let it rest for at least twenty minutes before carving. (Makes it easier to slice and keeps it juicy.) JAMES

YUMMY PUDS, CAKES & COCKTAILS

Forget all that healthy stuff we've been persuading you to eat. What we know you really, really want to cook are wickedly chocolatey cakes, puds and ice-creams. And shake a few cocktails. Bring it on...

MULLED CHRISTMAS CRUMBLE

SERVES 4

Here's a seasonal variation on apple crumble (which I think is better!). It's easy to make with a pack of frozen berries, some cranberry sauce and a slosh of port (making it perfect for mopping up Christmas leftovers). A vintage character or special reserve port is smoother and more drinkable than a basic ruby port. Own-label is fine, of which you should see plenty on special offer in the run-up to Christmas.

1 small jar of cranberry sauce or about
   3 large dollops homemade cranberry sauce
3 tbsp vintage character or special reserve port
1½ tsp mixed spice
a fine slice of orange peel
1 x 500g pack black forest fruits or other
   frozen red berries
extra sugar, to taste

For the crumble topping
175g plain flour
1 tsp cinnamon or mixed spice
100g chilled butter from the fridge
60g (about 4 tbsp) unrefined caster sugar

Tip the cranberry sauce in a saucepan, add the port and heat gently until it has melted. Stir in the spice, add the orange peel then tip in the frozen fruit, bring to the boil, stir then set aside to infuse. Measure the flour into a large bowl. Cut the butter into small cubes and tip into the flour. Keep cutting until you can't get the pieces of butter any smaller then rub the butter and flour together with the tips of your fingers, lifting it up and letting it fall back again into the bowl until the mixture is the consistency of coarse breadcrumbs. Stir in the sugar and carry on rubbing for another minute. (You can do this in seconds in a food processor.) Preheat the oven to 200C/400F/Gas 6. Remove the orange rind from the berries and check them for sweetness, adding more sugar if you think they need it. Tip them into a lightly buttered or oiled baking dish. Spread the crumble mixture evenly over the fruit, making sure you cover the whole surface then bake for about 30–35 minutes till the crumble is brown and the fruit juices are bubbling round the sides of the dish. Serve with vanilla ice cream or cream.

VARIATIONS

You can bulk up this filling you could add a peeled, finely sliced Bramley apple to the fruit. To make a plain apple crumble, peel, quarter and core 3–4 large Bramley apples and slice them thickly into a large saucepan. Sprinkle with ¼ teaspoon of ground cinnamon, 3 tablespoons of caster sugar and pour over 3 tablespoons of water. Cover the pan, place over a low heat and cook for about 12–15 minutes, shaking the pan occasionally until the apple pieces are soft but still holding their shape, then carry on with the recipe as above, leaving out the spice from the crumble topping if you want.

TOP STUDENT TIPS

 The trick here is to keep the crumble topping cold, so when it bakes in the oven it will turn crispy, rather than greasy or soggy. If you don't have a food processor, an easy way to add the butter to the crumble mixture is to grate it in, rather than cubing it. Make sure the butter is really cold though – it's worth freezing it for 15–20 minutes before you do this. If you want to vary the topping slightly, add some chopped almonds or hazelnuts. You can also replace a few tablespoons of plain flour with wholemeal flour: crumble topping made with a few tablespoons of oats or Weetabix makes another great variation to the classic crumble formula. Use what you have. **SIG**

OUR FAVOURITE CHEESECAKE

SERVES 8–10

A typical all-American cheesecake. Don't be daunted by the length of the recipe – it's dead easy. The only thing you need to remember is to equip yourself with a loose-bottomed cake tin, which you should be able to pick up quite cheaply, which makes it easier to get the cheesecake out without breaking it.

for the crust
110g digestive biscuits, crushed into fine crumbs
50g butter

for the first layer
2 x 200g packs Philadelphia cheese (the full-fat variety)
2 large eggs
100g caster sugar
$\frac{1}{4}$ tsp vanilla extract

for the second layer
1 x 284ml carton soured cream
150 ml Greek-style yoghurt
2$\frac{1}{2}$ tbsp caster sugar
1 tsp vanilla extract

for the topping
250g fresh or frozen berries, such as raspberries, blueberries and cherries
50–75g caster sugar
1 tsp arrowroot

you'll need a 20cm loose-based or spring-release cake tin

Preheat the oven to 190C/375F/Gas 5. Gently melt the butter in a saucepan, cool slightly and add the crushed biscuits. Press evenly into the base of the cake tin. Beat the ingredients for the first layer together thoroughly, pour over the biscuit base and smooth the top. Place the tin on a baking sheet and bake in the oven for 20 minutes or until just set. Set aside for 20 minutes to firm up. Mix the ingredients for the second layer and spoon evenly over the first layer. Return to the oven for 10 minutes then take out and cool. Refrigerate for at least 6 hours or overnight.

For the topping, heat 50g of sugar gently with 2 tablespoons of water until it dissolves. Turn up the heat, add the berries, cover and cook, shaking the pan occasionally for about 5 minutes until the berries are soft. Take off the heat. Mix the arrowroot with 2 tablespoons of water and tip into the blueberries. Stir over a gentle heat until the juice has thickened. Set aside to cool then check for sweetness, adding extra sugar to taste. About an hour before serving, ease a knife down the sides of the cake tin, then release the clamp or push up the base. Spoon the topping evenly over the cheesecake and return to the fridge until ready to serve.

VARIATIONS

You can make a sort of deconstructed cheesecake by baking the buttery biscuit crumbs on a baking sheet until crisp then putting them in the bottom of a glass dish, topping with mascarpone cheese mixed with sour cream or Greek yoghurt flavoured with a dash of vanilla and covering with fresh berries, sprinkled with a little caster sugar or sifted icing sugar.

TOP STUDENT TIPS

There's something about good old-fashioned nosh that just hits the spot, especially when it comes to puddings. Bread and butter pudding, crumble, or something like this – simple, delicious, sweet and indulgent. It's food that doesn't need mucking around with to make it special. JAMES

SIG'S CARROT, OAT AND CINNAMON MUFFINS

MAKES 9–12 MUFFINS

Rarely is a virtuous muffin a tasty muffin, yet this recipe will please even the most sweet-toothed buccaneer. The combination of carrots, toasted oats and wholemeal flour give the muffins extra fibre thus making them a sustaining snack for elevenses or that mid-afternoon slump, plus they taste so much better than boring old biscuits. The yogurt-infused milk plus honey add moisture, whilst a pinch of bicarb' ensures the muffins rise properly during baking. The cinnamon's a must, but you could try nutmeg, cardamom or mixed spice for a different twist. You can make in large batches, as muffins freeze really well and can be reheated in minutes, making them perfect for lazy weekend brunches.

55g porridge oats, plus a few more oats for decoration
55g butter
3 tbsp sunflower oil
4–5 level tbsp clear honey
200g carrots, trimmed and peeled
110g plain flour
55g plain wholemeal flour (not bread flour)
1 tsp baking powder plus $1/8$ tsp bicarbonate of soda
1 tsp cinnamon
a pinch of salt
2 medium eggs
1 tbsp plain yoghurt mixed with 75ml milk
$1/4$ tsp vanilla extract

You will also need a standard muffin tin lined with paper cups or brushed with a thin coating of oil (the mixture should make 9–10 muffins). Preheat the oven to 180C/350°F/Gas 4. Toast the oats for 5–6 minutes in the oven while it warms up. Melt the butter in a small saucepan with the oil and honey and set aside to cool. Sift the two flours, raising agents, and cinnamon into a large bowl, add the salt and mix thoroughly. Grate the carrots on the medium side of a grater and tip into a sieve to drain. Lightly beat the eggs then beat in the yoghurt, milk and vanilla. Lightly mix the toasted oats with the flour mixture, make a hollow in the middle then pour in the milk and eggs and melted butter and honey. Fold the mixture together swiftly with a large metal spoon, without over-mixing it, then carefully fold in the grated carrots. Spoon the mixture into the paper cases, taking it almost up to the brim if you want them to rise gratifyingly high. Sprinkle with extra porridge oats and bake for 20–25 minutes in the top half of the oven, until golden brown, firm and springy to the touch.

VARIATIONS

You could use grated apple instead of carrot, or ginger instead of cinnamon. You could also ice the muffins with a Philadelphia cheese icing. Take 75g of soft butter and cream with 40–60g of icing sugar (depending on how sweet you like your icing). Add a few drops of vanilla extract, then work in 150g of Philadelphia Cream Cheese (not the low-fat version!).

FIONA SAYS

Healthy baking sounds like a contradiction in terms but these muffins come as close to being virtuous as any of the recipes in this section – provided you don't eat the whole batch in one sitting! I like the fact that Sig doesn't make any of her cakes too sweet – it's worth reducing the amount of sugar you use in your recipes a little bit to shave off the few calories. The oats and wholemeal flower in the recipe will also give you a bit of an energy boost.

BANANA AND HONEY MUFFINS

MAKES 6 BIG MUFFINS, OR 10-12 SMALLER ONES

Muffins are one of the easiest and most delicious things to bake. You just need the kit (a muffin tin, a sieve and some paper cases if you can afford them) and the technique – light folding rather than energetic stirring or beating. If you want them to look like the ones they sell in the shops, buy a deep muffin tin rather than a shallow one.

150g plain flour
1½ level tsp baking powder
½ level tsp ground cinnamon
¼ level tsp salt
50g butter
2 tbsp runny honey (about 55g)
1 heaped tbsp natural unsweetened yoghurt
about 60ml milk
½ tsp vanilla flavouring
1 large egg, lightly beaten
1 medium ripe banana (yellow rather than green or speckled with black)
unrefined caster sugar, for topping

You'll need a muffin tin, preferably one with deep holes. Pre-heat the oven to 190C/375F/Gas 5. Line the tin with paper cups if you have some otherwise lightly grease the pan. Sieve the flour into a bowl with the baking powder, cinnamon and salt and hollow out a dip in the centre. Gently heat the butter in a pan with the honey. Set aside and cool slightly. Put the yoghurt in a measuring jug and mix in enough milk to bring it just over the 100ml mark. Stir in the vanilla extract. Pour the honey mixture, beaten egg and yoghurt and milk into the flour, mix in lightly and swiftly with a large metal spoon to get a rough batter. (This takes a few seconds.) Peel the banana, slice it thinly into the batter and stir lightly so that all the slices are coated. Spoon the batter into the muffin tin and sprinkle with a little caster sugar. Bake for 25–30 minutes (15–20 minutes if your muffins are smaller) or until fully risen and well browned. Leave in the tin or paper cups for 5 minutes then put on a cooling rack.

TOP STUDENT TIPS

These are great for a weekend bake if you have some funky ripe bananas that need eating. Making muffins is so simple, requiring a minimum of equipment, and no creaming or whisking, just gentle folding. The inclusion of honey, rather than caster sugar makes these muffins slightly more virtuous too – you can also replace half the flour with wholemeal flour. Enjoy with a cup of tea or glass of cold milk. **SIG**

'one of the easiest and most delicious things to bake'

SIG'S CHOCOLATE AND RASPBERRY BROWNIES

MAKES 16 BROWNIES

A happy marriage of two useful ingredients to the hard-up student: cocoa powder and frozen fruit! The high sugar content in this recipe gives the brownies their distinctive fudgy texture but feel free to drop the sugar content – the brownies will be less gooey and slightly less sweet.

250g butter at room temperature
7 level tbsp cocoa powder
2 tbsp strong coffee or 1 shot of espresso
4 medium eggs
400g caster sugar
1 tsp vanilla essence
150g self-raising flour
1/2 tsp salt
250g frozen raspberries

Preheat the oven to 180C/350F/Gas 4. Line a long rectangular baking tin or small roasting tin (about 20 x 30cm) with baking parchment. Melt the butter in a small saucepan, sift in the cocoa powder and stir until fully incorporated. Add the coffee and set aside. In a large bowl, beat the eggs with the sugar and vanilla until pale and fluffy (about 5–8 minutes) and then fold in the melted butter-cocoa-coffee mix. Sift the flour into the mix and stir with a spoon until just incorporated. Add the frozen raspberries, give the mix one or two stirs to incorporate the berries and then spoon the mix into the baking tin. Bake in the oven for 25–30 minutes – check with a skewer to see if there is any wet mixture remaining, if so leave for further 5 minutes. The top of the brownie mix should feel slightly soft to the touch, not hard – if hard, then the brownies have baked too dry!

Allow to cool, slice into squares and eat as they are or with a dollop of Greek yoghurt or fromage frais. Any leftover brownies (ha ha!) can be frozen.

FIONA SAYS

The great virtue of brownies – apart from the fact that they're one of the best chocolate cakes on earth – is that you can use them just as easily as a pud, as Sig suggests. Cocoa powder is well worth adding to your storecupboard to whip up a chocolate cake at any time. It has a better chocolate flavour than cheap bars of chocolate too. (See also Becca's Chocolate Cake on the next page.)

'add a teaspoon of vanilla essence'

BECCA'S CHOCOLATE CAKE

Becca says: 'This cake is excellent for birthday parties or any celebration. It only contains cocoa – no actual chocolate, so even if you've given up chocolate for Lent you can have this cake and it will taste exactly like real chocolate. Sneaky, huh?'

225g caster or granulated sugar
175g margarine (soft-tub or Vitalite)
3 eggs
1 tsp vanilla essence
175g low-fat natural yoghurt
225g self-raising flour
50g cocoa
1 tsp bicarbonate of soda

For the icing
50g margarine
50g cocoa
3 tbsp milk
350g icing sugar

you'll need a 20cm loose-based or spring-release cake tin

Preheat the oven to 170C/325F/Gas 3. Beat the sugar and margarine in a mixing bowl until smooth. Beat in the eggs, vanilla essence and yoghurt. Sift in the flour, cocoa and bicarbonate of soda and then stir until fully combined. Spoon the mixture into a cake tin (the inside of which has been pre-greased with a little butter/margarine) and level the surface. Bake the cake in the pre-heated oven until a skewer inserted into the centre of the cake comes out clean. Turn out the cake onto a wire rack to cool.

To make the icing, melt the margarine in a bowl until liquid. Stir in the cocoa, milk (3 tablespoons or as required) and the icing sugar. Once the cake has completely cooled, spread the icing over and around the entire cake.

FIONA SAYS

This wickedly indulgent cake from sixth-form student, Becca Carey, who won the Guild of Food Writers 'Write It!' competition for young food writers last year, proved the all-time favourite on our Facebook page so we just had to include it. Check out our fan page to see the video of Becca making it. She actually cooked it in a Remoska, a portable Czech cooker (available in the UK from Lakeland) which is handy if you don't have an oven in your student kitchen.

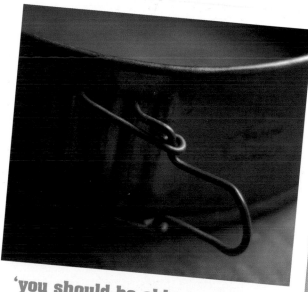

'you should be able to pick up a cake tin quite cheaply'

SIMPLE, BRILLIANT CHOCOLATE 'MOUSSE'

SERVES 6–8

You're simply not going to believe how easy this recipe is. Or how much fun it is to make. I originally found it in Heston Blumenthal's book *Family Food* (Penguin) shortly after he was awarded 3 Michelin stars. He, in turn, got it from a French chemist called Hervé This. Heston calls it Hervé's Chocolate Chantilly but to me it just tastes like the best imaginable chocolate mousse. A fantastic dessert for vegans.

230ml water
270g best-quality bitter chocolate

'all you need is very good quality chocolate'

You will need a handheld electric whisk or chef's balloon whisk for this. Measure the water carefully – quantities are critical in this recipe. (Measure to the 250ml mark then take out 1 tablespoons and 1 teaspoon of water). Break up the chocolate into squares, put it in a saucepan with the water and put it over a low heat, stirring occasionally until it has melted.

Meanwhile get two bowls, one slightly smaller than the other. Put some cold water and ice cubes in the larger one then place the smaller one inside it. Have your whisk ready. When the chocolate has melted pour it into the smaller bowl and start to beat it on the highest setting of your whisk or energetically by hand. After a few minutes (about 2–3) it will thicken and begin to go like whipped cream. Your beaters should leave a slight trail in the chocolate but it shouldn't be stiff.

Take the small bowl out of the big bowl and spoon the 'mousse' into small coffee cups or glasses. (That might sound mean but it is unbelievably rich!) If you do over-beat it, simply tip the chocolate back into the saucepan, melt it and start again.

TOP STUDENT TIPS

Thank God for recipes like this. All too often the idea of making a pudding just seems like a bridge too far. Not with gems like this kicking about it's not. A little trick just to add some sexiness to the dish, is to artfully lay a mint leaf on top, sieve over some icing sugar, then remove the mint – you'll be left with an incredibly elegant mint sprig stencil. Another fantastically quick and easy pud is achieved by melting a block of good white chocolate with whole milk and pouring it over frozen berries – a trick I learnt from chef Mark Hix. **JAMES**

SIG'S WHITE CHOCOLATE & PASSIONFRUIT MOUSSE

SERVES 2-4
(depending on how indulgent you're feeling)

This is a great dinner party dessert as it involves very little work and can be made a day ahead. You can use any kind of small glass dish, glass or ramekin to serve the mousse – in fact it looks great in a range of different dishes. White chocolate and passionfruit sounds a weird combination but I promise you it works. It makes a great dessert for a Valentine's date too.

75g white chocolate
2 medium eggs, separated
2 passionfruit, halved and pulp removed
pinch of salt

Place a heatproof bowl over a saucepan containing simmering water. Break the white chocolate into small pieces and allow it to melt in the bowl without letting the bowl touch the water. Add this to the separated egg yolks and stir thoroughly. Don't worry: it will look a bit firm and very yellow, but rest assured, the end result will be fine!

Next, whisk the egg whites in a large bowl for 1 or 2 minutes until the mixture holds a peak. (You should be able to pull your whisk upwards through the mixture and it will form a peak that won't flop over). Take a spoonful of this and add it to the chocolate-yolk mixture to loosen it. Then add the passionfruit pulp and the egg whites with a large metal spoon, mixing lightly but carefully so as not to knock the air bubbles out of the whites.

When you're finished mixing, spoon the mixture into small ramekins, cups, glasses or bowls. Cover with Clingfilm and store in the fridge for 4 hours minimum or overnight. When you're ready to serve these babies, add a little more passionfruit pulp on top, or some fresh berries.

FIONA SAYS

Once you can handle egg whites you can make a range of classy desserts like mousses, soufflés and meringues (see page 238). To separate an egg white, have two clean cups or bowls ready, crack the egg against the side of one and carefully pull the two halves apart letting the white fall into the bowl. Tip the yolk from one half of the shell into the other letting the rest of the white run into the bowl then put the yolk in the other bowl. Take another cup if you have more eggs to separate, otherwise, if one of the yolks breaks, it'll fall in your egg whites and they won't whisk properly.

'passionfruit and white chocolate make a great combination'

WARM CHOCOLATE CHIP COOKIES

MAKES ABOUT 30–35 COOKIES

Nothing compares to homemade cookies, straight from the oven so the chocolate is all warm and gooey.

125g dark luxury Belgian chocolate (from the baking section of the supermarket)
125g soft butter (at room temperature)
75g soft light brown sugar
50g granulated sugar
1 large egg
1/2 tsp vanilla extract (optional)
165g plain flour
1/2 tsp bicarbonate of soda
1/4 tsp salt

you will need a lightly greased baking tray – perferably two

Preheat the oven to 180C/350F/Gas 4. You'll need at least one, preferably two baking trays. Break the chocolate into chunks then cut it into smaller chips with a knife. Beat the butter and sugars together in a large bowl until light and fluffy. Lightly beat the egg in another bowl or mug, add the vanilla if using then add it to the butter mixture bit by bit, beating all the time. Mix in the flour, salt and bicarbonate of soda then add the chopped chocolate. Drop 8–9 teaspoons of the mixture on a baking tray leaving plenty of space in between each spoonful.

Bake for 10–12 minutes until browned. Remove the tray from the oven, leave for a couple of minutes then prise off the cookies with a knife and transfer them to a wire rack. (Use an oven shelf or the rack on a grill pan if you don't have one.) Repeat with the next batch of cookies. Serve warm on their own or with vanilla ice-cream.

• If you bake two trays at the same time the lower tray may cook more slowly than the top one, especially in a gas oven, so it will need extra time.

VARIATIONS

You can make white chocolate chip cookies by replacing the dark chocolate with white chocolate and adding a tablespoon of sifted cocoa to the flour.

TOP STUDENT TIPS

 My girlfriend, Claire, bakes these for stressful revision sessions. The recipe for these cookies is a great base that can be experimented with easily. We like to add a considerable dollop of crunchy peanut butter to the mix, along with the chocolate chips. The salty peanut flavour really goes well with the sweet chocolate, especially with a tall glass of milk. Plain chocolate chips can be replaced with diced mini-eggs or Smarties. **GUY**

DAIRY-FREE APRICOT MUESLI BARS

MAKES 16 BARS

It's good to have a bake you can make for dairy-intolerant friends. Because I've also replaced some of the usual golden syrup with dark muscovado sugar, they're softer than the typical flapjack but twice as delicious - and a good deal healthier. Or at least that's what I tell myself.

175g dairy-free margarine or spread
150g dark muscovado or Demerara sugar
2 tbsp golden syrup
100g dried apricots, preferably organic, cut into small pieces (easier to do with scissors!)
125g unsweetened Swiss-style muesli, preferably organic
125g porridge oats, preferably organic

you will need a small rectangular baking tin (about 27x17cm), lightly greased with the dairy-free spread

Preheat the oven to 160C/325F/Gas 3. Place the spread, sugar and syrup in a heavy-bottomed saucepan and warm over a low heat until completely melted, stirring occasionally. Add the dried apricots, muesli and rolled oats and mix thoroughly. Spread the mixture into the tin, making sure there's plenty around the sides which cook more quickly. Bake for about 35 minutes until golden brown. Remove from the oven and leave to cool for 15 minutes. Using a sharp knife, mark out the bars making one cut down the length of the tin then 8 cuts across to give you 16 bars. Leave the mixture in the tin until it has hardened completely (a good 2 hours) then carefully prise out the bars and store in an airtight tin.

• Never serve peanuts or other nuts to anyone without checking whether they're allergic to them.

TOP STUDENT TIPS

 My dad used to make these before long bike rides; he once dragged me on a 100-mile ride and one of the only upsides was surreptitiously grabbing these from the back of his jacket. Using raisins or dates also works well, but apricots give them a really good flavour. **GUY**

STRAWBERRY PAVLOVA

SERVES 4-6

This is one of those retro puddings whose appeal never seems to fade. I originally got the recipe from a cookery writer called Nicola Cox and I haven't found a better one. It just looks and tastes fantastic.

3 large egg whites (see tip, page 233)
175g caster sugar plus 2–3 extra tsp for sweetening the cream
1/2–1 tsp vanilla extract or essence plus a few extra drops for the cream
3/4 tsp white malt or wine vinegar
1 tsp cornflour
500g ripe strawberries
284ml carton of double cream

you will need some non-stick baking parchment – and a handheld electric beater, if you don't want to give yourself repetitive strain injury whipping the egg whites

Preheat the oven to 150C/300F/Gas 2. Roll out the baking parchment. Take a large plate, turn it upside down on the paper and draw round it with a pencil or pen then cut round the circle you've made. Place it on a baking sheet. Whisk the egg whites in a deep bowl until just holding their shape. Gradually whisk in one third of the sugar then keep whisking until the mixture is very stiff and shiny. Fold in* the remaining sugar, then finally fold in the vanilla essence, vinegar and cornflour (sieved over the top of the mixture to avoid lumps). Spoon the meringue onto the circle of paper hollowing out the centre slightly so the edges are higher than the middle. Bake for about 1 hour until the top is pale golden brown. When cool enough to handle (about 10 minutes) carefully peel off the baking parchment then leave to get completely cold. De-stalk and slice the strawberries.

Whip the cream (it should hold its shape but not be stiff). Add 1/2 teaspoon of vanilla extract and 2 teaspoons of caster sugar and fold carefully into the cream. Pile half the cream onto the Pavlova, top with half the strawberries then spoon over the remaining cream and arrange the rest of the strawberries artistically over the top.

* To 'fold' one ingredient into another, use a big serving spoon and take it down through the mixture in vertical movements, scooping the ingredients at the bottom up to the top.

CHEAT'S MINI-PAVS

If you want to make an easy version of this buy six meringue nests (Marks and Sparks do very good ones), fill them with sweetened whipped cream or vanilla ice cream and top with sliced strawberries.

TOP STUDENT TIPS

 Fabulously retro, yet timeless in its appeal, pavlova is an easy dessert with which to impress your friends or a hot date. With all that sweet meringue and whipped cream be as generous as you can with the fruit – you need some to break through the cloying creaminess otherwise you'll be waddling around from indigestion hours later. Strawberries are classic, but try raspberries, peaches, nectarines, apricots or passionfruit, or a mix of these. Pavs need not be confined to summer months. Try using frozen berries during winter and don't shy away from tinned fruit such as apricots. Served in individual glasses with broken-up meringue, pavlova evolves into 'Eton Mess', an even easier way to impress that date. **SIG**

GOLDEN MERINGUES

MAKES 8–10 MERINGUES

If you ever have any leftover egg whites it's always worth making a batch of homemade meringues. They cost next to nothing and taste truly wonderful. This is a slight adaptation of one of Delia's recipes I've been using for years.

2 large fresh, preferably free-range, egg whites (see tip on how to separate eggs, page 233)
110g golden (unrefined) caster sugar

you will need a large bowl, an electric or rotary whisk, a baking sheet and some non-stick baking parchment

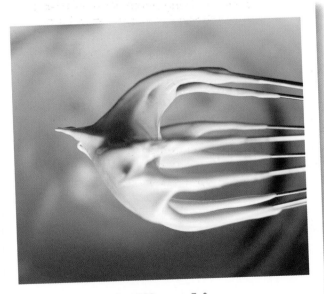

'stiff peak'

Preheat your oven to 150C/300F/Gas 2. Put the egg whites in a large, scrupulously clean bowl (clean because the whites won't beat up properly if there's grease on the surface) and whisk them with a handheld electric whisk or rotary whisk until stiff. (The whites should hold a peak when you draw the whisk up through them.) Add the sugar a heaped tablespoon at a time, beating the whites well between each addition. It should end up very stiff and shiny. Lay a sheet of baking parchment over the baking tray. Using two dessertspoons (the kind you use for cereal) take spoonfuls of the mixture with one spoon and scoop it out with the other onto the tray – you should get 8–10 meringues. Put the tray in the oven, shut the door then turn down the heat to 140C/275/F/Gas 1. Cook for 1–1½ hours then turn off the oven and leave the meringues to cool in the residual heat until completely cold. You can serve them as they are, or sandwich the halves together with whipped cream.

TOP STUDENT TIPS

The beauty of getting the hang of the meringue 'master recipe', as with so many master recipes, is that it gives you a lot of scope for creating other variations. You could, for example, make two big meringues and fashion yourself a Pavlova by sandwiching whipped cream and fresh fruit (I like passion fruit and kiwi) between the meringue wheels. Or you could go really old school and knock up a lemon meringue pie. That's the fun of cooking, in a nutshell: learn the basic techniques and then forge your own unique path. JAMES

BLACK MAGIC JELLIES

SERVES 6

If you're thinking of inviting friends over to celebrate Hallowe'en, these purply-black vodka jellies make a show-stopping dessert. The crème de cassis (blackcurrant liqueur) is a bit of an indulgence but it does improve the taste. You can find it in most supermarkets. (Make kirs with any leftovers – put a splash in a wine glass and top up with dry white wine or Cava.)

1 x 135g packet of blackcurrant jelly
a 75cl carton or bottle of red grape juice
about 225ml vodka
2 tbsp crème de cassis (French blackcurrant liqueur) – optional but good
about 300g black or dark red grapes
a small carton of double cream or some aerosol cream (optional)

you'll also need six glasses or small glass dishes (see below)

Cut the jelly in squares and put into a measuring jug. Add 3 tablespoons of the grape juice and microwave for 1–1½ minutes. Stir until dissolved. Add the vodka and enough grape juice to take the liquid to the 580ml (1 pint) mark. Stir in the cassis, if using, and set aside. Wash the grapes, then halve them and remove the pips (unless you're using seedless ones). Put a few grapes in the bottom of six small glasses or glass bowls and pour over the liquid jelly to cover. Put the glasses in the fridge until the jelly has set then scatter over the remaining grapes and pour over the remaining jelly (warming it slightly first if it's set) Return the glasses to the fridge until fully set. Spoon or squirt over the cream before serving.

• You can buy individual glass dishes really cheaply in charity shops – or make the jelly in one big glass dish if you prefer.
• If you haven't got a microwave heat the grape juice till almost boiling and pour over the jelly before you add the vodka.

VARIATIONS

If you wanted to be even more kitsch you could make a batch of orange jellies as well with orange jelly, orange or passionfruit juice, vodka, an orange liqueur like Cointreau or Grand Marnier and tinned mandarin oranges. Just follow the method above with roughly the same proportions of fruit juice, vodka, etc.

TOP STUDENT TIPS

 There's nothing naughtier than tarting up childhood favourites with a bit of booze. Slinging a glug of wine into a sauce is one thing – the alcohol cooks off as it boils anyway, so it has very little effect – but in its uncooked state, as in a tiramisu or a jelly, pudding takes on a whole new level of indulgence. That said, it's important to resist the urge to go for broke and hoi in as much grog as you can, tempting though it might be. A jelly swimming in vodka is (1) less likely to set, and (2) going to be fairly inedible. **JAMES**

SPARKLING PEACH, & BLUEBERRY JELLY

SERVES 2

A cute jelly for two that you can make for a Valentine or other romantic dinner (or scale up for a crowd). Don't be daunted by the idea of using gelatine (unless you're a vegetarian, obviously). It's really easy to use and gives you a much more natural set and flavour.

2–3 sheets of gelatine
275ml low-alcohol sparkling peach wine
   cocktail
1 small ripe nectarine
1 tsp lemon juice
50g fresh blueberries

Place the gelatine in a flat dish and pour over 2 tablespoons of cold water. Heat the peach cocktail in a microwave or saucepan until hot but not boiling. Tip the gelatine into the peach wine and stir to dissolve. Leave to cool then place in the fridge to for about an hour until beginning to set. When just about at setting point, cut round the nectarine and twist each half in opposite directions to pull them apart. Cut into small cubes and pour the lemon juice over it to stop it discolouring. Rinse the blueberries and stir them and the nectarine into the jelly, then spoon into individual glasses or glass dishes. Return to the fridge until set. Serve on their own or with a jug of cream.

• Sheets of gelatine vary in size, so check how much gelatine is required to set the amount of liquid in the recipe (allowing for the lemon juice). You can afford to use slightly less for a jelly that sets in a glass or bowl than one which you've set in a mould.

VARIATIONS

Once you've got into the jelly-making groove you can make great-looking jellies out of all kinds of drinks and fruit. I've made simple little jellies from clear apple juice with grapes and Granny Smith apples and more sophisticated sparkling jellies with pink Cava and strawberries and even with raspberry beer and raspberries. The key things to remember are that if you use a basically dry drink like wine you'll need to sweeten it (sugar syrup comes in handy here – see page 250) and that you must let the liquid begin to set before adding fruit otherwise it will all fall to the bottom. For perfect distribution, add fruit, cover with liquid jelly, set, then add the remainder of the fruit and liquid.

TOP STUDENT TIPS

 Often overlooked as a dessert, jelly is ideal for entertaining – you make it in advance, it looks pretty and you don't feel like a baby hippo after eating it. Be very careful not to overheat the gelatine as it will taste, for want of a better description, piggy. (You can use a vegetarian setting agent if you're veggie.) **SIG**

TOASTED WAFFLES
WITH BANANAS, VANILLA ICE CREAM AND YUMMY TOFFEE SAUCE

SERVES 3–4

Cooking is as much about presentation as anything. None of these ingredients are particularly out of the ordinary – shop-bought waffles, banana, vanilla ice cream but put them together and slather them with an indulgent home-made toffee sauce and you've suddenly got a great-looking dessert.

vanilla ice cream
3–4 waffles
3–4 small bananas

for the sauce
50g butter
4 tbsp light soft brown or Demerara sugar
6 tbsp double cream
a small pinch of salt

If your ice cream is not soft scoop, take it out of the freezer or freezer compartment to make it scoopable. To make the sauce, put the butter and sugar in a saucepan over a low heat until the butter has melted and the sugar completely dissolved. Stir in the cream and heat until almost boiling. Simmer for 2–3 minutes then take off the heat and stir. Toast the waffles on a low setting (they'll seem soggy at first and then crisp up) and slice the bananas. Put a waffle on each plate, with a scoop of ice cream alongside, top with sliced banana and pour over the warm sauce.

VARIATIONS

You could top this with a chocolate sauce instead. Put 100g of dark luxury Belgian chocolate (you'll find it in the baking section of most supermarkets) and 6 tablespoons of whipping cream in a bowl and set it over a pan of hot water without letting the base of the bowl touch the water. Stir occasionally until melted then sweeten to taste with caster sugar or sugar syrup. Add a tablespoon of water to thin, if necessary.

TOP STUDENT TIPS

Waffles are a staple dish in Norway. Seriously – they constitute a food group by themselves. Practically everyone in the country owns a waffle-iron. Expect to be proffered sour cream waffles topped with jam and sour cream wherever you go. Norwegians have a thing about sour cream, grannies make a porridge from it called '*rømmegrøt*' which is good for building stout Valkyrian hips and bosoms. Anyway, waffles are great sustenance for long cold winters or hikes through the mountains during short Norwegian summers. Short of investing in a waffle-iron, do as Fiona suggests and buy them for lazy weekend breakfasts and brunches. Warm through in the oven or toaster, and top waffles with bananas or other fresh fruit, compôtes, jam, spices such as cinnamon, etc. Maple syrup's also a popular topping. **SIG**

NIGEL SLATER'S EASY BANANA ICE CREAM

SERVES 3–4

I don't know anyone who isn't a Nigel Slater fan. His recipes are so deliciously simple – none more so than this unbelievably easy banana ice cream – a perfect way to use up leftover, overripe bananas. Depending on how ripe your bananas are you might want to add a little soft brown sugar or honey

3 medium-sized, ripe bananas
300g natural yoghurt
soft brown sugar or honey, to taste (my addition)

To make the ice cream, peel the bananas, chop them into short chunks and drop into a blender. Pour in the yoghurt and blitz until smooth. Add a little brown sugar or honey, if the mixture is too tart for you. Pour the mixture into either the bowl of an ice-cream machine and churn till frozen or into a plastic container and put it in the freezer. If you do the latter, give it a good beat every hour, bringing the frozen edges in with the more liquid centre.

VARIATIONS

Another great instant ice cream from food writer, Xanthe Clay: beat a tin of condensed milk with 300ml double cream until thick, fold in 250g of puréed strawberries. Freeze. Bingo.

TOP STUDENT TIPS

This recipe is incredibly handy for situations where you need to whip up an easy but impressive pudding. Adding walnuts to the mix will give some crunchiness that is well suited to the honey. You should definitely use this ice cream in order to make the ultimate banana split. Peel and slice a banana lengthwise, add a couple of scoops of this ice cream along with some whipped cream, melted chocolate and another handful of walnuts. **GUY**

'a perfect way to use up leftover overripe bananas'

SIG'S VIRGIN MOJITO GRANITA

SERVES 4

A slightly complicated but brilliant recipe inspired by a Heston Blumenthal recipe in *The Sunday Times*. Granitas are basically roughed-up sorbets.

juice and zest of 3 limes (about 6 tbsp)
50g mint leaves – blanched in boiling water until they turn bright green, then immediately refreshed under cold water
50g fructose (fruit sugar)

Put the lime juice in a measuring jug and top up to 250ml with cold water. Pat the mint leaves dry, place in a blender or food processor and blitz with the lime zest, juice, water and fructose until very smooth. Pass through a fine sieve with a piece of muslin or a J-cloth over it pressing as much of the liquid out of the mixture as possible. Place this in a shallow container, seal and then freeze. After an hour or so, take out the mixture and break up with a fork. Return to the freezer and repeat every half-hour. The more the granita mixture is forked through, the smoother the result, unless you like large ice crystals! After 3–4 stirs, freeze for one hour and serve. You can fork through once more before serving to create a rougher texture.

FIONA SAYS

You can use this technique with any good-quality natural fruit drink you enjoy to make a sophisticated kind of Slush Puppie! Lemon works particularly well. Just freeze and fork through.

'wonderfully refreshing mint and lime'

SIG'S GUIDE TO MAKING YOUR OWN ICE CREAM

 Much like making your own bread, homemade ice cream depends on a limited number of ingredients – milk and/or cream, eggs, sugar and flavouring – and a bit of know-how. Don't be intimidated by the prospect of making your own vanilla or chocolate ice cream: it won't require any fancy gadgets and really is quite simple....

But why would you go to the trouble of even making your own ice cream when there are so many available at supermarkets? For the same reason you'd make your own bread, yoghurt, or muesli: there is a tremendous satisfaction to be gained from creating something with a smattering of ingredients, using your own fair hands. The added benefit, of course, is you'll know exactly what goes in your mouth, something that can't be said of commercial ice cream. Plus ice cream-making is fun, so get your mates round and start experimenting.

Ice cream, in fact, was the reason I applied to work as a stagière at the legendary Fat Duck. Seriously, seeing Heston Blumenthal enthuse about ice cream and reading his observations about how to perfect its technique was an inspiration to learn about the science of ice cream. Plus, of course, I love eating the stuff.

The peculiarity of ice cream lies in its liminal nature – neither liquid nor food, but instead a semi-solid foam frozen to just the right level of coolness so that it refreshes without losing its taste or texture. Commercial ice creams are generally full of stablisers, emulsifiers, artificial colours and flavourings, not to mention any number of weird-sounding additives which you don't need to make your own ice cream.

There are a few rules to bear in mind, as corralled from my three sources on ice cream: Heston Blumenthal's *Big Fat Duck Cookbook*

(Bloomsbury), Harold McGee's *McGee on Food and Cooking* (Hodder & Stoughton) and Peter Barham's *The Science of Cooking* (Springer). The first step is to make a basic mixture and in most cases this will be a cooked custard consisting of egg yolks, milk and/or cream, sugar and some flavouring such as vanilla, coffee or chocolate.

According to the food scientist, Harold McGee, cooking your ice cream custard base will improve both texture and minimise the size of ice crystals in the end result. Minimising the size of ice crystals in ice cream is key, hence the beating of your mixture while it's freezing. In a nutshell, the various ingredients and your technique will have an effect on the molecular structures in your ice cream – too much sugar will make the ice cream 'chewy' and affect its freezing point, and too little will result in crunchy ice. Different sugars have different effects, so watch out if you're thinking of substituting table sugar (sucrose) with fruit sugar (fructose) as this will have a marked effect on your ice cream. Too much milk fat can result in buttery ice cream, and impair flavour-release, so follow the recipe and you'll have, in Heston's words, 'an ice cream which is clean-tasting and has a quick-flavour release, with a refreshing character'.

Once you've made the custard base, ideally you should subject it to what McGee calls 'quiescent cooling' before churning – this will crystallise the fat and improve the consistency. Start at least 8 hours before you want to freeze the ice cream and refrigerate the custard base between 8 and 24 hours for maximum 'maturation'. This may seem time-consuming but all you have to do is plan ahead and once the custard is made, you just leave it in the fridge, though if you forget about it and remember a week later that you have custard in the fridge, you should throw it away – eggs and dairy can give you a very dodgy tummy if they go off!

When you're ready to tackle the final stage of ice cream production, you have three options:

1) Use an ice cream machine. This will churn and cool your custard base within 30 minutes. Job done; go and make yourself a cocktail.

2) If you're without a machine (as most of us are) the first alternative is to put your custard base in a freezer-proof bowl and place in the freezer. Take this out every 15 minutes or so, and stir well, bringing in the mixture from the edges to break up the ice crystals starting to form on the perimeter of the bowl. This distributes the cooler liquid on the outside edges throughout the custard so you get an even 'freeze'. Depending how cold your freezer is, this will take a couple of hours.

3) Alternatively, Peter Barham suggests you use a 'freezing mixture' which is the speediest option for those without a fancy machine. All you do is get 1kg of ice, crush it and place in a large plastic washing bowl, then add 200g of salt dissolved in 300ml of water. Salt lowers the temperature of the ice and creates an instant ice bath for freezing your custard mixture, which is ideal, as the faster the custard freezes the better the texture will be. So, place your custard mixture in a metal baking tin and float on top of the ice bath, making sure you don't get any salty water in your custard! Carefully scrape the bottom of the baking tin every few minutes to circulate the cooler liquid and break up those ice crystals, and, *voila!*, within 30 minutes you have ice cream.

In principle, ice cream – like baking – is easy. The chemistry of ice cream is complex but all you have to do is follow the formula of an ice cream recipe. Test recipes, try different flavours (suggested below) and, if you're a keen bean, check out the three books mentioned opposite, they're all invaluable guides to the science and art of ice cream.

SOME FLAVOUR IDEAS

• Instead of infusing your custard with vanilla or chocolate, how about herbs such as fresh bay leaf or rosemary?

• Experiment with spices. Try cinnamon, cardamom, nutmeg or star anise – infusing these in the custard for the required time and then sieving them out before you freeze and beat the mixture.

• Try adding a fruit purée – though be careful they don't have a high water content as this will result in watery, and potentially crystal-dense ice cream. It's worth cooking the purée and allowing all excess liquid to evaporate so you get a concentrated fruit taste. Try summer berries, peach, apricot, apple, banana (this won't really require cooking, just mash and add to the custard), passionfruit, rhubarb. These can also be made into sorbets.

• Add praline mixtures, marshmallows, bits of cookies, brownies or leftover Christmas cake. The latter makes a great post-Christmas treat, a bit like rum-and-raisin ice cream.

• You can add alcohol to the mixture, though be wary of adding too much as this will impair freezing. A great example of this is Heston's Kirsch ice cream (see his *Big Fat Duck Cookbook*) – a really delicate flavour, and the custard is made with sour cream instead of regular cream.

• Last, but not least, savoury ice creams are seriously good – these take a bit of getting used to, but if you can get your head around eating salty ice cream (think salted butter caramel, but with less sugar) then give it a go. Chefs have been doing it for years and they're proving increasingly popular.

ICED LEMON VODKA SORBET

SERVES 2

A sophisticated instant dessert that looks fantastic in frozen martini glasses. Pick up a couple of cheap ones and leave them in the freezer compartment until you're ready to serve up (or if there isn't room fill them with ice and a little water then chuck it out and dry them).

2–3 tbsp frozen vodka (keep in the freezer
   compartment until you need it)
a carton of good-quality lemon sorbet

Take the sorbet out of the freezer and put it in the fridge about 15 minutes before you plan to serve it. (This makes it soft enough to scoop.) Spoon out a couple of generous scoops and place them in the frosted glass. Pour over the frozen vodka. Await gasps of admiration.

VARIATIONS

You can obviously make this with other sorbets. Raspberry goes well with vodka too.

TOP STUDENT TIPS

 Mix a generous pinch of ground piri-piri chilli with the frozen vodka before pouring over the sorbet. The chilli's heat contrasts with the icy vodka and sour lemon to produce an unforgettable taste sensation. **GUY**

'pick up a couple of cheap martini glasses'

COCKTAILS: SPIRIT+SUGAR+LIME

Even if you don't cook it's fun making cocktails. That doesn't mean you should go mad and pour in everything but the kitchen sink. The best cocktail recipes are quite simple – relying on two or three well-balanced ingredients. Ideally, you should make cocktails individually, but that's not really practical when you're making them for more than two or three people. In which case, mix them in a large jug. As well as a jug then, you'll need the following:

• Ice – and far more than you think. A good cocktail needs to be shaken with ice or at least poured into a jug full of ice. Buy a big bag (or two) for any cocktail session. If you haven't got enough room in your freezer you can keep it cold for a couple of hours in a cool box (essential for parties – and picnics).
• A shaker or a large jam jar and a fine strainer – a tea strainer will do – to strain out bits of broken ice and fruit. If you use a jam jar you'll also need a measuring spoon (2 tablespoons equals a shot). Otherwise, use the top of the shaker as a measure.
• A rolling pin – for making crushed ice (wrap it in a clean tea-towel then bash it) and for 'muddling' (i.e. crushing) mint leaves and fresh fruit.
• Martini glasses (if you want to show off).
• Freshly squeezed lime and lemon juice. Certainly in any cocktail where they're a key ingredient. Just prior to using, roll them under the palm of your hand on a flat surface to maximise the amount of juice.
• And sugar syrup...

SUGAR SYRUP

This will make your drink sweet without making it gritty. Measure 125g of unrefined (golden) granulated sugar and put into a pan with 125ml of water. Warm it over a very low heat, stirring occasionally until all the sugar crystals dissolve. boil for 2 minutes without stirring. Cool the syrup then pour into a clean jam jar and put it in the fridge. It should keep for a couple of weeks.

BARGAIN BOTTLES

These few tips should help keep costs down.

• Own-brand spirits are a good £3–4 cheaper than the well-known brands. Check the strength though – most cocktail recipes are based on using spirits that are 40% ABV.
• Vermouth – so out of fashion it's ridiculously cheap. Secco is the type you use with a classic martini (just a whisper). Sweeter Bianco and Rosso can be mixed 50/50 with other ingredients for a long refreshing drink (try Bianco with soda and Rosso with cranberry juice).
• Ginger wine – great for winter drinking. Mix it with whisky for a warming Whisky Mac.
• Own-brand Irish cream liqueur. Much cheaper than Bailey's. Serve straight from the fridge.
• White port – quite scarce, but worth picking up if you can find it at a reasonable price. Dilute with tonic to taste (about 50/50) and serve it over ice, the way the Portuguese do.
• Montilla – from the same part of Spain as sherry but even cheaper. The medium-dry is especially appealing.

SPIRIT+SUGAR+LIME = A UNIVERSAL FORMULA

These three ingredients are at the heart of the world's most popular cocktails, notably the Margarita (tequila), Daiquiri and Mojito (rum) and Caiprinha (made with the Brazilian national spirit, cachaça). If you can make these well, you can make anything.
The recipes on the following pages all serve one. Feel free to alter the amounts of lime juice and sugar to your own taste.

MARGARITA

The world's most popular cocktail.

50ml (3 tbsp) tequila
25ml (1¹/₂ tbsp) lime juice
25ml (1¹/₂ tbsp) Cointreau or triple sec
coarse sea salt (optional)

Place the ingredients in a shaker or jam jar with 1 tablespoon of water. Fill the shaker with ice. Shake vigorously and strain into a glass. To make a frozen Margarita, blend the ingredients with crushed ice (you need a powerful blender for this). It's traditional to serve a Margarita in a salted glass but don't feel bound to.

• To salt a glass, run half a lime round the rim of the glass then press it into a plate of salt.
• You can also make fresh fruit Margaritas – strawberry is particularly good.

DAIQUIRI

Pronounced *die-kerree*. A Cuban classic.

50ml (3 tbsp) light or dark rum
20ml (1¹/₄ tbsp) freshly squeezed lime juice
1¹/₂-2 tsp sugar syrup (see page 250)

Follow the method for the Margarita, above. You can make frozen Daiquiris the same way as a frozen Margarita.

MOJITO

Pronounced *mo-heatoe*. Another Cuban favourite. Great summer drinking.

2 sprigs of fresh mint
1¹/₂-2 tsp sugar or sugar syrup (see page 250)
25ml (1¹/₂ tbsp) lime juice

'a mojito – great summer drinking'

50ml (3 tbsp) rum
soda water
Angostura bitters (optional)

Strip the leaves off the stalks of the mint sprigs. Place in the bottom of a chunky glass, add the sugar and 'muddle' or pound (gently) with a pestle, or the base of a rolling pin, to crush the mint leaves. Add the lime juice, 3 cubes of crushed ice and the rum and a few drops of Angostura bitters, if you have some. Stir and top up with soda.

CAIPIRINHA

Pronounced *ky-pireenya*. Brazil's national drink.

1 lime, preferably unwaxed
1¹/₂-2 tsp sugar syrup (see page 250) or sugar
50ml cachaça or white rum

Wash the lime and cut into 8 pieces. Put in the bottom of a glass with the sugar syrup and pound to extract the oils from the skin (see Mojito, above). Add 3 crushed ice cubes, pour in the cachaça and stir.

COCKTAILS: SOME EASY JUG DRINKS

Each of the following recipes makes roughly a litre (enough for 4–6 glasses). Filling a jug – or glass – with ice is not as extravagant as it sounds. The colder your drink stays, the less diluted it will get and the better it will taste.

SEA BREEZE

Just about the best summer cocktail to have been invented in recent years.

300ml vodka
400ml cranberry juice
300ml grapefruit juice

Pour the ingredients into a large jug full of ice. Stir.

RUM PUNCH

The classic formula for a Jamaican rum punch is one of sour (lemon or lime juice), two of sweet (sugar syrup or grenadine), three of strong (rum, of course) and four of weak (some kind of fruit juice or water). Personally I prefer a slightly less sweet drink, so I make the sweet component the same as the sour, but it's up to you.

100ml freshly squeezed lemon juice
100ml sugar syrup (see page 250) or grenadine*
300ml golden or dark rum
400ml tropical fruit juice

Follow the method for Sea Breeze. Float some slices of orange, lemon or apple in, if you want.

* Grenadine is a non-alcoholic (or occasionally low-alcohol) syrup made from pomegranates which gives a lovely deep colour to cocktails.

SIG'S SUPER-SPICY BLOODY MARY

 My favourite cocktail for brunch – probably because of the big umami hit. A great way to get over a hangover!

1 litre tomato juice, clamato juice or V8 veggie juice
splash of Worcestershire sauce
slightly less generous splash of Tabasco Sauce
1½ tbsp horseradish cream or grated horseradish
250ml vodka (or aquavit if you're a Scandi)
salt and pepper
celery sticks for garnish (failing that, cucumber sticks work fine)

Mix all the ingredients in a large jug and fill with ice. You can replace the horseradish with wasabi. (For a non-alcoholic 'Virgin Mary' see page 255)

WHITE SANGRIA

A bit like a floating fruit salad but brilliantly refreshing.

1 bottle basic dry Spanish – or French – white wine, chilled
5cl miniature of Cointreau or other orange-flavoured liqueur
2 tbsp caster sugar
½ orange and ½ lemon, finely sliced
¼ of a ripe honeydew melon, peeled and cut into cubes
chilled soda water, to taste

Pour the wine into a large jug with the Cointreau and sugar and stir till the sugar has dissolved. Add the orange and lemon slices and leave to infuse for an hour or so. Add the melon and 10–12 ice cubes then top up with soda to taste.

'bloody mary –
a classic brunch cocktail'

TOP STUDENT TIPS

Always store your vodka in the freezer. You'd be amazed at how easily it slips down when ice cold – it's actually quite a pleasant beverage. Obviously if you're drinking it only to get blind drunk then it matters little how you serve it, but you'll find it becomes a really enjoyable aperitif if sipped super-cold and with a sliver of lemon peel. While most ingredients are at their best when at room temperature or above, vodka, when ice-cold, loses the alcoholic sharpness and takes on a really lovely sweetness. *Na zdrowie*! JAMES

My favourite cocktail is a Spritz. It is most famous in Venice where outside every bar you will see people sipping this colourful drink. One part Prosecco, one part Aperol and one part sparkling water. Aperol is a bitter aperitif that is orange in colour – you can substitute Campari. The cocktail is really refreshing and brilliant for the summer. GUY

HOT TODDIES AND MULLED DRINKS

MULLED WINE

MAKES 6–8 SMALL GLASSES OR MUGS

You can, of course, buy ready-mixed mulled wine – or *glühwein* – but this tastes better. Double (or treble) up for a crowd

75cl bottle of full bodied red wine (a cheap Spanish red would be ideal)
150 ml Vintage Character, Special Reserve or other inexpensive ruby port
150ml water
4–5 tbsp granulated or caster sugar, preferably unrefined
1–2 mulled wine sachets
1 orange

Pour the red wine, port and water into a saucepan. Add 4 tablespoons of the sugar and 1 sachet of the mulled spice. Pare 3 thin strips of orange rind off the orange with a vegetable peeler or a sharp knife and add to the saucepan. Heat very slowly until the sugar has dissolved, check for sweetness adding more sugar or spice to taste. Turn up the heat until the wine is almost at boiling point but DON'T LET IT BOIL or you'll lose the alcohol and your mulled wine will taste bitter Cover the pan and leave for 30 minutes for the flavours to infuse.

* You can use any leftover port (joke) for the mulled Christmas crumble. Or maybe you should make that first...

JAMES' MULLED CIDER

SERVES 8

 A delicious, and cheaper, alternative to mulled wine.

1½ litres cider
2 cinnamon sticks
1 bay leaf
3 cardamom pods
100g sugar
juice of 1 orange
500ml water

Put all ingredients in a saucepan over a gentle heat and whisk to dissolve the sugar. Warm gently (not boiling) for about 20 minutes. Add a couple of shots of rum for that extra kick.

* You can cook red cabbage with mulled cider. Put 250ml in a saucepan with sliced red cabbage, cover and simmer for 1-2 hours. Brilliant with roast pork.

BLV (AKA BLACKCURRANT, LEMON AND VODKA)

SERVES 1

You can of course make this without vodka.

2 tbsp Ribena Original
1 tbsp vodka
1 tbsp freshly squeezed lemon juice

Pour all the ingredients in a mug or tough glass and pour over 200ml boiling water.

HOT WHISKY WITH LEMON, HONEY AND GINGER

SERVES 1

The classic hot toddy – a great drink for when you're feeling fluey or coldy, but don't save it up till then.

2 tbsp blended whisky
2 tbsp Stone's ginger wine
1 tbsp freshly squeezed lemon juice
1 tsp runny honey
stick of cinnamon, for garnish (optional)

Pour the whisky, ginger wine and lemon juice in a mug or strong glass. Add the honey and pour over 200-225ml boiling water. Stir and serve with a cinnamon stick.

VERVEINE (LEMON VERBENA)

This is my favourite night time drink. You can buy lemon verbena from health food shops and some specialist tea shops. You need a small handful of dried lemon verbena leaves or a lemon verbena teabag. Put the leaves in a pot or jug and pour over 250ml boiling water. Cover and leave to infuse for 5 minutes. Strain into a mug and serve.

'the classic hot toddy'

NO- AND LO-ALCOHOL OPTIONS

JAMES' SPRITZER WITH A TWIST

SERVES 1

 White wine spritzer has a bit of a reputation for being a girly drink (not that there's anything wrong with that), but this is an incredibly refreshing version that could almost pass as Prosecco – ideal for a special occasion when you don't want to break the bank. Needless to say your ingredients ought to be refrigerated.

125ml dry white wine
125ml soda water
a dash of elderflower syrup

Pour the wine into a wine glass, add the soda water and a dash of the elderflower syrup, stir and serve.

VIRGIN MARY

I actually think this non-alcoholic version is better than the original Bloody Mary. Adjust the seasoning to taste but it should be good and spicy.

tomato juice
Worcestershire sauce
Tabasco
salt and pepper
a slice of lemon

Pour the tomato juice into a glass full of ice cubes. Add a shake (about $\frac{1}{2}$ a teaspoon) of Worcestershire sauce and a few drops of Tabasco hot pepper sauce and season with salt and pepper. Serve with a slice of lemon (or a stick of celery, if you have some).

ST CLEMENTS CITRUS PUNCH

SERVES 4

A refreshing very low-alcohol punch that makes the perfect start to a lazy Sunday. You can buy freshly squeezed juices rather juicing fruit yourself, though you may want to adjust the proportions depending on the brand you use.

250ml chilled freshly squeezed orange juice
150ml chilled freshly squeezed pink grapefruit juice
250ml chilled lemon refresher or traditional lemonade
1 tbsp orange liqueur e.g. Grand Marnier or Cointreau (optional)
a fresh orange and a lemon

Pour the chilled juices into a jug and top up with the lemon refresher. Add the Grand Marnier, if using, and stir. Add a few slices each of orange and lemon and serve.

TOP STUDENT TIPS

 There's no need to spend money on expensive mineral water. Simply buy one large bottle then when it's empty fill it up with cold water from the tap. (If you're doing this first thing in the morning let the tap run for a minute so the water is as fresh as possible) Then keep the bottle in the fridge so you have a supply of lovely cool water. Add a couple of ice cubes and a slice of lemon or lime to the glass before you pour it in. GUY

'makes a great lassi'

MANGO LASSI

SERVES 2

Wonderfully refreshing and tasty.

1 medium-sized ripe mango (about 300g)
150ml very low fat yoghurt
1–2 tbsp freshly squeezed lime juice

you'll need some kind of blender or food processor for this

Hold the mango upright and cut vertically down each side as near as you can get to the stone. Peel the slices you've made then cut away the rest of the flesh from around the stone. Place in a blender or liquidiser with 1 heaped tablespoon of the yoghurt and whizz until smooth. Add half the lime juice and remaining yoghurt and whizz again. Pour into a jug and gradually dilute to a drinkable consistency with chilled water (about 75ml) adding a little more lime juice if you think it needs it.

ULTIMATE STRAWBERRY MILKSHAKE

SERVES 2

Awesome. And it contains one of your '5 a day'!

a small carton of strawberries
2–3 scoops strawberry ice cream
a mug (about 225ml) cold milk
grenadine (optional)

Remove the stalks and any unripe white flesh round the stalk from the strawberries and slice. Put in a blender or food processor with the ice cream – or you can use a handheld blender. Whizz till smooth then gradually add the mug of cold milk. Add a little grenadine, if you have some, to intensify the colour and sweeten. Or just a bit of sugar. Accompany with home-baked cookies

HOW TO MAKE A DECENT CUP OF TEA

Among the skills to acquire as a fresher is the art of making a decent cup – or rather mug – of tea. Why do you need to be told how? Because so many people make rubbish tea and tea-making skills impress, as Masterchef James Nathan recently confessed in the *Guardian*.

1. Buy decent teabags. It's not worth buying from a budget range, though there's nothing wrong with own-brand. Look out for big brand discounts.
2. Use fresh not longlife milk. By fresh I mean in date and that's not been hanging around out of the fridge for half a day. Personally, I prefer semi-skimmed milk but it's up to you.
3. Discard any water that's stagnant in the kettle and refill with fresh water. This is important because water that's already been boiled lacks oxygen and will make your tea taste flat. Bring to the boil, being certain that the water does actually boil.
4. Put teabags in mugs and pour in the boiling water. (Don't let the boiled water start to get cold. And never add the milk first!)
5. Now LEAVE IT for a couple of minutes to infuse. That's what brings out the flavour. Don't be tempted to swish the teabag around in the water and squeeze it against the side. (I know, everyone does it, but it will taste so much better if you don't). Only if you're drinking your tea black with lemon (i.e. without milk) should you leave it for less time.
6. Now, finally add sugar and milk to taste. Some people like their tea very milky like a latte. Some people (mention no names) are strange....
7. Finally, be sure to reseal the teabags carton so that the air can't get to them. Better still, transfer them to a tin. And don't forget the biscuits!

LOOSE-LEAF TEA

The next step is using loose tea which will give a much, much better flavour and enable you to try all sorts of different teas that you can't buy in bag form. You'll obviously also need a teapot and a strainer.

Warm the pot first: swish hot water around in it, then discard the water and add the tea (about 1 rounded teaspoon per person). Pour over freshly boiled water, stir and leave to infuse as with bags before straining into cups or mugs. **Note:** different teas need different water temperatures and infusing periods. Take a look at one of the specialist tea sites like www.tea.co.uk to find out more.

MOROCCAN MINT TEA

A great tea to drink after a meal to aid digestion.

1 green tea bag
a sprig of fresh mint
$^1/_2$ –1 tsp runny honey

Put the green tea bag and the mint in a mug and pour over boiling water. Cover with a saucer and leave to infuse for 5 minutes. Remove the mint and tea bag and sweeten to taste with honey.

SIG'S ICED TEA
SERVES 2

 Plain builders tea works fine, but try Earl Grey, Lady Grey or green tea for a change.

2–3 tea bags
a few cubes of ice
lemon, cucumber and mint, to taste

Measure 450ml of water into a measuring jug, submerge the teabags, cover and leave for an hour to infuse (better than pouring boiling water over the teabags as it makes a less tannic drink). Remove the bags, cooling the liquid if necessary then add ice, lemon, cucumber and mint. Think of it as mock-Pimms. If you've got a sweet tooth sweeten with sugar syrup (see page 250).

HOW TO MAKE REAL COFFEE & GREAT HOT CHOCOLATE

These useful tips from one of my favorite coffee companies, Union Hand Roasted, will set you on the route to the perfect cup.

1. Start by using freshly drawn cold water.
2. When using a cafetière, allow the kettle to stand for a few seconds before pouring as boiling water scalds the delicate coffee flavours and causes bitterness.
3. Use about one rounded dessertspoon of ground coffee per person. If you find this too strong, add hot water to the cup (not the cafetière) afterwards and dilute to your taste. Do not use less coffee as this causes over-extraction and bitterness.
4. Keep your coffee brewing equipment clean, as built-up coffee oils will get stale and cause a taint in your cup. Try and clean the mesh on your cafetière once a week.
5. Make coffee fresh each time you serve it and only prepare as much as you plan to drink. Do not reheat coffee you made earlier.
6. Remember, roasted coffee is perishable and once the pack is opened should be kept in a cool airtight container and consumed within two weeks.

SIG'S PERFECT HOT CHOCOLATE

You want equal parts (say 2 teaspoons each) cocoa and dark chocolate. Allow that to melt with a bit of water, add a splash of vanilla extract and then fill up with wholemilk, bring to the boil and drink as it is, or with some cream or even (my waistline does not thank me for this) a scoop of vanilla ice cream. Heaven. Always use whole milk. Never compromise with semi-skimmed. For non-dairy (soy or oat milk) just use one extra teaspoon of dark chocolate and fill up with a bit more water, creating a molten brew.

ULTIMATE COCOA

Put 2 level teaspoons of cocoa into a mug. Add 4 tablespoons of Baileys and 1 tablespoon of Tia Maria or Kahlua coffee liqueur (optional, but good) and stir well. Top up with semi-skimmed milk and stir. Microwave for 1 minute, stir again then microwave for a further 30 seconds. Stir and indulge yourself with the best cocoa ever!

TOP STUDENT TIPS

If you would like to support third-world producers, Fairtrade tea, coffee and cocoa is a good place to start – all widely available in supermarkets and charity shops for just a touch more than you'd usually pay. Fairtrade Fortnight in early March is a good time to find them on promotion. **SIG**

'go on... indulge yourself'

OTHER USEFUL STUFF

Where we've put all the other extremely useful things we couldn't fit in anywhere else: food styling tips (you want to be a telly chef, don't you?); a list of our favourite recipes, for those of you who can't make up your mind what to cook; how to cook various veg; and an index that will tell you where to find everything.

HOW TO MAKE YOUR FOOD LOOK GREAT

One of the things that sets good cooks – or people who are regarded as good cooks – apart is that they know how to make their food look good. By that I don't mean elaborate cheffy presentation – simply making it look appetising.

The main mistake that most people make – especially hungry students – is to pile on too much food. Piled-high food, whether it's pasta or chips can look like a whole pile of unappetising stodge. (Remember when you were a kid how daunting it was to be given a plate with more food on it than you could eat? You don't? Well remember how it put off your fussier friends.) Here are five points to bear in mind for all budding Jamie Olivers:

1. Think about colour. Try not to end up with it all looking beige or, let's face it, poo-coloured (a hazard with veggie food like with brown rice and lentils) Most savoury dishes benefit from a bit of green whether it's in the form of a scattering of herbs, a few salad leaves or a bright-coloured veg such as broccoli, asparagus or peas.

2. Break up the surface of smooth food like soup. Again, herbs are useful or add a swirl of cream or yoghurt and/or a few croûtons.

3. Use a bit of creativity in the way you cut fruit and veg. Slice carrots or courgettes on the slant rather than in rounds, for example. Cut cucumber thinly. Chop up a salad like a salsa for a change (see page 114). Cheese also looks sexier crumbled or shaved (with a cheese slicer or veg peeler) than cut in cubes or hefty wedges.

4. Create some height in your dishes. a little mound of salad leaves or a pile of beans looks much better than the same ingredients spread flat over the plate.

5. Be imaginative about the plates and bowls you use. You can pick up cheap plates and glasses for next to nothing in charity shops. Take a basic tumbler, put a layer of cooked fruit in the bottom, top with a layer of fromage frais and spoon or shake a little granola over the top and you've got a really great looking and healthy breakfast. Takes no time at all.

Take a look at one of the glossy food mags or a good cookery website (as well, of course, as the fabulously creative photography in this book!

TOP STUDENT TIPS

 When I eat in restaurants, I'm quite picky about the presentation of food. I'm always looking for a variety of colour and a 'clean', unfussy presentation. That may seem a little pretentious, but I think any chef worth his or her salt should be able to cook seriously good food whilst presenting it in a visually appealing manner. Too much fuss on a plate and food looks contrived, overwrought. As Fiona argues, a mound of food carelessly lumped together just isn't very appetizing – just don't keep your mates waiting ages while you construct and de-construct a tower of Bolognese. Comfort food should be served in generous quantities, with a bit of garnish to add colour. Desserts are where you can really go crazy with creative ideas – a drizzle of raspberry coulis, a glistening jelly, a scattering of candied citrus zest... the dessert plate is your canvas, so be bold. **SIG**

'a sloppy mess will always look less appealing...'

'...than a dish you've taken a bit of care over'

HOW TO COOK VEG WITHOUT DROWNING THEM

If you are going to attempt to eat healthily you need to know how to cook and prepare a few different veg, so you don't bore yourself witless eating peas and carrots all the time.

ASPARAGUS

Cheap in season (April–May). Cut off the woody end of the stem about a third of the way up. Place in a microwaveable dish with a little water and a damp piece of kitchen towel (run a sheet under the tap and shake off the water), or use cling film. Microwave on high for 3–4 minutes. You can also steam the spears or put them in a frying pan with a little boiling water and roll them around until they're lightly cooked. Drain and serve with melted butter or allow to cool and use in a salad (see page 184).

• Asparagus makes your pee smell weird. Don't worry – you haven't got a deadly disease.
1 bunch will serve 2 as a main dish

BEANS (GREEN)

Cut off the stalk and the wiggly bit at the end. Leave small (dwarf or Kenya) beans whole otherwise cut into thick slices. Place in a saucepan and cover with boiling water. Bring back to the boil, add salt and cook for about 5-6 minutes until you can easily stick a knife through them. Drain in a colander or sieve and run cold water over them to keep them green. Return to the pan with a little butter or olive oil and crushed garlic and heat through gently for 3–4 minutes. **A 250g pack will serve 3–4**

'lightly steam for 3–4 minutes and serve with melted butter'

BROCCOLI

Cut each head of broccoli into small florets. Rinse. Either microwave or steam for 4–5 minutes. Or stir-fry adding a little water and garlic and soy sauce to taste.
1 head will serve 2–3 as a vegetable

CABBAGE AND GREENS

Remove the outer leaves then cut into quarters, removing the tough white stalk in the centre. Shred the rest of the leaves finely and rinse. Cook in a little boiling salted water for about 2–3 minutes, stirring occasionally. Drain and serve with plenty of butter and black pepper. Or stir-fry with a little soy sauce – a better method for oriental greens like pak choi.
Half a cabbage will serve 3–4

CARROTS

Scrub clean and peel if necessary (supermarket carrots are usually washed). Cut off any leaves or stalks. Slice into rounds or diagonal slices (you may need to halve or quarter them if they're particularly large). Heat a little butter or oil in a large saucepan and add a pinch of ground coriander or cumin and a pinch of sugar. Stir the carrots around in the melted butter then pour over half a glass of water, cover with a lid or foil and cook for about 10–12 minutes. New carrots (which tend to be sold with their leaves still on) will take a little less. You can also steam them.

Allow 1 medium-sized carrot per person

'new carrots will take a little less time to cook'

CAULIFLOWER

Cut the white, creamy florets off the stalk, cut into even-sized pieces and either steam or cook in boiling water for about 6–8 minutes, depending on the size of the florets. Use for cauliflower cheese (page 133) or fry up with onion, garlic, Moroccan Spice Mix and cooked potato for a tasty curry.

A medium cauliflower serves 3–4

CORN ON THE COB

Cut off the stalk and tear off the outer husk. Plunge each cob into a large saucepan of boiling water (don't salt it – it makes them tough) and cook for about 7–8 minutes. Drain and smother with soft butter. See page 75 for a great Thai-style Sweetcorn and Spring Onion Chowder.

Allow 1 cob per person

COURGETTES

Easily go soft or soggy so best fried or steamed. Trim each courgette at the ends and slice. Grate the courgettes coarsely and throw them into a frying pan in which you've heated a tablespoon of oil and a good chunk of butter. Stir-fry for 1 minute then season with salt and pepper. Add some chopped fresh parsley if you like.

Allow 1 medium courgette per person

TOP STUDENT TIP

My favourite way of cooking veg with a short cooking time, like asparagus, broccoli, cauliflower, courgettes and mange-tout. If you don't have a steamer, put them in a metal colander over a pan of boiling water covered with a lid or a piece of foil.

CUCUMBER

Whether or not you peel cucumber is a matter of taste. Ditto whether you eat the seeds. A quick way of removing them is to cut the cucumber lengthways and run the tip of a teaspoon down the centre to remove the seeds, leaving you with nice arc-shaped pieces.

LEEKS

Trim off any roots and the coarse green leaves off the top of the leek (about a quarter of the way down). Slice thickly in rounds then wash thoroughly under running water. (If you buy them from a market stall they're likely to have quite a bit of earth still on them.) Stir-fry in a little oil and butter for 5–6 minutes until soft, then season. You can use leeks in the place of onions.
Allow 1 medium-sized leek per person

LETTUCE

Simply remove any coarse outer leaves, wash and dry in a salad spinner or with a clean tea-towel. Add any salad dressing just before serving (page 68–69) Store any leftover leaves in a plastic bag in the fridge – they should keep for up to two days if your lettuce was fresh in the first place.
One small round lettuce will serve 2-3, a larger cos or iceberg lettuce about 4-6

MANGE-TOUT/SUGARSNAP PEAS

Easy. Rinse and microwave or steam for 2 minutes. (Sugarsnap peas will take 3 minutes.)
A small pack will serve 2-3

MUSHROOMS

Small white button mushrooms are best eaten raw in a salad or as part of a stir-fry. Just wipe clean and slice. Bigger, fatter portabella mushrooms are better baked or grilled with garlic butter (see page 56).
A small pack of mushrooms will serve 2. With big mushrooms you need 1-2 a head

PARSNIPS

Trim each parsnip at the top and bottom and peel. If they're large cut into quarters then cut out the woody core. Best as part of a dish of roast vegetables or as a mash – cook in boiling, salted water until soft (about 15 minutes), drain thoroughly then whizz in a food processor with butter and a little cream. Season with black pepper and a little grated nutmeg if you have some. You can also boil them for just 5 minutes then drain and grill them, trickling over a little runny honey.
Allow 1 medium-sized parsnip each

Roast Winter Vegetables
• For four people cut up two medium to large potatoes, carrots, onions and parsnips into even-sized chunks. Lay in a roasting tin and pour over a good glug of olive oil and mix well so the veg are thoroughly coated. Tuck 4-5 smashed garlic cloves in between and a few sprigs of rosemary if you have some. Roast at 200C/400F/Gas 6 for about 45 minutes to an hour, turning them half the way through.

PEAS

Check the instructions on the packet. No point in shelling peas unless you're a masochist.
You need about 50g of peas per person

POTATOES

The simplest way of cooking potatoes is to boil them. You can peel them or not as you prefer (generally I would with older potatoes and not with new potatoes), if they're old cut them into even-sized pieces – halved or quartered depending on size – cover them with cold water and bring to the boil then cook for about 20 minutes until you can stick a knife into them without any resistance. Drain and add a knob of butter and some chopped parsley and/or chives if you have some. New potatoes are better cooked in boiling water, and only take about 10 minutes. (See also perfect mash, page 154; baked potatoes, page 164; and roast potatoes, page 152.)
You need about 3-4 small, 2 medium or 1 large potato per person

SPINACH

Spinach comes in microwaveable bags these days but it's pricey. If you buy it loose, tip the leaves into a sinkful of cold water and wash thoroughly. Pull off the stalks and central rib of any particularly large leaves. Drain off the water and press the spinach down into a large lidded saucepan. Place over a low heat and cook until the leaves start to collapse. Turn over and cook for a couple of minutes, then drain thoroughly in a colander or sieve. Return to the pan with a good chunk of butter, reheat and season with pepper.
500g of spinach will serve 2-3 people

SPROUTS

Cut across the base and remove the outer leaves. If the sprouts are very big cut a cross in the base to help them cook more quickly. Cover with boiling water, add salt and bring to the boil. Cook for about 8-10 minutes until you can stick a sharp knife through them. Drain, return to the pan and add a knob of butter.
500g sprouts will serve 4-5 people

TOMATOES

Two issues: Are they ripe? (Don't bother if they're not.) And do you mind the skin? If you do, simply make a small cut near the stem end, put them in a bowl and pour over boiling water. Leave them for a minute then drain and rinse them in cold water. The skin should come away easily.

'to skin or not to skin?'

THE WEBSITE, FACEBOOK PAGE & TWITTER...

Since the first *Beyond Baked Beans* book was published 6 years ago we've had our own website – radical at the time. It's still going strong at www.beyondbakedbeans.com – along with the Beyond Baked Beans Facebook fan page we added last year and a Twitterstream we decided to call StudentsCanCook.

If you think all this means you (or possibly your kind and thoughtful parents or grandparents) don't have to buy the book, think again... There's far more info and many more recipes here than there are on the website (we're not daft) plus it still remains the case that it's easier to read and cook from a book than it is from a site.

The website does, however, give us the ability to highlight recipes and subjects that are topical and seasonal so that you can make the best of the cheapest ingredients that are around at any given time of year. There are also more discursive articles on subjects such as healthy eating than we have room for in a book, including some excellent advice from nutritional therapist Kerry Torrens who has been involved with our student cookery project for many years.

The Beyond Baked Beans Facebook page enables us all to post whenever we feel inspired by something we've cooked and for you to upload your own recipes and tips. Apart from Sig (the queen of the step-by-step technique and a mean photographer to boot), Guy and James who've made some great videos, we've acquired a number of regulars who have really made the page the lively forum that it is. (Particular thanks to Nicola, Verity, Charlie, Gemma and Clare.)

The StudentsCanCook Twitterstream encapsulates our philosophy that anyone can cook if they want to and enables us to connect with students all over the world. We'll post the odd tip and useful link on that as well – to other sites as well as our own, so do follow us (and, provided you don't look like a porn, star we'll follow you back).

There may well be a new must-join social media site by the time this book has been out for a year or so. Rest assured, we'll be on it....

'log on to keep up to date with what's going on'

AND GOOD OLD BOOKS...

All this doesn't mean that we don't read cookery books any more. We have those as well – in Fiona's case, hundreds. Not all of them are written with a student budget in mind but here are our favourites that we think will inspire you once you've got into your stride (or started earning...).

SIG

Leith's Simple Cookery, Jenny Stringer and Viv Pidgeon (Bloomsbury Publishing)
Ottolenghi: The Cookbook, Yotam Ottolenghi (Ebury Press)
The Scandinavian Cookbook, Trina Hahnemann (Quadrille Publishing)

GUY

Rick Stein's Mediterranean Escapes, Rick Stein (BBC Books)
Wagamama: Ways with Noodles, Hugo Arnold (Kyle Cathie)
In Search of Perfection, Heston Blumenthal (Bloomsbury Publishing)

JAMES

The Kitchen Diaries, Nigel Slater (Fourth Estate)
Black Pudding and Foie Gras, Andrew Pern (Face Publishing)
Darina Allen's *Ballymaloe Cookery Course* (Kyle Cathie)

FIONA

Jamie's *Ministry of Food*, Jamie Olive (Michael Joseph)
Anything by Nigel Slater
A New Book of Middle Eastern Food, Claudia Roden (Penguin)

Charity shops are a great place to pick up cheap cookery books. On newer titles check out the 'Used and new' category on Amazon or AbeBooks (www.abebooks.co.uk).

OTHER STUDENT TITLES BY ME

Beyond Baked Beans £8.99
Beyond Baked Beans Green £8.99
Beyond Baked Beans Budget £6.99

'The perfect present... I regretted that there was nothing around like this when I was a student and that it was Fiona who had the idea for this book and not me.' **Antony Worrall-Thompson**

THE BEST OF THE BEST

If you don't know where to start with this book here are the recipes for the dishes we know students have most enjoyed together with our own personal faves.

QUICK & EASY MEALS FOR 1 OR 2

CHEAP & TASTY MEALS TO SHARE FOR 3, 4 & MORE

'page 78'

'page 13

FLASHY, SHOW-OFF RECIPES

YUMMY PUDS, CAKES & COCKTAILS

'page 213'

'page 231'

INDEX

A

B

'charred aubergine and tomato salad, page 174'

Baking

Bananas

Beef

'banana and honey muffins, page 227'

Bread

Broccoli

C

cake, Becca's chocolate 231
Caipirinha 251
capers, Guy's spaghetti with tuna,
    tomatoes and 86

Carrots
Carrot and apple slaw 66
Carrot and coriander soup 70
carrot and peanut butter,
    Wholemeal wraps with grated 62
carrot, oat and cinnamon muffins,
    Sig's 225

casserole, James' sausage 160
Cauliflower cheese 133
celery and apple salad, Cheese, 66
Charred aubergine and tomato
    salad 174
Cheat's Christmas pudding 219
Cheat's hummus 178

Cheese
blue cheese, sour cream and
    bacon, Baked potato with 164
Brie and mushroom melt 54
camembert, Baked 183
cheese and onion toastie, Pan-
    fried 53
cheesecake, Our favourite 224
cheese, Cauliflower 133
Cheese, celery and apple salad 66
cheese, Classic macaroni 133
cheese fondue, Gorgeous
    gooey 208
Cheese, onion and bacon stuffed
    baked potatoes 165
cheese on toast, Easiest ever 52
cheese salad, Mixed bean and
    crumbly white 65
cheese sauce, Classic 131
cheese sauce, How to make a 131
cottage cheese tzatziki, Baked
    potato with 164
garlic and herb 'roulé' cheese,

'chicken pot pie, page 195'

Baked potato with soft 164
goat's cheese and sundried
    tomatoes, Salmon burgers
    with 193
goat's cheese, Baked potato with
    roast peppers and 164
goat's cheese risotto, Spring
    vegetable and 184
gorgonzola, James' pearl barley
    risotto with sausage, spinach
    and 186
gorgonzola sauce, Creamy 200
gorgonzola tart, Red onion, chicory
    and 198

chicory and gorgonzola tart, Red
    onion, 198

Chicken
chicken, Bang bang 118
chicken, Beer-can 217
chicken broth with coriander and
    noodles, Asian-style 92
chicken korma, Easy 116
chicken, lentil and butternut
    squash korma, James' 187
chicken, Mexican salsa 147

chicken, No-carve roast 149
chicken (or turkey), Sweet and
    sour 119
Chicken pot pie 195
chicken salad, Spicy 118
chicken with garlic and lovely
    lemony potatoes, Baked 150
chicken with herbs, Roast 151
chickpeas with spinach,
    Moroccan-spiced 107

Chillies
chilli and garlic pasta, Broccoli, 89
Chilli beef hash 157
chilli, Black bean 138
Chilli con carne 80
chilli con carne, Baked potato with
    Bolognese sauce or 164
chilli con carne, Guy's 137
chilli or barbecue sauce, Baked
    potato with baked beans and 164
sweet chilli salsa, Fish fingers with
    cucumber and 110

chocolate and passionfruit
    mousse, Sig's white 233
chocolate brownies, Sig's

D

'sig's raspberry and chocolate brownies, page 228'

'extremely easy stir-fry, page 98'

E

Eggs

F

Fish

G

Garlic

garlic and herb 'roulé' cheese, Baked potato with soft 164

garlic and lovely lemony potatoes, Baked chicken with 150

garlic mayo and buttered spinach, Fish fingers with 110

Garlic mushrooms on toast 56

garlic pasta, Broccoli, chilli and 89

garlicky yoghurt dressing, Stuffed pitta breads with falafel, salad and 61

Ginger

ginger, Hot whisky with lemon, honey and 254

ginger, Pan-fried apple with honey, lemon and 122

ginger smoothie, Sig's energising raspberry and 50

granita, Sig's virgin mojito 245

Gravy 219

gravy, Sausage and mash with onion 159

Greekish salad 65

Greek(ish) shepherd's pie 143

Golden meringues 238

Good Italian dried egg pasta 183

Gorgeous gooey cheese fondue 208

guacamole, Authentic rough-crushed 179

Guinness, Cottage pie with 146

goulash, Pork, pepper and potato 207

Guy's chilli con carne 137

Guy and Claire's peanut noodles 94

Guy's spaghetti with tuna, tomatoes and capers 86

Guy's honey-sesame stir-fry 97

Guy's winter vegetable soup 126

H

Hair-dried duck 201

hash, Chilli beef 157

hash, Salmon and leek 156

herbs and lemon, Spring lamb stew with 206

herbs, Roast chicken with 151

Homemade barbecue sauce 217

Homemade hummus 178

Homemade subs 59

Honey

honey and ginger, Hot whisky with lemon, 254

honey, lemon and ginger, Pan-fried apple with 122

honey muffins, Banana and 227

honey porridge, Banana and 44

Honey-roast duck with stir-fried greens 203

honey roughie, Banana, yoghurt and 50

honey-sesame stir-fry, Guy's 97

Hot buttered sprouts with almonds 219

hot chocolate, Sig's perfect 257

Hot whisky with lemon, honey and ginger 254

How to barbecue 214

How to cook a steak 199

How to cook boiled eggs 38

How to cook fried eggs 38

How to cook pasta 76

How to cook poached eggs 38

How to cook rice 100

How to cook scrambled eggs 38

How to cook turkey and other Christmas tips 218

How to make a cheese sauce 131

How to make a decent cup of tea 256

How to make real coffee and the best hot chocolate 257

How to make perfect mash 154

How to make pizza 211

How to make your own muesli 45

How to stir-fry 96

hummus, Cheat's 178

hummus, Homemade 178

'guy's chilli con carne, page 137'

'keralan-style prawn curry with mussels, coconut and coriander, page 188'

M

'south african-style pork chops with apricots, page 121'

'apple and raisin muesli, page 44'

N

O

P

'guy's winter vegetable soup,
page 126'

*'prawn and pea pilau,
page 102'*

Prawns *see* **Shellfish**

Puddings

R

Raspberries

Rice

S

Salads

'spaghetti with bacon and cockles, page 84'

'spring vegetable frittata, page 43'

U

V

'ultimate fry-up, page 40'

Vegetarian

'american breakfast pancakes, page 47'

Yoghurt

ACKNOWLEDGEMENTS

I've never written a book with a collaborator
before, let alone three, but James, Guy and
Sig have made it a breeze. Their knowledge,
wit and enthusiasm shines through every page.
There's also been a brilliant collaboration
chez Absolute Press where art director Matt
Inwood has turned his hand to photography,
working alongside Andrea O'Connor who
briefly put PR and editorial duties on hold to
turn home economist and food stylist. Claire
Siggery worked tirelessly through assorted
computer crises, designing, re-designing
and ensuring everything was in place.
Thanks too to Jon, my publisher, and Meg,
my commissioning editor, for agreeing to all
our crazy ideas, casting their eagle eyes over
the text and keeping us all on track. If there's
anything you want to know that you can't find
in this book do check out our regularly
updated website www.beyondbakedbeans.com
and Facebook page where you could even
upload some recipes and tips of your own.